THE INTELLECTUAL VERSUS THE CITY

From THOMAS JEFFERSON
To FRANK LLOYD WRIGHT

THE INTELLECTUAL VERSUS THE CITY

From THOMAS JEFFERSON
To FRANK LLOYD WRIGHT

MORTON and LUCIA WHITE

GREENWOOD PRESS, PUBLISHERS
WESTPORT, CONNECTICUT

Library of Congress Cataloging in Publication Data

White, Morton Gabriel, 1917-
   The intellectual versus the city.

   Reprint. Originally published: Oxford ; New ~~~ .
Oxford University Press.
   Includes bibliographical references and index.
   1. Sociology, Urban--Addresses, essays, lectures.
2. Cities and towns--United States--Addresses,
essays, lectures.   I. White, Lucia.   II. Title.
[HT113.W53   1981]   307.7'6'0973   81-1755
ISBN 0-313-22786-1 (lib. bdg.)   AACR2

Reprinted in 1981 by Greenwood Press,
a division of Congressional Information Service, Inc.
88 Post Road West, Westport, Connecticut 06881

Printed in the United States of America

10 9 8 7 6 5 4 3 2 1

TO OUR SONS

FOREWORD FOR 1977

The decay of the American city dramatically reached a serious danger-point only a year before our nation celebrated its two-hundredth anniversary. During the fifteen years since this book was first published, the crisis of American cities had deepened until a climax came in the winter of 1975, when New York City announced that it would be forced into bankruptcy unless the federal government were to come to its rescue. When the President of the country at that time began to lecture New York petulantly on the errors of its ways, it became all too clear—to New Yorkers, at any rate—what he had meant when he once announced on television that he was a Ford and not a Lincoln. And some readers of the present book may see an even deeper meaning in Gerald Ford's effort at self-deprecatory witticism when they find on p. 201 the words of Henry Ford: "We shall solve the City Problem by leaving the city." In the pronouncements of the automotive Ford and his politically motivated namesake we certainly find no Lincolnesque effort to deal with a two-hundred-year-old antipathy to the American city which has been expressed not only by thinkers on the level of the Fords, but also by Thomas Jefferson, Ralph Waldo Emerson, Henry Adams, and Henry James —to mention only a few of the more important American writers treated in this book. Of course, by linking the name of the thirty-eighth President of the United States with that of the third, we do not imply that the thirty-eighth was an *intellectual* versus the city but there is little doubt in our minds that Ford's latter-day scoldings of New York City are causally linked by complicated chains, of course, with the fears, prejudices—and it must be said—the reasonable criticism that some of our best-known and ablest writers have expressed about the city for two centuries.

This antipathy to the *American* city of *major American writers* in the broadest sense of that term is our main concern in the present work, which we are happy to see in this new edition. We have made only minor corrections of the original text but we have no doubt that if we were writing the book today we should write it differently. We are also aware that related topics might be treated in other books. For example, it might be worthwhile to study the reactions of lesser intellectuals as well as non-intellectuals, to study the American city itself while assessing the claims of its critics, and to compare the attitudes of American writers toward their cities with those of European writers toward theirs in the same period.

Those, however, are books that we have *not* written and, so far as we know, books that no one else has written. We mention them in the hope that other scholars will write them and in order to let the reader of the present book know what *not* to expect in these pages. Because we concentrate on the persistent antipathy of *major* American writers toward the American city, we cheerfully acknowledge that Oliver Wendell Holmes called Boston the hub of the universe, that O. Henry thought of New York as Bagdad on the Subway, that Ben Hecht wrote affectionately of a thousand and one afternoons in Chicago, that Floyd Dell wrote his "Ballad of Christopher Street," and that George M. Cohan gave his regards to Broadway. And because our book is a study of the antipathy of major *American* writers toward the *American* city, we are not fazed by the fact that Samuel Johnson once said "when a man is tired of London, he is tired of life; for there is in London all that life can afford." Since we not only acknowledge but dilate on Henry James's love of London, the reader will see that we do not deny that some writers of American origin admired *foreign* cities and that we do not assert that all of our writers hated the city *as such*. On the contrary, we distinguish explicitly between disapproving of the city as such and disapproving of the American city while we recite the charges leveled against it.

Those charges, we should say quickly, were various in nature. Therefore, our reader will discover that we share John Stuart Mill's view that a phenomenon like the antipathy toward the American city may spring from what he calls a plurality of causes. Different attitudes have led different writers to disapprove of the American city: dislike or fear of crowds, of crime, of dirt, of noise, and of certain ethnic groups, to mention only a few of the factors we list on p. 222 below. And we dare say that the millions of ordinary Americans whom Gerald Ford sought to arouse were against helping their greatest city for different reasons, just as millions of ordinary Americans voted against Gerald Ford for different reasons. In saying so we do not wish to be dogmatic about what further study of our materials may reveal. For all we know, some enterprising scholar of the future may find one bright thread that runs throughout the different reasons which different American writers have had for disliking the American city. And when such a scholar convincingly reveals that thread we shall be the first to offer our congratulations.

One further word about our method. When we started our work we did not anticipate the degree of ambivalence or antagonism toward the American city that we found. We had not *looked for* anti-urbanists but we found a lot of them simply by reading American writers who were chosen because they were distinguished. We also found gradations of anti-urbanism. Many writers who appear in these pages—for example, William James, Robert Park, John Dewey, and Jane Addams—expressed sincere hope that the American city could be reclaimed, and were eager to root out the evil and preserve the good they saw in urban life.

All of this may at first seem irrelevant to people who are eager to solve the crisis of the American city: the city-planners, the financiers, the administrators, and government officials, as well as all of the rest of us who are confronted with urban crises every day of the week. But this history of reflection on the quality of urban life in America should persuade not only general readers and historians but all seekers after quick solutions that the remedies for the ills of the American metropolis will have to include long-term solutions of basic problems of American society. It will become evident to the reader of these pages that our most serious thinkers from Jefferson to Dewey tell us that habitable and enjoyable American cities cannot be built without educating all of our people to participate in our democratic society, to develop their individuality, and to communicate in ways that increase their understanding of each other. As Emerson would have said, the rebirth of the American city will depend less on the kind of automobiles, skyscrapers, freeways, or airports we produce than on the kinds of men, women, and children we turn out.

Princeton, N. J.   LUCIA WHITE
January 1977   MORTON WHITE

PREFACE

It is a pleasure to acknowledge with gratitude the aid and encouragement that many friends and associates have given us. Jean Gottman first stimulated us to investigate the problems that concern us in this study; and if it were not for the cordial interest of Martin Meyerson we might never have continued our investigations. Frank Freidel and Louis Hartz not only encouraged us while we were in the earliest stages of writing, but were generous enough to read the final manuscript. Harry Austryn Wolfson kindly advised us on several matters of style and content.

We are also indebted to the Twentieth Century Fund, the Joint Center for Urban Studies of the Massachusetts Institute of Technology and Harvard University, and the Center for Advanced Study in the Behavioral Sciences for providing us with leisure, secretarial assistance, and the opportunity to benefit by exchange with other scholars. At the Center for Advanced Study in the Behavioral Sciences, in the year 1959–1960, we profited especially by discussions with Sigmund Diamond, Albert Guérard, Jr., and Carl Schorske. In the winter of the same year the Joint Center for Urban Studies circulated an earlier version of our manuscript and arranged an afternoon's discussion of it, thereby permitting us to receive useful comments and suggestions from John Burchard, Albert Bush-Brown, Alan Heimert, Reginald Isaacs, Kenneth Lynn, Perry and Elizabeth Miller, Elting Morison, Lloyd Rodwin, and Arthur M. Schlesinger.

We want to thank members of the staff of Widener Library, especially Thomas F. O'Connell, for their remarkable capacity to make books available to us when we needed them. And we want to express our appreciation to several ladies who typed various sections of the manuscript in its different stages: Elizabeth Hooper, Letitia

McClure Potter, Ruth Smith, Joan Warmbrunn, and especially Dorothy Trefry, who typed the final version.

In conclusion we wish to express our gratitude to the Henry P. Kendall Foundation for its generous support of our research. Without that support it would have taken much longer to bring the research to a conclusion.

Cambridge, Mass.   LUCIA WHITE
October, 1961   MORTON WHITE

CONTENTS

xiii

CONTENTS

THE INTELLECTUAL VERSUS THE CITY

From THOMAS JEFFERSON
To FRANK LLOYD WRIGHT

I

OPENING THEME

THE decay of the American city is now one of the most pressing concerns of the nation. Every day we hear of a continuing flight from the central city; of explosions into the suburbs and more distant places; of sprawling supercities; of automobiles crawling through and around the city on roads that strangle it; of a city-based culture that is allegedly destroying our spiritual life; and of lonely crowds of organization men. But in spite of all this complaining about the city's defects and deficiencies, it is now fashionable for many American intellectuals to express tender concern for the city's future, to hope that its decay may be arrested, and to offer plans for its revitalization. No week passes without some new university conference on the future of the city, without some effort on the part of educated men to deal sympathetically with the problems of urbanization.

Yet enthusiasm for the American city has not been typical or predominant in our intellectual history. Fear has been the more common reaction. For a variety of reasons our most celebrated thinkers have expressed different degrees of ambivalence and animosity toward the city, attitudes which may be partly responsible for a feeling on the part of today's city planner that he has no mythology or mystique on which he can rest or depend while he launches his campaigns in behalf of urban improvement. We have no persistent or pervasive tradition of romantic attachment to the city in our literature or in our philosophy, nothing like the Greek attachment

1

to the *polis* or the French writer's affection for Paris. And this confirms the frequently advanced thesis that the American intellectual has been alienated from the society in which he has lived, that he has been typically in revolt against it. For while our society became more and more urban throughout the nineteenth century, the literary tendency to denigrate the city hardly declined; if anything, its intensity increased. One of the most typical elements in our national life, the growing city, became the bête noire of our most distinguished intellectuals rather than their favorite. It would therefore be extremely difficult to cull from their writings a large anthology of poetry or social philosophy in celebration of American urban life. No matter what ordinary people may have been feeling about Boston, Chicago, or New York; no matter what chamber of commerce boosters and Fourth of July orators may have shouted, America's major writers did not rise up in a body to greet the American metropolis with enthusiasm.

Of course there were some like Walt Whitman and William James who could at times speak affectionately about New York, but they were on such occasions voices crying in "the city wilderness," to use a phrase of their time. The volume of their voices did not compare with the anti-urban roar produced in the national literary pantheon by Jefferson, Emerson, Thoreau, Hawthorne, Melville, Poe, Henry Adams, Henry James, and William Dean Howells. Therefore today's admirers of the American city would do well to realize that the American anti-urbanist has not lived only in the Kentucky mountains, in the Rockies, on the farm, in the Ozarks or in the Cracker country. He has also lived in the mind and heart of America as conceived by the intellectual historian. The intellect, whose home is the city according to some sociologists, has produced the sharpest criticism of the American city.

That criticism, it must be repeated, has come from some of our most talented and most influential minds. To concentrate on their views is, of course, not to imply that they typify the spirit of America's reaction to the city. The spirit of America's reaction to one hundred and seventy-five years of urban life is as elusive as spirits usually are, and it is idle to ask whether the municipal planner embodies it more truly than the novelist or the philosopher. But the negative attitude of the intellectual toward the American city is of interest in its own right, especially because it is voiced in unison by figures who represent major tendencies in American thought: by Jefferson, the child of the Enlightenment; by Emerson and Thoreau, the Transcendentalists; by Hawthorne, Poe and Melville, who represent what Harry Levin calls "the power of blackness";[1] by Henry Adams and Henry James in reaction to the Gilded Age; by Howells, Dreiser, and Norris, spokesmen of literary realism and naturalism; by John Dewey and Jane Addams in what Richard Hofstadter calls "The Age of Reform"; by Louis Sullivan and Frank Lloyd Wright, America's best-known architects; by Robert Park, its most influential urban sociologist. Because these figures dominate or sum up certain phases of American intellectual development, they form a body of intellectual lore and tradition which continues to affect thought and action about the city today. There is a contemporaneity about some of their views which is not obscured by the fact that they speak from the past; they continue to be read by those who are interested in the general history of the United States and also by those who are curious about our literary and philosophical tradition. They virtually constitute our intellectual tradition as it is known today. They make up the core of our intellectual history and one must go to them if one wishes to know what the articulate American conception of urban life has been.

Faced with this powerful tradition of anti-urbanism in the history of American thought, the contemporary well-wisher of the American city may take one of two opposing attitudes. He may turn his back on the literary and philosophical traditions of the nineteenth and early twentieth centuries and thus treat some of the American city's most profound critics as irresponsible literary men or as idle metaphysicians who fled the city instead of facing its problems realistically. Or he may regard this critical tradition as a repository of deep, though troubling, wisdom and as a source of sometimes justified, sometimes baseless, fear and anxiety about urbanization. We

3

have little doubt that the second is the more advisable course. The student and reformer of contemporary urban life would do well to examine and weigh the charges that American intellectuals have levelled against the American city: to know what some of the most intelligent and most sensitive Americans have said and felt about it. Much of what they said was the product of doctrinaire ideology, of blindness, ignorance, and prejudice; but it is also true that they were responding to urban situations which were really objectively bad. The main purpose of this study is to describe, analyze, and classify some of the major intellectual reactions to the American city from the eighteenth century to the first part of the twentieth century, and to examine the intellectual roots of anti-urbanism and ambivalence toward urban life in America. We shall be mainly concerned with writers who are explicitly hostile to American city life and who may be called anti-urbanists without any doubt. But we shall also examine writers who are less extreme in their indictment of American cities. It is not our purpose to show that every writer treated in this study rejects the city as such. The anti-city party in American thought has its wild men and its wise men, and both will be represented in this story.

Since we shall be inquiring into more than a century and a half of reflection about American cities, it is well to say at once that American cities changed radically in this period. The colonial city was— in important respects—different from the city that grew up between the War of 1812 and the Civil War, and the metropolis that followed the Civil War was not the supercity which came into being after the first World War. For that reason it might be said that earlier writers who were critical of American cities understood something different by the general term "city" from what was understood by later writers. That may be so, but the fact is that the writers with whom we deal are concerned essentially with the same few places —with Boston, Philadelphia, New York, Washington, and Chicago —which they call cities and which they distinguish from the surrounding countryside even when they are not prepared to give a clear definition of what they mean by the term "city." The geographical extension of the term "city" remains roughly the same, to use the language of the logicians, even though its intension is vague and shifting in the literature under consideration. It would be folly to suppose that one could extract from the writings of Emerson, or Henry James, or John Dewey some airtight definition of what they understood by the word "city." Indeed, even the scientifically minded Robert Park does not provide us with such a definition, nor do his successors in urban sociology seem to have come to any clear consensus on the use of the term.[2] It is sufficient for our purposes, therefore, to think of the writers treated in this book as primarily critical of specific places, notably Boston, New York, and Chicago in the nineteenth and early twentieth centuries, for many reasons that will emerge in the succeeding chapters. And now, without further elaboration of our concern, we turn back to the eighteenth century where our story begins.

II

THE IRENIC AGE

FRANKLIN, CRÈVECOEUR, AND JEFFERSON

ALTHOUGH the nineteenth century was dominated by a powerful intellectual tradition of anti-city feeling in America, it was preceded by a very different kind of period in the history of American thought. The eighteenth-century American city had not become large enough or unattractive enough to stir men into passionate ideological argument about the virtues and vices of urbanization, or into identification with the country or the city as *the* place in which the good life was to be lived. The great eighteenth-century towns-man, Benjamin Franklin, was not opposed to rural life;[1] the agrarian writer, J. Hector St. John Crèvecoeur, was not anti-urban; and Thomas Jefferson lived long enough to say that his apparently anti-urban *Notes on Virginia* had been misconstrued and that the American city was an indispensable part of American life. Franklin's *Autobiography,* which told the story of the greatest urban intellectual of the period, is a record of civic devotion but not a contentious or carefully contrived celebration of urban culture. And while Crèvecoeur's *Letters from an American Farmer* are passionately sympathetic in their descriptions of inland farm life, they were written by a man who also spoke with unmistakable pleasure about American cities at the end of the eighteenth century.

In the eighteenth century the American city had developed few of the objectionable qualities that came to characterize it by the end of the nineteenth. Commerce, industry, and massive immigration had not yet marked the American city with the blemishes and the

6

scars that were so offensive to later generations of writers. And that is one reason why the eighteenth-century city was not the problem for intellectuals that its successors were to become. Even at the end of the century what were then called cities were tiny dots in the immense wilderness of the continent of North America. Land ruled supreme and seemingly limitless untamed nature, rather than the city, was the gigantic obstacle that confronted the five million people who populated the United States of America in 1800. Not Wall Street bears, but real ones, filled their more anxious thoughts.

In 1800 the population included about one million white male adults and about one million Negro slaves. Two-thirds of the total population was concentrated along the eastern seaboard within fifty miles of tidewater. The largest cities, all coastal seaports, were —in order of approximate size—Philadelphia, 70,000 (about the size of Liverpool); New York, 60,000; Boston, 25,000; and Charleston, 18,000; while Washington, the new national capital, was just becoming established as a town. Some four or five hundred thousand settlers had already penetrated the country west of the Alleghenies, making Kentucky the largest western community and Tennessee next in size, while Cincinnati had become a town of 2,300 people by 1810. Thus the western thrust of the settlers formed a wedge pointed toward the center of the continent, but between the eastern seaboard communities and the western settlements there was a separation running north and south of one hundred miles of densely forested mountains. In the northern part of the country Albany was a concentration of 5,000 people and western New York state still a wilderness. On the outer fringes of the thinly scattered settlements warfare with Indian tribes was still frequent. Within the inhabited regions, where the foremost pursuit was agriculture, there were only thin strips of cultivated land, and mineral deposits remained underground. In spite of the fact that the thirteen states had formed a political union, they remained very separate primarily because overland transportation continued to be a stubborn problem as it was in Europe.

The transportation facilities of the United States in 1800 were

7

not developed much beyond what they had been in the colonial period around 1750. As through the centuries, ships were the best vehicles for travel and trade, and the liveliest commerce of the new republic remained tied to Europe. Even along the Atlantic coast shipping between the states was slow and uncertain, and there was no regular packet even between New York and Albany. Along the Ohio River there were flat-bottom barges for downstream transport, but only light rowboats could effect an upstream passage. Besides this kind of navigation on the rivers and streams there were three main wagon roads which had been laboriously constructed across the Allegheny mountains: one from Philadelphia to Pittsburgh; one from the Potomac to the Monongahela River; and one passing through Virginia to Knoxville, Tennessee, with a branch through the Cumberland Gap into Kentucky. However, over the main wagon routes it took ten days to three weeks to travel inland from Philadelphia to Nashville, whereas the trip by light stagecoach along tolerably good coastal highways was quite rapid—three days between Boston and New York, and about two days from there to Philadelphia.[2]

Looking backward to the year 1800 Henry Adams wrote in his *History of the United States* that "if Bostonians for a moment forgot their town-meetings, or if Virginians overcame their dislike for cities and pavements, they visited and admired, not New York, but Philadelphia." This city, which had been the national capital between 1790 and 1800 "surpassed any of its size on either side of the Atlantic for most of the comforts and some of the elegancies of life."[3] At the end of the eighteenth century Jefferson had found Philadelphia much handsomer than London.[4] The terrible scourge of yellow fever had stimulated sanitary precautions, so that the city was well-paved with brick sidewalks and curbstones, had an elementary sewage system, and brought in its water supply through wooden pipes. It was also the best-lighted city in America. And besides a model market, it supported several flourishing industries, including ironworks and paper, gunpowder and carriage manufactures. Even after the seat of government was removed to Washington, Philadelphia continued to house the Bank of the United States and several private banks. Philadelphia, and the state of Pennsylvania, besides being the wealthiest part of the republic, boasted the most active public spirit of any region in the country. The region was especially noted at the time for its roads and canals, and the new turnpike from Philadelphia to Lancaster. The most important artery of national life ran between Philadelphia and Pittsburgh.

Philadelphia, of course, was the town of Benjamin Franklin who "personified" the American city of the Enlightenment.[5] But in his *Autobiography,* Franklin was neither a theorist of city life nor a controversialist preoccupied with showing its virtues by comparison to the country. He faced the problems of the city in a highly practical way, devising schemes for dealing with street paving, fire, sanitation, hospitals, government, crime, and education. And more than any of our great intellectual figures, he participated in the urban life of his time. But one finds in Franklin no sense of philosophical commitment to the city as a way of life; he had little consciousness of a need to join an ideological or literary party of the city. Franklin, the city-builder, was also one of the most active agrarian pamphleteers of his time and not overly concerned to fight in any intellectual war between town and country. There are references in his *Autobiography* to the kind of urban corruption that came to haunt later American writers, but Franklin did not make much of the fact that Philadelphia, as he knew it, was inhabited by strumpets, drunkards, and many who engaged in sharp business practices.

There are also places in the *Autobiography* at which a more sentimental admirer of the city might have become enthusiastic in its behalf or critical of its enemies, but Franklin engaged in no such partisanship. At one point he spoke of his early partner, Meredith, who had decided to break up their partnership because, as Meredith said, he was bred as a farmer and had been ill-advised to come to town and enter a new trade at the age of thirty. Franklin simply reported that he bought out Meredith on generous terms and that Meredith went to North Carolina. But Franklin did not use the opportunity to debate the relative merits of city and country. On

9

the contrary, he closed the incident by reporting the later receipt from Meredith of "two long letters containing the best account that had been given of [North Carolina's] climate, soil, husbandry, etc.," which Franklin printed and which "gave great satisfaction to the public."[6] At another place in the *Autobiography,* Franklin avoided an even more obvious opportunity to debate the issues of city versus country in general terms. He told of the country representatives in the Assembly who did not relish subscribing to a hospital for the poor in Philadelphia because, as Franklin said, "it could only be serviceable to the city."[7] But the objection did not become the occasion for Franklin to sound the theme of rural-urban strife. At the end of the eighteenth century, Franklin the city-builder was as broad-minded about the country as Crèvecoeur, the New York farmer, was about the city.

J. Hector St. John Crèvecoeur lived in Ulster County, New York, where he gathered the materials for his celebrated *Letters.* He was, he tells us, no philosopher, no politician, no divine, no naturalist, but only a simple farmer.[8] However, he insisted, a farmer may engage in studious reflection. His minister encouraged him to do so by telling him of the excellent sermons that may be composed while following the plough: "The eyes not being then engaged on any particular object, leave the mind free for the introduction of many useful ideas. It is not in the noisy shop of a blacksmith or of a carpenter, that these studious moments can be enjoyed."[9] And yet Crèvecoeur's notion that the intellectual life may best be lived in the country is no basis for supposing that the differences between Franklin and Crèvecoeur, great as they are, may be incorporated into a romantically conceived contrast between pragmatic urban man and emotional rural man, of the kind suggested by D. H. Lawrence. Lawrence was of course fascinated by Crèvecoeur's love of the soil and he disliked Franklin—"middle-sized, sturdy, snuff-colored Doctor Franklin, one of the soundest citizens that ever trod or used 'venery.' "[10] Lawrence, the irrationalist, adored Crèvecoeur because he had "blood knowledge"[11] and because he "spotted [nature] long before Thoreau and Emerson worked it up."[12] When

10

Crèvecoeur broke into tears as he contemplated his wife by the fireside spinning, knitting, darning, or suckling their child,[13] Lawrence hailed him as the man of emotion in contrast to Franklin, "the real *practical* prototype of the American."[14] In setting up this contrast between practical Citizen Franklin and emotional Farmer Crèvecoeur, Lawrence simply disregarded Crèvecoeur's own image of the farmer as a man who interests himself primarily in the *use* of things. The farmer's feelings, Crèvecoeur says, are those of a man "who daily holds the axe or the plough."[15] If any contrast is to be drawn between Franklin and Crèvecoeur, it is not between practical city man and emotional rural man. If we accept Lawrence's oversimplification, his romantic stereotype, we are too likely to fall into thinking of Franklin, scientism, pragmatism, utilitarianism, and urbanism on the one side, arrayed against Crèvecoeur, blood-knowledge, feeling, anti-intellectualism, and ruralism on the other; a dichotomy in which Crèvecoeur is then pictured as a colonial agrarian who glowers across a philosophical gulf at Franklin, the pragmatic urbanite. However, this conception, when projected onto the eighteenth-century American scene, creates a misleading impression. True, Crèvecoeur was a farmer and Franklin was a townsman, and there were enormous temperamental differences between them. But Crèvecoeur "was . . . never guilty of the fanciful idealization of Indian life that was characteristic of some of the French followers of Rousseau"[16] and his candid recitation of the farmer's troubles showed that he did not idealize agricultural conditions in the new world.

Moreover, Crèvecoeur's admiring description of New York City in the years between 1770 and 1781 shows how little he thought of the American city as a deplorable contrast to the American countryside of the period. He speaks of it as a handsome city in which Dutch neatness is combined with English taste and architecture, of its clean and well-lighted streets. In this town of 3,400 houses and 28,000 inhabitants, he found a well-built college with an excellent library and many costly mathematical instruments. And like so many later visitors, he reported that "nothing is more

11

beautiful, and nothing gives the reflective spectator a higher idea of the city's wealth, or of the nature of its free and happy commerce, than the multitude of ships of all sizes, which continually tack about in the bay." Crèvecoeur found New York's merchants intelligent, able, and rich, and its artisans very skillful. "Let those who like myself have experienced the hospitality of New York praise it as it deserves," he adds in gratitude. Such hospitality was, he announced to prospective visitors to America, an example of the "simple and cordial friendliness they are to expect in other cities of this continent."[17]

Crèvecoeur's feelings toward cities in Europe were not so sympathetic. In the eighteenth century, to like American cities was one thing, to like those in Europe was another. Crèvecoeur admired the towns of the North American continent, but he also remarked on how lucky America was to be spared cities such as he knew in Europe. "How I hate to dwell in these accumulated and crowded cities!" he exclaimed as he spoke of European cities. "They are but the confined theatre of cupidity; they exhibit nothing but the action and reaction of a variety of passions which, being confined within narrower channels, impel one another with the greatest vigor."[18] This combination of distaste for European cities and affection for American cities in the late eighteenth century makes it easier to understand the more complex and more interesting reaction of Thomas Jefferson to the city.

Like Crèvecoeur, Jefferson was made uneasy by pictures he formed of the impact of the Industrial Revolution on European cities, and these pictures did not become rosier when he visited Europe in the years between 1784 and 1789. In trying to understand Jefferson's complex reaction to urban life in America, it is important to keep in mind three of his main attitudes. First of all, he dearly loved the farmer's life as he conceived it and he thought of the farmer as the bulwark of democracy. Secondly, Jefferson was a talented, many-sided child of the Enlightenment, who took delight in all of the things he associated with civilized urban life: varied sociability, gaiety, philosophical conversation, architecture, painting, and music. And finally, he was influenced by all considerations affecting the national interest. More than any figure to be dealt with in this study, Jefferson was actively and responsibly concerned with the internal and foreign politics of the American republic. His agrarianism, his cultivation, and his patriotism must all be taken into account in any effort to understand the development of his thinking about the city.

That story is best begun with the anti-urban *Notes on Virginia* of 1784 and concluded with his conciliatory letter to Benjamin Austin in 1816, when he admits that we can no longer depend on England for manufactures and must therefore have our own cities. In 1784 Jefferson's preference for the health, virtue, and freedom of the farm was pitted against his passion for the "elegant arts," and when he had only this choice to make, his agrarianism usually triumphed over his esthetic taste. This is most evident in the fact that his visit to Paris, which he loved in many ways, did not lead him to revise the recommendations of the already written *Notes on Virginia*. When faced with a choice between the elegant arts of some future American Paris and the yeoman's health, virtue, and freedom, Jefferson bit his lip and, as it were, urged the nation to stay down on the farm. But later, when the international political dangers of 1812 made clear that the formation of manufacturing centers was necessary for the preservation of that very freedom which he identified with life on the farm, he abandoned his opposition to the encouragement of cities in America. What Paris could not do, the War of 1812 did decisively. Jefferson was first a patriot, then a lover of the soil, and then a lover of chamber music; and this ordering of his values helps illuminate the development of his views on the city.

The *Notes on Virginia* contain the best-known and most frequently cited of Jefferson's animadversions on urban life. Contrasting the European situation with the American, he says that in Europe manufactures were needed to support the surplus of people,

13

but in America the immensity of the land eliminated this need. When he asked himself whether all Americans should be employed in improvement of the land or whether half of them should engage in manufacture and handicraft, Jefferson replied that *all* should cultivate the land, except carpenters, masons, and smiths, who are themselves needed by farmers. The most famous relevant passage is: "For the general operations of manufacture, let our workshops remain in Europe. It is better to carry provisions and materials to workmen there, than bring them to the provisions and materials, and with them their manners and principles. The loss by the transportation of commodities across the Atlantic will be made up in happiness and permanence of government. The mobs of great cities add just so much to the support of pure government, as sores do to the strength of the human body. It is the manners and spirit of a people which preserve a republic in vigour."[19]

In his book, *Farming and Democracy*,[20] A. W. Griswold makes it easier to understand Jefferson's views in the *Notes*. Griswold reminds us that Jefferson loved the soil and its people, that he had a horror of the effects of the Industrial Revolution, that he believed in the ownership of private property as conducive to individual freedom in an age when farm land was the most typical and useful form of private property. So strong were these beliefs and attitudes that Jefferson wanted to prevent the transatlantic crossing of the European mob. When Jefferson was composing the *Notes on Virginia,* he later reported, American industry had not engendered the spirit of which he complained when he looked at European cities. In the *Notes on Virginia* he was not attacking the American city of the seventeen-eighties, he said, but rather the European city he feared it might come to resemble. For, like Crèvecoeur, he was worried by the possibility that our cities might imitate the great cities of Europe, where "want of food and clothing necessary to sustain life has begotten a depravity of morals, a dependence and corruption, which renders them an undesirable accession to a country whose morals are sound."[21]

In this first round of the American city's battle for Jefferson's mind, his love of the farmer's life triumphed and took precedence even over the economic disadvantages that might come with sending raw materials to Europe and bringing them back in finished form. The second, more difficult round began when Jefferson went to Paris and his agrarianism was put to a sterner test. Yet once again Jefferson remained firm in his conviction that America should do without cities. He was not converted by Paris' charms. In fact he was so indifferent to its blandishments as to appall one of his (French-born) biographers, Chinard, who speaks of his "utilitarian" and "puritanical" attitude toward the pleasures of Paris, of his narrowness and almost Philistine outlook.[22] At least one highly relevant letter written by Jefferson from Paris is worth quoting at length. It was sent to Mrs. William Bingham and deals with the typical day of an upper-class Parisian lady. He begins by speaking of the "empty bustle" of Paris, which he contrasts with the "tranquil pleasures of America," and then says: "At eleven o'clock it is day chez Madame. The curtains are drawn. Propped on bolsters and pillows, and her head scratched into a little order, the bulletins of the sick are read, and the billets of the well. She writes to some of her acquaintance and receives the visits of others. If the morning is not very thronged, she is able to get out and hobble around the cage of the Palais Royal: but she must hobble quickly, for the Coeffeur's turn is come; and a tremendous turn it is! Happy, if he does not make her arrive when dinner is half over! The torpitude of digestion a little passed, she flutters half an hour thro' the streets by way of paying visits, and then to the Spectacles. These finished, another half hour is devoted to dodging in and out of the doors of her very sincere friends, and away to supper. After supper cards; and after cards bed, to rise at noon the next day, and to tread, like a mill-horse, the same trodden circle over again. Thus the days of life are consumed, one by one, without an object beyond the present moment: ever flying from the ennui of that, yet carrying it with us; eternally in pursuit of happiness which keeps eternally before us. If death or a bankruptcy happen to trip us out of the circle, it is matter for the buzz of the evening, and is completely forgotten by the next morning."[23] Jefferson contrasts this life of Madame with a woman's life in America where she enjoys the society of her husband, the fond care of her children, the arrangement of the house, and the improvement of the grounds. And his praise of American domesticity reminds one of Crèvecoeur's affecting description of an American woman's life with her husband and baby.

Life "chez Madame" was apparently not a great lure to Jefferson. The "savage from the mountains of Virginia," as he called himself in a letter to Charles Bellini, apparently did not take to the Parisian society he described to Mrs. Bingham. Intrigues of love occupied Paris' young people, he said, while intrigues of ambition occupied the older. Satisfaction of the "bad passions" offers them "only moments of extasy amidst days of restlessness and torment." So far the mountains of Virginia still had the advantage. It was not until Jefferson thought of the literary and artistic life of the French capital that he began to show signs of weakening. Then, and only then, did he acknowledge the unqualified advantages of Paris for a cultivated man. "Were I to proceed to tell you how much I enjoy their architecture, sculpture, painting, music, I should want words. It is in these arts that they shine. The last of them particularly is an enjoiment, the deprivation of which with us cannot be calculated. I am most ready to say it is the only thing which from my heart I envy them, and which in spite of all the authority of the decalogue I do covet."[24]

It should not be thought, however, that Paris caused Jefferson to abandon some of his reservations about importing cities to America, even cities with concert halls. However much he coveted the arts of Paris, he did not covet them enough to overcome his medical, moral, and political opposition to cities for America. Not for all the chamber concerts in Paris would he bring its urban woes to America, and this emerges by implication in a letter to Benjamin Rush about an outbreak of yellow fever in 1800. Jefferson writes: "When great evils happen, I am in the habit of looking out for what good may arise from them as consolations to us, and Providence has in fact so established the order of things, as that most evils are the means of producing some good. The yellow fever will discourage the growth of great cities in our nation & I view great cities as pestilential to the morals, the health and the liberties of man. True, they nourish some of the elegant arts, but the useful ones can thrive elsewhere, and less perfection in the others, with more health, virtue & freedom, would be my choice."[25]

This was a strong statement, of course, but Jefferson was not so doctrinaire or so silly as to hope that the problem of urban disease would not be dealt with rationally. For during the very same year in which he wrote to Rush in such theological tones, Jefferson was proposing scientific methods for preventing the spread of yellow fever in cities by the improvement of ventilation. He proposed that new cities be constructed in the form of checkerboards whose black squares alone would be reserved for buildings and whose white squares would be covered with turf and trees. Such a plan, he said, "will be found handsome, & pleasant, and I do believe it to be the best means of preserving the cities of America from the scourge of yellow fever."[26] By the time Jefferson began to propose such schemes for avoiding urban disease he may have started to relent about the city. For once he came to view yellow fever as avoidable, at least in newly planned cities, a powerful anti-urban argument had been met in his mind. He still disliked the European city's spirit, manners, and principles, and he would have done without those if he could, but he would not abandon the American city to disease in the name of Providence or ideological commitment.

Nor was he prepared to abandon the nation to foreign domination by depriving it of manufacturing centers in times of war or national emergency. In the War of 1812 Jefferson's most basic value, his patriotic concern for national survival, was affected in a way that at last called forth from him a defense of the American city. Writing to Benjamin Austin in 1816, Jefferson points out that he can no longer say, as he did in the *Notes* that we should depend on England for manufactures. For in the seventeen-eighties, when he wrote the *Notes*, those who supplied raw materials to manufacturing nations in exchange for finished products were welcomed

17

as customers in a peaceful and friendly way. "But who in 1785," he asks, "could foresee the rapid depravity which was to render the close of the century the disgrace of the history of man? . . . We have experienced what we did not then believe, that there exists both profligacy and power enough to exclude us from the field of interchange with other nations: that to be independent for the comforts of life we must fabricate them ourselves. We must now place the manufacturer by the side of the agriculturist . . . Shall we make our own comforts, or go without them, at the will of a foreign nation? He, therefore, who is now against domestic manufacture, must be for reducing us either to dependence on that foreign nation, or to be clothed in skins, and to live like wild beasts in dens and caverns. I am not one of these; experience has taught me that manufactures are now as necessary to our independence as to our comfort."[27]

So by 1816 Jefferson was no longer as adamantly opposed to the American city as he had been in 1784.[28] His mind had been changed, however, not by his love of music but by his concern for national survival. He disliked the city's spirit, its manners, and its principles. He disliked its manufactures and its banks, but the international situation ultimately forced him to regard the city as an indispensable element of American life. He accepted the city, but he never really came to admire it. The famous qualifying letter was written to Austin on January 9, 1816, but it was followed by one written to William H. Crawford on June 20th of that year, and there Jefferson indicated that he would go so far in behalf of the city, but no further, in his concessions to expediency. "The exercise, by our own citizens of so much commerce as may suffice to exchange our superfluities for our wants, may be advantageous for the whole. But it does not follow, that with a territory so boundless, it is the interest of the whole to become a mere city of London, to carry on the business of one half the world at the expense of eternal war with the other half. The agricultural capacities of our country constitute its distinguishing feature; and the adapting of our policy and pursuits to that, is more likely to make us a numerous and happy people, than the mimicry of an Amsterdam, a Hamburgh, or a city of London."²⁹ Jefferson accepted the city without loving it wholeheartedly. The country and its yeomen he loved; the manufacturer's city he came to accept only as a source of independence and comfort in the world of 1812. And therefore, while the American city found in Jefferson a great intellectual defender at the beginning of the nineteenth century, the terms on which he defended it were not such as to encourage any enthusiastic, romantic celebration of urban life. In Jefferson's eyes the republic and the city joined hands only in a marriage of convenience, with no thoughts of love at all. Even in 1823 Jefferson at the age of eighty wrote from Monticello to William Short: "A city life offers you indeed more means of dissipating time, but more frequent, also, and more painful objects of vice and wretchedness. New York, for example, like London, seems to be a Cloacina of all the depravities of human nature. Philadelphia doubtless has its share. Here, on the contrary, crime is scarcely heard of, breaches of order rare, and our societies, if not refined, are rational, moral and affectionate at least."³⁰

However, because Jefferson was a practical statesman, he could not indulge in the luxury of a purely emotional assessment of urban life. Practical politics and empiricism weighed more heavily in his reflections than they did with most intellectual commentators on the American city. In a later generation, writers whose political concerns were less serious, or whose metaphysical aspirations were more abstract and more romantic, could not control their anti-city animus as easily as Jefferson controlled his. Emerson and Thoreau were confronted by a growing American reality, while Jefferson was haunted by a transatlantic image. Moreover, the two Transcendentalists were not active political men. The War of 1812, which had produced Jefferson's more favorable view of the city, had also increased the resemblance between the American city and the European city that Jefferson distrusted. And so the early nineteenth-century American city provided those who lacked Jefferson's political responsibility with an occasion for freely expressing their anti-urbanism, unchecked by his concerns for national safety. The age of Crèvecoeur, Franklin, and Jefferson ended on an irenical note; but soon the trumpets of a militant anti-urbanism filled the intellectual air, played by romantic metaphysicians with little sympathy for colonial ways of thought and feeling, and with no inclination to serenade the American city.

III

METAPHYSICS AGAINST THE CITY

THE AGE OF EMERSON

AFTER the War of 1812 the American city rapidly resumed the expansion that had been interrupted by hostilities, and expansion inevitably magnified the problems of city life.[1] Worries like Franklin's about water, fire, crime, and health continued in greater degree, but the spurt in urban population and beginning industrialization dramatically transformed the city and its role in the life of the nation. The age of the nineteenth-century city was opening before Jefferson's eyes. Pittsburgh and Cincinnati, at first centers for the distribution of seaboard goods, became market towns in which local manufacturers and farmers exchanged their products.[2] At the fall line of rivers in the East, new cities came to use water power for manufacture. The urban imperialisms of New York, Philadelphia, and Baltimore, as Arthur M. Schlesinger has called them, struggled with each other for control of trans-Appalachian trade as they searched and scrambled for new routes to the interior of the country. Baltimore constructed a turnpike to the eastern end of the Cumberland Road and Pennsylvania encouraged more wagon roads from Philadelphia. And when the Erie Canal was built as a water route from the Hudson River to Lake Erie, it combined with railroads to the West and a wonderful harbor to establish the preeminence of New York among American cities.[3]

In 1800 the population of New York City was 60,000; in 1860 it was 600,000. The *Charleston Mercury* complained that during this period Norfolk, Charleston, Savannah, and Mobile had become suburbs of New York,[4] while New York boosters took pride in its commercial supremacy and power. One of them, E. P. Belden, who is said to have written the most accurate and most complete mid-century guide to the city,[5] unabashedly affirmed in 1849 that the settlement of other American cities was stimulated by religious or political intolerance abroad, whereas New York was founded in the hope of commercial gain. It was, he said, the unrivalled metropolis of America, a "comprehensive emporium" in which representatives of all races from the world over were gathered together, a gas-lit nirvana of parks, shops, docks, and aqueducts. But Belden did not wish to wrangle with the city's moral critics; he freely acknowledged New York's spiritual limitations. It was not only a comprehensive emporium and a sunlit seaport but also a city of moral shadows.[6]

"Large cities," booster Belden admitted, "never present a pleasing view to the eye of the moralist. Where multitudes, of all opinions, characters and pursuits, congregate, vice is more open in appearance and more successful in operation. Companions are found to suit every taste, and individual turpitude escapes, in the mass, its merited disgrace." Addressing himself to the city's detractors, Belden granted that youth was constantly drawn into whirlpools of vice. Such newcomers, he said, are perhaps educated in correct principles but they are no match for wily traders in sin. "The theater presents its gorgeous pageantry; the haunts of fashionable intemperance exhibit their glittering decorations; the gaming table allures with its enticing arts; debauchery sets before [the inexperienced newcomer] its gilded pleasures; his eyes are dazzled, he becomes dizzy, and falls." Of course, Belden admitted that New York was morally superior to European cities of a comparable size. But this unusually honest advertiser was also constrained to say that New York's moral advantage over European cities was traceable to the superiority of the national character and not to anything peculiar to the city. Even this devoted admirer of New York was inclined to think that the same population, scattered through the towns and villages of the country, would conform to higher standards of conscience and of religion.[7]

If the author of an advertisement for New York acknowledged its great intellectual, literary, and religious failings at the midpoint of the nineteenth century, it is not surprising that Alexis de Tocqueville was fearful about the disturbing tendencies he saw in the American city before the Civil War. As a political observer he focused on other troubling aspects of city life. While Belden worried about vice and debauchery, de Tocqueville feared political insurrection in the city and urban tyranny over the rest of the country. The French visitor knew that in the eighteen-thirties the American city was still small by comparison to the rural element, but he expressed Jeffersonian fears about the city's menacing future even after Jefferson himself had managed to conquer some of them. Writing in 1835, de Tocqueville argued that the fact that America then had no dominating metropolis was one of those circumstances which tended to maintain a democratic republic in the United States. But he warned that "in cities men cannot be prevented from concerting together and awakening a mutual excitement that prompts sudden and passionate resolutions. Cities may be looked upon as large assemblies, of which all the inhabitants are members; their populace exercise a prodigious influence upon the magistrates, and frequently execute their own wishes without the intervention of public officers."[8]

While de Tocqueville observed that the United States had no dominating metropolis, he pointed out that it did have several large cities by the standards of the day and that these constituted a political menace. Speaking of Philadelphia with its 161,000 inhabitants and of New York with its 202,000, he admonished: "The lower ranks which inhabit these cities constitute a rabble even more formidable than the populace of European towns. They consist of freed blacks, in the first place, who are condemned by the laws and by public opinion to a hereditary state of misery and degradation. They also contain a multitude of Europeans who have been driven to the shores of the New World by their misfortunes or their mis-

23

conduct; and they bring to the United States all our greatest vices, without any of those interests which counteract their baneful influence. As inhabitants of a country where they have no civil rights, they are ready to turn all the passions which agitate the community to their own advantage; thus, within the last few months, serious riots have broken out in Philadelphia and New York." In spite of his fears about these riots de Tocqueville made clear that he did not view the city of the eighteen-thirties as an overpowering force in American social and political life. He pointed out, after mentioning the riots: "Disturbances of this kind are unknown in the rest of the country, which is not alarmed by them, because the population of the cities has hitherto exercised neither power nor influence over the rural districts." Still, de Tocqueville concluded ominously: "I look upon the size of certain American cities, and especially on the nature of their population, as a real danger which threatens the future security of the democratic republics of the New World." And, he gravely continued, "I venture to predict that they will perish from this circumstance, unless the government succeeds in creating an armed force which, while it remains under the control of the majority of the nation, will be independent of the town population and able to repress its excesses."[9]

If such an admonitory prediction could be issued by one of the most astute and controlled foreign observers ever to visit our shores, we should not be surprised to hear that some of our major literary figures expressed a less than admiring view of American urban life between the Revolution and the Civil War. Ralph Waldo Emerson said that he shuddered when he approached New York. The growth of northern cities made him even more anxious than Jefferson was made by European cities. Emerson's first philosophical work, *Nature*, appeared in 1836, right in the middle of the period that witnessed an eleven-fold increase in our urban population, and it was written partly in protest against nature's most palpable opposite, the growing American city. If Jefferson had cause for concern about urban culture in the seventeen-eighties, Emerson had eleven times that cause for concern a half-century later. Yet, while Jefferson, the empiricist, could see by 1816 that the manufacturing city was a political necessity in the nineteenth century, Emerson's transcendentalism made a similar insight very difficult.

Jefferson was a philosopher of the Enlightenment and the eighteenth century, but Emerson, following Coleridge's version of idealism, was in reaction against the traditions of British empiricism and French materialism. With the details of Emerson's metaphysics and theory of knowledge we need not be concerned; they are not very clear. But it is important to observe that his theory of knowledge was linked by him with his distaste for the city. Emerson distinguished sharply between the Understanding and Reason. The Understanding, according to Emerson, "toils all the time, compares, contrives, adds, argues; near-sighted but strong-sighted, dwelling in the present, the expedient, the customary," while Reason, which was for him the highest faculty of the soul, "never reasons, never proves; it simply perceives; it is vision."[10] Reason was the soaring faculty of the philosopher and the poet, while Understanding was that of the ordinary, lumbering scientist. And therefore, he said, Reason is characteristically exercised in the country, while the Understanding is an urban faculty: "the city delights the Understanding. It is made up of finites: short, sharp, mathematical lines, all calculable. It is full of varieties, of successions, of contrivances. The Country, on the contrary, offers an unbroken horizon, the monotony of an endless road, of vast uniform plains, of distant mountains, the melancholy of uniform and infinite vegetation; the objects on the road are few and worthless, the eye is invited ever to the horizon and the clouds. It is the school of Reason."[11]

In the essay *Nature*, Emerson tells us that empirical science is apt to cloud our sight and that by its concern with functions and processes may "bereave the student of the manly contemplation of the whole." The scientific savant, he said, becomes unpoetic, whereas the student of Nature, using his Reason, will see that his relation to the world will not be learned by "any addition or subtraction of

25

known quantities" but rather by "untaught sallies of spirit." There are far more excellent qualities than preciseness and infallibility; "a guess is often more fruitful than an indisputable affirmation"; and "a dream may let us deeper into the secret of nature than a hundred concerted experiments."[12] Although one may find many passages in which Emerson praised science and experiment, in the essay *Nature* he conceived of experiment as inferior to rational speculation, and regarded the products of experiment and artifice as less valuable than items in untouched Nature. The city was the home of artificial operations and was itself man's most imposing artificial construct. It was also the home of commerce, convention, custom, expediency, all of which Emerson distrusted.[13]

Unlike many romantic writers, however, Emerson did not identify the city with civilization and so he could praise the values of civilized life even though he attacked the American city. Neither the census, nor the size of cities, he argued, was the true test of civilization. It was "the kind of man the country turns out" and "not New York streets, built by the confluence of workmen and wealth of all nations, though stretching out toward Philadelphia until they touch it, and northward until they touch . . . Boston." And the kind of men Emerson valued, wherever they were, were "self-directed," "gifted," and "virtuous." They, rather than great cities of enormous wealth, made up the certificate of America's civilization.[14]

However much he distrusted the city, Emerson was too sociable, too inquiring, and too instinctively democratic to shun cities altogether, no matter how defective or insignificant they might appear *sub specie aeternitatis*. He was always more than willing to join a club in Boston since society, he said, was the most cordial tonic he knew.[15] His chosen club companions were men of culture with a wide range of experience, who had seen aspects of life unknown to gentlemen.[16] He recommended that men should not only enjoy congenial discourse while in cities, but that they should also educate their sympathies by mixing in different classes of society.[17] His related advice to the writer was to learn the essentials of his craft by mingling with the people in the streets and public squares.[18] He recognized too that cities have a magnetic attraction for men of genius[19] and that only the city is likely to provide certain educational institutions like the swimming school [!], the opera, the museum, the library, and the club, as well as orators and foreign travelers.[20] And since Emerson defined the task of civilization as partly a problem of giving every man access to the masterpieces of art, he admitted that some of the time every man should be in or near a large city.[21]

So Emerson had his urban tastes, and they produced a conflict in him. In 1844 he confided to his *Journal:* "I wish to have rural strength and religion for my children, and I wish city facility and polish. I find with chagrin that I cannot have both."[22] If he resolved this conflict, he resolved it primarily in favor of the country, because he held that for all of the city's stimulation and educational value, its atmosphere must be inhaled with caution and in very limited quantities. The Boston of Emerson's boyhood, where he played in gardens on Summer and Chauncy Streets and where he had driven his mother's cow to pasture along Beacon Street,[23] had been a pleasant mixture of city and country. But Boston's air had changed considerably in Emerson's own lifetime. In the early eighteen-thirties the railroad invaded Boston with the opening of lines to Lowell, Providence, and Worcester; and at the same time the spacious mansion of Gardiner Greene on Tremont Street, with a hillside garden that was one of the wonders of the first third of the nineteenth century, was sold to land speculators.[24] In 1834, two years before *Nature* appeared, Emerson finally moved to Concord at a time when he felt that a country environment was the most compelling need of his spirit. His conflicting feelings about the city were best expressed when he complained: "Whilst we want cities as the centers where the best things are to be found, cities degrade us by magnifying trifles. The countryman finds the town a chop-house, a barbershop. He has lost the grandeur of the horizon, hills and plains, and with them sobriety and elevation. He has come among a supple, glib-tongued tribe, who live for show, servile to public opinion."[25] Like

27

Jefferson before him, Emerson distrusted the moral environment of cities while recognizing some of their civilizing qualities. "They must be used," he admitted, "yet cautiously and haughtily, and will yield their best values to him who can do without them. Keep the town for occasions, but the habits should be formed to retirement. He who should inspire and lead his race must be defended from traveling with the souls of other men."[26] In the last analysis Emerson believed that the country, where man is closer to nature and God, was the better influence on a man's character, for there he learned the importance of tranquility, innocence, and patience, and there, Emerson added characteristically, he gained endurance from "plenty of plain food," unwatered milk, and cheaper and better sleep than is possible in the city.[27]

The way of life that Emerson preferred in spite of the minor advantages of the city is conveyed in that famous passage in which he describes his joy in a lonely, natural setting: "Crossing a bare common, in snow puddles, at twilight, under a clouded sky, without having in my thoughts any occurrence of a special good fortune, I have enjoyed a perfect exhilaration. I am glad to the brink of fear. In the woods, too, a man casts off his years, as the snake his slough, and at what period soever of life is always a child. In the woods is perpetual youth."[28] Readers who focus on the fact that Emerson was here reporting his experiences not only in the woods but also in a *common*—which is after all part of a town—might argue that the passage shows no antipathy to the city. But Emerson wrote in his *Journal* on December 8, 1834: "I do not cross the common without a wild poetic delight, notwithstanding the prose of my demeanor. Thank God I live in the country."[29] The point is that Emerson delighted in the common not because it was an artificial, cultivated, quasi-urban piece of ground but rather because he associated it with the country and the woods.

In the woods, according to Emerson, reason and faith operated at their best, in cooperation with nature. "There I feel nothing can befall me in life—no disgrace, no calamity (leaving me my eyes), which nature cannot repair."[30] And the woods as the scene of faith, Emerson contrasted with the city as the scene of artifice conceived as a form of deception. He wrote to Carlyle in 1840: "I always seem to suffer some loss of faith on entering cities. They are great conspiracies; the parties are all maskers, who have taken mutual oaths of silence not to betray each other's secret and each to keep the other's madness in countenance. You can scarce drive any craft here that does not seem a subornation of the treason."[31] In 1854 he returned to the same theme of urban deception, writing in his *Journal:* "Rest on your humanity, and it will supply you with strength and hope and vision for the day. Solitude and the country, books, and openness, will feed you; but go into the city—I am afraid there is no morning in Chestnut Street, it is full of rememberers, they shun each other's eyes, they are all wrinkled with memory of the tricks they have played, or mean to play, each other, of petty arts and aims all contracting and lowering their aspect and character."[32]

To avoid conspiracy and trickery Emerson's poet and good man was to go to the woods. There he would not need to employ artifice or deception (if only because there would be no one there to deceive). In the woods Emerson became the celebrated "transparent eye-ball," who *is* nothing and who sees all, who is part or parcel of God, and through whom the currents of Universal Being circulate. To this eye-ball the names of his nearest friends sound foreign. His acquaintances, brothers, masters and servants create trifling disturbances. Customary relations of the city dissolve in the wilderness, where Emerson found "something more dear and connate than in streets and villages."[33] And these facts, and others, Emerson concludes, "may suggest the advantage which the country-life possesses for a powerful mind, over the artificial and curtailed life of cities." The poet-orator who is bred in the woods will learn a lesson that he will never lose "in the roar of cities or the broil of politics."[34] The artificiality of the city will not conquer such natural men, Emerson assures us.

Emerson's writing is filled with this kind of feeling. He thought that the city was artificial, that it destroyed solitude, poetry, and

29

philosophy. In his lecture, "The Transcendentalist," delivered in January of 1842, he observes that it is a sign of the times that many intelligent and religious persons are withdrawing from the competition of the market and the caucus, and that they adopt a solitary and critical way of thinking. These are the Transcendentalists, he tells us as if he were describing the first Christians, who hold themselves aloof and who "prefer to ramble in the country and perish of ennui, to the degradation of such charities and such ambitions as the city can propose to them."[35] They are lonely men who repel influences and shun general society; "they incline to shut themselves in their chamber in the house, to live in the country rather than in the town."[36] And in his essay "Farming," first delivered as a lecture in 1858, he declares: "That uncorrupted behavior which we admire in animals and in young children belongs to him, to the hunter, the sailor—the man who lives in the presence of Nature. Cities force growth and make men talkative and entertaining, but they make them artificial."[37]

In his remark on uncorrupted behavior, Emerson might have been talking about his friend, Henry David Thoreau. At Thoreau's funeral in 1862, he complimented him by quoting the Greek saying that "one who surpasses his fellow citizens in virtue is no longer a part of the city. Their law is not for him, since he is a law to himself."[38] Thoreau "loved Nature so well, was so happy in her solitude, that he became very jealous of cities and the sad work which their refinements and artifices made with man and his dwelling. The axe was always destroying his forest. 'Thank God,' he said, 'they cannot cut down the clouds!' "[39] Thoreau's *Walden, or Life in the Woods,* is a bible of anti-urbanism, but it is also a diatribe against the life of the village and the farm. The values it espouses are essentially those of the isolated individual, living in nature and free of all social attachments. Emerson might have been describing Thoreau when he said of the Transcendentalists that they withdrew from conversation and the labors of the world; that they were not good citizens or good members of society; that they did not willingly contribute to public charities, nor participate in public religious rites, in the enterprises of education or in missions. "They do not even like to vote," he added.⁴⁰ In this spirit Thoreau retreated to Walden from which he shouted: "Simplicity, simplicity, simplicity! I say, let your affairs be as two or three, and not a hundred or a thousand; instead of a million count half-a-dozen, and keep your accounts on your thumb-nail."⁴¹ Understandably, Thoreau reported that he was "ever . . . leaving the city more and more and withdrawing into the wilderness" and that he "must walk toward Oregon and not toward Europe."⁴²

The distrust of the American city that Emerson and Thoreau shared was typical of the literature of American transcendentalism. Whatever differences existed among transcendentalists on this topic were differences of degree. Most of them distrusted or hated the city, but some, like Thoreau, fled from it to the woods alone; some, like Emerson, went to Concord where they could take sociability or leave it for the nearby woods; and some, like the Brook Farmers, went to the woods in socialist phalanxes. One of the transcendentalist Brook Farmers, Elizabeth Peabody, asked: "What absurdity can be imagined greater than the institution of cities?" Cities, she asserted, "originated not in love but in war. It was war that drove men together in multitudes, and compelled them to stand so close, and build walls around them. This crowded condition," she continued as she sounded the familiar theme of Nature versus Artifice, "produces wants of an unnatural character, which resulted in occupations that regenerated evil, by creating artificial wants." Then, as she laid out a task for future scholars, she announced: "The growth of cities, which were the embryo of nations hostile to each other, is a subject worthy the thoughts and pen of the philosophic historian." And at the end of her "Plan of the West Roxbury Community" she epitomized the protest of the Brook Farmers as a jeremiad against the "thraldom of city life."⁴³ Though Emerson shared many of Miss Peabody's feelings about the city, he would not allow himself to be bullied by his friends into *collective* farming. Emerson would not follow Miss Peabody or George Ripley to the cooperative hideout in Roxbury,⁴⁴ nor did he find himself walking with Thoreau to Oregon. He therefore occupied a middle position among the transcendental anti-urbanists. When he summarized his attitude toward the New England reformers in a lecture in 1844, he concluded that, for all of the lunacy of utopianism, it had engendered "a good result, a tendency to the adoption of simple methods, and an assertion of the sufficiency of the private man."[45] It was their search for both simplicity and privacy that led him and Thoreau to deplore both Boston and Brook Farm. The point that must be emphasized here is that the transcendental individualists, Emerson and Thoreau, could combine with the transcendental socialists in a united front against the American city.

As we have seen, however, Emerson's individualism was not as extreme as that of Thoreau, for Emerson did make some concessions to the city, while Thoreau did not. In Emerson's correspondence with the elder Henry James, one may observe Emerson's appreciation of aspects of the city; but this is coupled, as we might expect, with expressions of distaste for it. He reported to James that, like all solitary men, he shuddered as he approached New York. The hotels of New York were a "mortification" to him. The people oppressed him with their excessive virility, he noted in his *Journal,* "and would soon become intolerable if it were not for a few friends, who like women, tempered the acrid mass." So worried by the city was Emerson that he wrote to James in 1843: "I live in Concord, and value my nest, yet I will not promise to myself or another that I shall not in a year or two flee to Berkshire from so public and metropolitan a place as this quietest of country towns." Nevertheless, as we have seen, Emerson believed that Boston could be used by men of sensibility—from a distance. For him and the elder Henry James, the city was a meeting place for visiting intellectuals. Both of them undertook often to bridge the blank social gulfs they dreaded in the city by introducing each other to congenial friends. In 1849 Emerson remarked that James was an "expansive, expanding companion and would remove to Boston to attend a good club in a single night," and so, unlike Thoreau, would be a proper candidate for a new circle that would later become the Saturday Club.[46]

Thoreau was a very different person, and would make concessions neither to socialist Brook Farm nor to social Boston. When he was invited to visit the Saturday Club he responded characteristically: "The only room in Boston which I visit with alacrity is the Gentlemen's Room at the Fitchburg Depot, where I wait for cars sometimes for two hours, in order to get out of town."[47] By contrast to Emerson, Thoreau not only disliked the city but civilization itself. So we find him saying: "I wish to speak a word for Nature, for absolute freedom and wildness, as contrasted with a freedom and culture merely civil—to regard man as an inhabitant, or a part and parcel of Nature, rather than a member of society. I wish to make an extreme statement, if so I may make an emphatic one, for there are enough champions of civilization: the minister and the school-committee and every one of you will take care of that."[48] No wonder that the younger Henry James described Thoreau as a "sylvan personage." And the fact that this description appeared in James' critical study of Hawthorne may be connected with Hawthorne's frequent application of the word "sylvan" to his character Donatello in *The Marble Faun*. It is tempting to suppose that James regarded Thoreau as a sort of Donatello of American literature; and Hawthorne's Donatello, as we shall see in the next chapter, did not know sin or evil before he came to the decaying and corrupting city of Rome.

Our discussion so far has made abundantly clear that before the Civil War the main figures in American philosophical thought were persistently critical of the American city, and that when they made kind remarks about urban life, they usually made them grudgingly on grounds of the city's usefulness. Jefferson thought we needed cities as arsenals for the young republic; and Emerson admired them mainly, it would appear, for providing hotel rooms in which the Saturday Club might meet. Of the two, Jefferson reflected in more empirical terms about the city, while Emerson seemed to think of his anti-urbanism as a theorem in a metaphysical system. Emerson's opposition to the American city was elaborately linked with his world-view and epistemology, and typical of that "little epoch of fermentation," to use the younger Henry James' phrase, in which American transcendentalism flourished. By contrast, Jefferson's anti-urbanism seemed more peripheral to his thinking as well as to the spirit of Enlightenment of which he was such a distinguished representative. As a child of the eighteenth century, and as a deist in theology, Jefferson could not have thought as little of artifice nor of empirical science as Emerson did. For after all, God himself is the great artificer whose existence the deist can establish only by induction from the signs of design in the world. And therefore the sheer artificiality of the city could not have supplied Jefferson with the metaphysical objections to city life that it supplied to the romantic Emerson. In Emerson we find the beginnings of a more elaborate anti-urban ideology than we find in Jefferson, one that influences much of our literature to the present day.

The fact that Jefferson and Emerson were both suspicious of urban life shows that we cannot subsume all American anti-urbanism under romanticism or transcendentalism. The empiricist Jefferson and the transcendentalist Emerson could easily forget their philosophical differences as they made common cause against urbanism. By the middle of the nineteenth century at least two great intellectual debates had been conducted in America, one over the nature of knowledge and the other over the nature of the good society; but those who participated in them always found time to suspend their attacks on each other in order to train their guns on their common enemy, the city. Empiricist and transcendentalist, individualist and utopian socialist, all disliked the American city that was spreading across the nation and threatening to become one of the most powerful forces in American life. If Jefferson was prepared to encourage the growth of the American city, that was partly because he had not lived long enough to see it become like the European cities he distrusted. But Emerson faced a much more menacing American city, and his militant reaction to it set the tone of a great deal of American literature in the middle of the nineteenth century. Above all, it is certain that three famous philosophical minds—Jefferson, Emerson, and Thoreau—did nothing to encourage the American to love the American city. They preferred life in Monticello, in Concord, or beside Walden Pond. From these retreats they looked with suspicious eyes on Philadelphia, Boston, and New York.

IV

BAD DREAMS OF THE CITY

MELVILLE, HAWTHORNE, AND POE

THE animadversions in the writings of Jefferson, Emerson, and Thoreau are easily matched by those in the novels and stories of Herman Melville, Nathaniel Hawthorne, and Edgar Allan Poe. The philosophical statesman, the metaphysical essayist and the nature-lover were joined in their campaign against the evils of urbanism by the most gifted writers of fiction in the period before the Civil War. Jefferson and Emerson were comparatively optimistic about man's nature and his capacities, but literary men with darker thoughts agreed with them about the failings of the European city. The anxiety they all shared about the future of the American city demonstrated that theoreticians and novelists, optimists and believers in original sin—writers in different genres and of diverse doctrinal persuasions—all feared that the American city would go the wicked way of London, Liverpool, and Rome.

Whereas Jefferson was a political critic of the American city who could change his mind about it under altered circumstances, and whereas the metaphysically minded Emerson saw it as a menacing artifact, writers like Melville, Hawthorne, and Poe viewed the city from perspectives that were not primarily political or metaphysical. They were more interested in the mood and the atmosphere of city life. Their concern is more subjective than Jefferson's, more concrete and more dramatically articulated than Emerson's. Their pictures of city life are more darkly painted, and seldom relieved by Jeffersonian admissions of the city's value as an industrial center, or by acknowledgment of the virtues Emerson saw in its clubs and swimming schools. Being men of imagination and sensibility, Melville, Hawthorne, and Poe were disturbed and offended by the American city's effect on the human spirit in the period before the Civil War. And so for them the city scene was a backdrop for frightening experiences, personal defeat, icy intellectualism, heartless commercialism, miserable poverty, crime and sin, smoke and noise, dusk and loneliness. Often they confronted the city in bad dreams and nightmares. "For our dreamers," Harry Levin tells us, "America was a garden, an agrarian Eden, which was losing its innocence by becoming citified. Melville had located his City of Woe in London or Liverpool; Poe had tracked down imaginary crimes in the streets of an imagined Paris; and Hawthorne had exposed sins most luridly among the ruins of Rome."[1] They agreed with Jefferson that the American city was not yet as wicked as some European cities, but they too feared that it might repeat the histories of crime and sin enacted in London, Paris, Rome, and Liverpool.

Liverpool was typically seen by Melville's character Redburn in the misty twilight. When he first came to it he caught sight of "distant objects on shore, vague and shadowy shapes, like Ossian's ghosts."[2] Redburn's "isolation in Liverpool and the monstrous poverty of the place furnish glimpses of the growing conflict in the nineteenth century between man and the modern city," according to the Melville scholar, William Gilman. Melville had already attacked the evils of civilization in his earlier novels, *Typee* (1846) and *Omoo* (1847); but, as Gilman points out, Redburn "in his love of historical tradition . . . is the civilized Westerner who seeks to assimilate and be assimilated by his own culture." Liverpool hardly satisfied this desire, for "in Liverpool Redburn finds a commercial and relatively new metropolis, blind to the past and interested only in profit, inhuman in itself and dehumanizing its swarming populace. It allows widows and children to starve, and except for its churches, it thrusts Redburn out of doors. In Redburn's awareness of the way a large city crushes both body and spirit in man, Melville makes one of the earliest statements of the cleavage between the individual and his environment in the modern world."[3]

In *Redburn* one finds horrifying descriptions of the pestilential lanes and alleys of Liverpool, as well as a nightmarish picture of a London interior. Redburn was shocked to see death by starvation witnessed by Liverpool's inhabitants with indifference. In the chapter called "A Mysterious Night in London" Redburn speaks of the "unreality" of what he saw. The filth and degradation of Liverpool, and the gaudiness of London have further disturbing effects on young Redburn, who records his fear and uneasiness in a London gambling-house: "In spite . . . of the metropolitan magnificence around me, I was mysteriously alive to a dreadful feeling, which I had never before felt, except when penetrating into the lowest and most squalid haunts of sailor iniquity in Liverpool. All the mirrors and marbles around me seemed crawling over with lizards; and I thought to myself, that though gilded and golden, the serpent of vice is a serpent still." Redburn continues: "It was now grown very late; and faint with excitement, I threw myself upon a lounge; but for some time tossed about restless in a sort of nightmare."[4] In Liverpool and London the uneasy Melville not only sees the serpent of vice, but is upset by the transitoriness of urban life. His father's guidebook to Liverpool is no longer truthful: old sites and scenes have been destroyed or covered up and, predictably, Redburn's English sojourn is at its happiest in Chapter XLIII, entitled "He Takes A Delightful Ramble into The Country." In the country he says, "every blade of grass was an Englishman born. Smoky old Liverpool, with all its pitch and tar, was now far behind; nothing in sight but open meadows and fields."[5]

Melville's own experience in Liverpool dated from 1839, when he shipped to it as a common sailor out of New York. The New York of that day did not approach the dock sections of Liverpool in degree of "poverty and beggary." But when Redburn strolled through the wealthier quarters of Liverpool he discovered that "Liverpool, away from the docks, was very much such a place as New York. There were the same sort of streets pretty much; the same rows of houses with stone steps; the same kind of sidewalks and curbs; and the same elbowing, heartless-looking crowd as ever."[6] The theme of elbowing heartlessness in New York City was developed by Melville in *Pierre,* which appeared in 1852. There he more explicitly attacked commercialism, the city's greedy and grasping ways. Pierre was no match for this, for it was his "choice fate to have been born and nurtured in the country, surrounded by scenery whose uncommon loveliness was the perfect mould of a delicate and poetic mind."[7] He is the product of semifeudal family tradition which, Melville says, is impossible in the cities, where "families rise and burst like bubbles in a vat."[8] On the other hand the "country is not only the most poetical and philosophical, but it is the most aristocratic part of this earth, for it is the most venerable."[9] Poetical, philosophical, and aristocratic Pierre is out of place in the plebeian city. His beloved Lucy Tartan, although resident in the city, "did not at all love [it] and its empty, heartless, ceremonial ways."[10] Her feelings are echoed by other ladies in the novel, notably Isabel, Pierre's half-sister, and Delly, the girl they befriend. When that curious trio flees from the country to New York, Melville presents their flight in a chapter that is called "First Night of their Arrival in the City." The ladies are first of all struck by the hardness of the pavements. "Are they so hard-hearted here?" asks Isabel. And Pierre replies: "Ask yonder pavements, Isabel. Milk dropped from the milkman's can in December, freezes not more quickly on those stones, than does snow-white innocence, if in poverty it chance to fall in these streets."[11] Isabel complains: "I like not the town" and asks "Thinks't thou, Pierre, the time will ever come when all the earth shall be paved?" And Pierre answers: "Thank God that never can be!"[12] The city is represented in *Pierre* as the hard-hearted, paved home of intellect, and the novel is dotted with invidious comparisons between the metropolitan head and the rural heart.[13]

It should be said that Melville's distrust of the city was not invariably associated with anti-democratic feelings, even though in *Pierre* he calls the town the earth's "plebian portion," a fact plainly "evinced by the dirty unwashed face perpetually worn by the town."[14] His view of the democratic process has been rightly called paradoxical. At times he confesses to a "dislike to all mankind—in the mass," but at others he speaks as an egalitarian.[15] Like Emerson he did not indulge in the bigoted nativism of the mid-nineteenth century. Emerson exclaimed, "I see with joy the Irish emigrants landing at Boston, at New York, and say to myself, 'There they go—to school.' "[16] With equal democratic conviction Melville said passionately, "If they can get there, they have God's right to come; though they bring all Ireland and her miseries with them."[17] His hero, Redburn, was pleased by the friendly attitude toward the Negro in Liverpool where he had encountered his ship's "black steward, dressed very handsomely, and walking arm in arm with a good-looking English woman," while, "in New York, such a couple would have been mobbed in three minutes; and the steward would have been lucky to escape with whole limbs."[18] Melville did not fear the alien in the city, but he feared the city itself. It was one element in a great complex of ideas and attitudes that were distasteful to him.

Henry A. Murray, in his illuminating essay on *Pierre* tells us that Melville's decision to allow himself to be possessed by passion, intuition, and spirit "required, according to his dualistic logic, the complete rejection of everything that seemed to be opposed to it." And therefore, Murray says, "an uncompromising dichotomy was established." On the favored side of the spirit, which was symbolized by the sea, the boundless deeps, and Virgin Country, Melville put: "open space, freedom, adventure, danger, the Heart, spontaneity, selfless benevolence, single-hearted dedication, passionate undirected thought, truth-seeking, zeal for heaven and immortality, God and insanity." And "on the opposite side, symbolized by the land (*especially the city*), or by 'vulgar shoals' he put: closed or structured space, slavishness, family obligations, domestic comforts, safety, the Head, cool directed thinking, the calculations of self-interest, propriety, the World, and conventional commonsense. Over and over again, in multifarious rhetorical forms, Melville contrasts these two clusters of values and always champions the former, though his partiality is sometimes qualified . . ."[19] It is not surprising, then, that the commercial, intellectual, plebeian, smoky city contributes to the downfall of poor Pierre, who in his effort to support three women becomes a struggling writer, ultimately victimized and destroyed by the city's commercialism. Nature may have favored Pierre by birth in the country, but the city helps to ruin him in the end.

* * *

Although Melville despised the commercialism of the city, he did not look to utopian socialism for a solution of the problems created by urbanization. At the end of *Pierre* Melville satirizes a group of writers called "the Apostles," who are New York versions of New England reformers. In resisting utopianism Melville resembled not only Emerson but also Hawthorne, another anti-urbanite who did not think that socialism was the way out.[20] *The Blithedale Romance,* published as *Pierre* was in 1852, records Hawthorne's critical reaction to Brook Farm, where he lived for a while. He makes clear that the members of the Blithedale community were united in their distaste for certain aspects of city life and that their common reason for establishing the farm was negative rather than affirmative. "We had individually found one thing or another to quarrel with in our past life, and were pretty well agreed as to the inexpediency of lumbering along with the old system any further. As to what should be substituted there was much less unanimity."[21] Many of the more obnoxious aspects of the "old system" Hawthorne identified with the city. His hero complains of its duskiness and its bad air, of its hothouse warmth and excessive luxury, of its smoke, of the monotony of its buildings, of its slums. To these sensuously perceived limitations Hawthorne adds the more abstract defects of artificiality and conventionalism.

It would be wrong, however, to see nothing but anti-urbanism in *The Blithedale Romance,* for there is an extended section in which the hero, Coverdale, sets down his pleasure with Boston after re-

41

turning to it from Blithedale. He seeks relief in Boston and upon his arrival there remarks: "Whatever had been my taste for solitude and natural scenery, yet the thick, foggy, stifled element of cities, the entangled life of many men together, sordid as it was, and empty of the beautiful, took quite as strenuous a hold upon my mind. I felt as if there could never be enough of it."[22] He was most fascinated by the city's sounds—the stir of his hotel, the loud voices of its occupants, footsteps on the staircase, porters thumping their baggage on the floors, chambermaids scurrying through the halls, the tumult of the pavements outside, including a military band, fire engines, church bells, the noise of a nearby public hall which gave forth music and applause. "All this," he says in a passage that is notably concessive so far as the city is concerned, "was just as valuable, in its way as the sighing of the breeze among the birch-trees" at Blithedale.[23] And he even goes so far as to remark on a family he has observed in the city: "I bless God for these good folks! . . . I have not seen a prettier bit of nature, in all my summer in the country, than they have shown me here, in a rather stylish boarding-house. I will pay them a little more attention by and by."[24]

Coverdale's point of view in his boarding house, as Harry Levin has remarked, is that of an eavesdropper.[25] And as soon as Coverdale acknowledges his passive curiosity about city people, he adds a defense of it: "I felt a hesitation about plunging into this muddy tide of human activity and pastime. It suited me better, for the present, to linger on the brink, or hover in the air above it."[26] Coverdale, then, is the disembodied spectator of the city rather than the active participant in its life. His desire for isolation makes rural Blithedale too sociable for him and he abandoned his comrades periodically for the deepest woods. "Though fond of society," Coverdale admits, "I was so constituted as to need these occasional retirements, even in a life like that of Blithedale, which was itself characterized by a remoteness from the world. Unless renewed by a yet further withdrawal towards the inner circle of self-communion, I lost the better part of my individuality."[27] No wonder Hawthorne's New York contemporary, Evert Duyckinck, said of him:

"He is purely romantic, conscious all the while of the present world about him, which he lingers around without the energy of will to seize upon and possess."[28] And Levin[29] reminds us that Hawthorne in his story "Sights from a Steeple" suggested that "the most desirable mode of existence might be that of a spiritualized Paul Pry, hovering invisible round man and woman, witnessing their deeds, searching into their hearts, borrowing brightness from their felicity and shade from their sorrow, and retaining no emotion peculiar to himself." Unfortunately, Hawthorne adds, "none of these things are possible; and if I would know the interior of brick walls, or the mystery of human bosoms, I can but guess." His guessing, like that of his character Coverdale, was symbolically done in a steeple far above the city of Boston, whose obscured and desolate streets he saw as "a city of the dead."[30]

Understandably, the dead city could induce nightmares in Hawthorne as it did in Melville. In "My Kinsman, Major Molineux" Hawthorne tells of a country boy who comes by ferry to Boston one night in search of an affluent relative who has offered to help establish him in life. The boy walks through a fantastic city, which is represented in a ghostly manner. There he meets a variety of disturbing night-time figures from whom he seeks information about Major Molineux's whereabouts, "with stronger hopes than the philosopher seeking an honest man, but with no better fortune." At one point he tells of "a sensation of loneliness stronger than he had ever felt in the remotest depths of his native woods." After many strange encounters he falls asleep and meets his kinsman in a dream. The old gentleman has been tarred and feathered and sits in a cart which is dragged through the streets of Boston by a weird night-town crowd. When the boy awakes, he reports, "I have at last met my kinsman, and he will scarce desire to see my face again. I begin to grow weary of a town life, sir. Will you show me the way to the ferry?"[31]

In "The New Adam and Eve" Hawthorne focusses more on urban artificiality than on urban terror. In that story Adam and Eve return to Boston after all of its inhabitants have disappeared.

While walking through the town they visit a dry goods store, a church, a courthouse, a hall of legislature, a prison, a mansion on Beacon Street, a bank, a jeweller's shop, Harvard College Library, and finally the Mount Auburn Cemetery. Slowly they come to realize that the place was once inhabited. Hawthorne implies that they were innocently observing the remains of a race which paid a price for its "revolt against nature." But this criticism was not incompatible with Hawthorne's disapproval of Brook Farm, for it had afforded his hero Coverdale "some grotesque specimens of artificial simplicity" and was full of "Arcadian affectation."[32] The commercial city and the socialist farm had both departed from nature. Both were in this sense unreal.

Despite their worries about the American city, neither Hawthorne nor Melville regarded it with the degree of repugnance they reserved for certain European cities. In this respect they typify intellectual anti-urbanism before the Civil War, when the American city was between its period of colonial charm and its period of industrial chaos. But they have fears about the future of the American city, even while they accept de Tocqueville's conclusion that the adverse features of urbanism had not yet come to tyrannize American life. As we have seen, the New York described in *Pierre* was not as awful as the Liverpool described in *Redburn,* and, similarly, Hawthorne's treatment of Boston was very different from one of his treatments of Rome. The American city in the period before the Civil War was at some intermediate point on Hawthorne's "Celestial Railroad" in his story of that name, somewhere between his Celestial City and his City of Destruction, whereas Rome, as treated in *The Marble Faun,* was very close to the terminal at the less attractive end of the Bunyanesque line.

In the preface to *The Marble Faun,* Hawthorne made a famous statement about American life which Henry James was to amplify and modify in a more complex and more famous lament. Hawthorne complained of the lack of shadow, of antiquity, of mystery, of picturesque and of gloomy wrong, all of which, he said, "fill the mind everywhere in Italy, and especially in Rome," where most of the story in *The Marble Faun* takes place. Appropriately enough, therefore, *The Marble Faun* contains a catalogue of anti-urban expletives. Rome is a town of "evil scents," "hard harsh cries," "guilty shadows," "uneasy streets," "evil streets," "stony-hearted streets," "sin," "crime," "hard pavements," "mouldiness," "ancient dust," "cold formalities," "nervousness," "labyrinthine intricacies"; it is a "heap of broken rubbish," a "long decaying corpse"; it is "chilly," "gloomy," "melancholy," "sickly," "bloodstained," "dreary," "dreamy," "filthy," "foul," "corrupt," "wicked," "dissolute." Above all, it is "dusky," a word which is so overworked by Hawthorne in his descriptions of both Boston and Rome that Henry James apologized to William Dean Howells for using it too much in his book on Hawthorne.[33]

It is significant that Donatello in *The Marble Faun* loses his innocence in the dusky city; that "sickly Rome" steals away "his rich, joyous life." It is also significant that Hawthorne should often symbolize freedom from the awful aspects of Rome by life in a tower, high above the horrid noises, the evil scents and the wicked actions of the town. Both Donatello and Hilda are never happier than when they are in their respective towers, and so it is with Hawthorne in his steeple. "Oh that I could soar up into the very zenith," he exclaims there; and in the preface to *The House of the Seven Gables* he hopes that "the book may be read strictly as a Romance, having a great deal more to do with the clouds overhead than with any portion of the actual soil of the County of Essex." Coverdale, Donatello, Hilda, and Hawthorne himself are all eager to disentagle themselves from the city in which they are involved, either by the method of a spiritualized Paul Pry or by the method of flight to clouds and "aerial chambers" from which their vision of the city below could be dreamy, misty and disapproving. So disapproving that Hawthorne advises at one point in *The Marble Faun* that "all towns should be made capable of purification by fire, or of decay, within each half-century. Otherwise they become the hereditary haunts of vermin and noisomeness, besides standing apart from the possibility of such improvements as are constantly introduced into the rest of man's contrivances and accommodations. It is beautiful, no doubt, and exceedingly satisfactory to some of our natural instincts, to imagine our far posterity dwelling under the same roof-tree as ourselves . . . we may build almost immortal habitations, it is true; but we cannot keep them from growing old, musty, unwholesome, dreary, full of death-scents, ghosts and murder stains."[34]

In saying this Hawthorne closes the ideological pincers on the city, attacking it from two opposite directions. He attacks it as artificial and hence as lacking the permanence of nature; he finds newer countries like America wanting because they lack shadow, antiquity, mystery, and picturesque, gloomy wrong; but then when he finds a city which is possessed of all these lugubrious qualities, Hawthorne urges that it be burned to the ground. He cannot live in such a city, but he cannot live without it either. He hates its mustiness, its noise, its murder-scents, and its death-stains; but he admits that they are precisely what make it fascinating to him. Indeed he explicitly resolves any suspected contradiction in this combination of feelings when he tells us that "there is reason to suspect that a people are waning to decay and ruin the moment that their life becomes fascinating either in the poet's imagination or the painter's eye."[35] The moralist Hawthorne says one thing about the sickly city, the poet another. And the resolution of the conflict between them takes place in the steeple and the tower, which are connected with the fascinating plain of the decaying city but also removed from that plain. In the steeple and the tower, vision and imagination are still possible. From them the poet, like the painter, may look at the decaying city to his romantic heart's content, through dark and dreamy clouds.

Edgar Allan Poe could see cities of even lower repute through an even denser medium. In his poem, "The City in the Sea," in earlier versions entitled "The Doomed City" and "The City of Sin," a city is buried by water. It is a town in which "Death has reared himself a throne."

No rays from the holy heaven come down
On the long night-time of that town;
But light from out the lurid sea
Streams up the turrets silently.

The whole scene is ghostly and filmy. Suddenly a wave is created by the sinking towers of the city.

And when, amid no earthly moans,
Down, down that town shall settle hence,
Hell, rising from a thousand thrones,
Shall do it reverence.

We are not told by the poet what town this is, but it has been suggested that the origin of this poem is to be found in lines from Poe's longer poem, "Al Araaf":

Friezes from Tadmor and Persepolis—
From Balbec, and the stilly, clear abyss
Of beautiful Gomorrah! O, the wave
Is now upon thee—but too late to save![36]

Like so many romantic writers, Poe was fascinated not only by the lurid quality of ruined cities in the past but also by cities in his own day.[37] His story "The Man of the Crowd" shows London under a wave of people, and like Gomorrah it may be too late to save it from crowd and crime. One autumn evening, as the story opens, a man is sitting in his London hotel, looking out of the window at a principal thoroughfare of the city. As darkness approaches, he is struck by a "tumultuous sea of heads" outside, and this, we are tempted to think, is the counterpart of the sea over Gomorrah. At first, the narrator tells us, his "observations took an abstract and generalizing turn." He "looked at the passengers in masses, and thought of them in their aggregate relations." But soon he "descended to details and regarded with minute interest the innumerable varieties of figure, dress, air, gait, visage, and expressions of countenance."

Like Hawthorne, Poe is intrigued by all of this, but also like Hawthorne he does not admire it. As the night deepens, the harsher features of the crowd emerge just as the "City in the Sea" becomes

47

visible in lurid light. The late hour "brought forth every species of infamy from its den." "The rays of the gas-lamps, feeble at first in their struggle with the dying day, had now at length gained ascendancy, and threw over everything a fitful and garish lustre."

And now, after first seeing the crowd in masses and then in distinguishable subclasses, the person telling the story finally comes upon the "Man of the Crowd." With his brow to the windowpane, he suddenly spies a decrepit old man of sixty-five or seventy whose countenance arrests and absorbs his entire attention "on account of the absolute idiosyncrasy of its expression." Its effect is to convey "the ideas of vast mental power, of caution, of penuriousness, of avarice, of coolness, of malice, of bloodthirstiness, of triumph, of merriment, of excessive terror, of intense—of supreme despair." At once this face arouses the narrator's curiosity. He puts on his hat and coat, seizes his cane, makes his way into the street, and pushes through the crowd in pursuit. At length he comes within sight of his man, and follows him closely without attracting his attention. The pursued is short, very thin, and apparently very feeble. His clothes are filthy and ragged. His linen, although dirty is beautiful in texture. Through a tear in his clothing, the pursuer gets a glimpse of a diamond and a dagger. "These observations heightened my curiosity, and I resolved to follow the stranger whithersoever he should go."

The moral of the chase that follows is that this old man *needs* to be in a crowd. The narrator emphasizes the fact that whenever the old man comes to a relatively quiet or uncrowded street he walks more slowly, hesitates, is impatient and looks around him anxiously, becomes pale, is agitated or even agonized. But in the most crowded sections, which he constantly seeks out, his eyes roll wildly with pleasure, he shrieks with joy. The narrator follows him to a bar in a slum. The old man has to leave it at daybreak and retraces his steps to the most populous part of London near the hotel where the chase began. He spends the day walking to and fro in this crowd, watched by his now exhausted pursuer, who concludes his labors with the following remark: "As the shades of the second evening came on, I grew wearied unto death, and stopping fully in front of the wanderer, gazed at him steadfastly in the face. He noticed me not, but resumed his solemn walk, while I, ceasing to follow, remained absorbed in contemplation. 'This old man,' I said at length, 'is the type and the genius of deep crime. He refuses to be alone. *He is the man of the crowd.*' "

It is because the man of the crowd refuses to be alone that he must, the narrator thinks, be filled with some secret horror, some mystery that can never be revealed. The need to be in the crowd is identified by Poe with some problem of conscience, some failing, a "burden so heavy in horror that it can be thrown down only into the grave." So it is that the epigraph of the story is quoted as coming from La Bruyère: "Ce grand malheur, de ne pouvoir être seul." Poe, it should be emphasized, does not celebrate the city for its capacity to grant relief from such horrors of the soul. Rather, he leaves us with the impression that the city is *the* home of "the genius of deep crime."

"The City in the Sea," "The Man in the Crowd," "The Murders in the Rue Morgue" deal with buried cities of the distant past or with nineteenth-century London and Paris, but Poe was of course also concerned with the American city of his own day. He shared Hawthorne's and Melville's premonitions and fears about it. In one of his letters of 1844 to the newspaper, the *Columbian Spy,* he reports that in Manhattan some of "the most picturesque sites for villas to be found within the limits of Christendom" are "doomed." "The spirit of Improvement has withered them with its acrid breath. Streets are already 'mapped' through them, and they are no longer suburban residences, but 'town-lots.' In some thirty years every noble cliff will be a pier, and the whole island will be densely desecrated by buildings of brick, with portentous facades of brownstone."[38] By that time, we are led to think, the Man of the Crowd will have taken up his residence in Manhattan. "I could not look on the magnificent cliffs, and stately trees, which at every moment met my view, without a sigh for their inevitable doom—inevitable and swift. In twenty years, or thirty at farthest, we shall see here

THE INTELLECTUAL VERSUS THE CITY

nothing more romantic than shipping, warehouses and wharves."[39] Wonderful opportunities for the Man of the Crowd were already developing. Poe complains that "Entire districts . . . are left, for weeks, in outer darkness, at night; the lamp-lighting functionaries flatly refusing to light up; preferring to appropriate the oil to their own private and personal emolument, and thus have a penny in the pocket, with which to console themselves for the dismissal which is inevitable. Three quarters of a mile on the Third Avenue, one of the most important and most thronged thoroughfares, have been thus left in darkness visible for the last fortnight or more."[40] What would Poe have said of Third Avenue's darkness during the decades in which the Elevated covered it? How the Man of the Crowd could have cavorted down it to the Bowery, Chatham Square, and Park Row!

Poe did not limit his criticism to Manhattan. He saved his most forceful language for Brooklyn, of which he complained: "I know few towns which inspire me with so great disgust and contempt. It puts me often in mind of a city of silvered-gingerbread; no doubt you have seen this article of confectionery in some of the Dutch boroughs of Pennsylvania. Brooklyn, on the immediate shore of the Sound, has, it is true, some tolerable residences; but the majority, throughout, are several steps beyond the preposterous. What can be more sillily and pitiably absurd than palaces of painted white pine, fifteen feet by twenty?—and of such is this boasted 'city of villas.' . . . In point of downright iniquity—such sin, I mean, as would consign a man, inevitably, to the regions of Pluto—I really can see little difference between the putting up of such a house as this, and blowing up a House of Parliament, or cutting the throat of one's grandfather."[41]

Poe was, of course, speaking facetiously when he said that poor Brooklyn in 1844 was a City of Sin, that its architects' crimes were as iniquitous as the crimes of London's man of the crowd, and those of the Parisian "man of the woods" (in Malay "orangutan") who slits someone's throat in "The Murders in the Rue Morgue." For the sins of Brooklyn in the *Doings of Gotham* are more like the sins of Boston in *The Blithedale Romance,* far less awful than those of London, Paris, Liverpool, and Gomorrah. The doings of Gotham, as Poe visualizes them, were no more wicked than the shouting of fishwomen, charcoal-men, monkey-exhibitors, and clam-and-cat-fish-venders, no more reprehensible than the rumblings of vehicles over "unmeaning round stones—than which a more ingenious contrivance for driving men mad through sheer noise, was undoubtedly never invented."[42] Perhaps that is why Poe transferred the murder of Mary Rogers from Staten Island to Paris when he came to describe it in "The Mystery of Marie Rogêt." Paris must have seemed like a much more appropriate place than Staten Island for a mystery of such dimensions, and a Paris *grisette* seemed like a more appropriate victim than Mary Cecilia Rogers of Richmond. In 1844 the wrongs of New York, then, were not as gloomy as Poe thought they were to become, for at that time he tended to identify them with round stones, brownstones, black streets, blue boards and harsh cries. Along with other writers of fiction before the Civil War, Poe saw atrocities occurring mainly in European cities while he contented himself with seeing handwriting on the walls of American cities. This handwriting could not be erased from Poe's mind by the optimism and pragmatism of the older Jefferson. For during the half-century between 1816—when Jefferson penned his irenicon on the American city—and the end of the Civil War, things were happening of which Jefferson did not dream in his philosophy. As they studied these events, professional dreamers like Poe wrote fantasies about urban problems of the future.

In his story "Mellonta Tauta" Poe looks at the nineteenth century from a position which is far removed from its cities. The narrator is aboard a balloon in the year 2848 (Poe's balloon may be the counterpart of Hawthorne's tower), looking at country once inhabited by a portion of the "Knickerbocker tribe of savages," much as Poe had looked at the doomed city in the sea. The balloonist finds that, absurdly enough, the "Amriccans" governed themselves. He also reports that just when philosophers were coming to recognize the limitations of Republican political doctrine, "a fellow of

51

the name of *Mob* . . . took everything into his own hands and set up a despotism, in comparison with which those of the fabulous Zeros and Hellofagabaluses were respectable and delectable. This *Mob* (a foreigner, by the by), is said to have been the most odious of all men that ever encumbered the earth. He was a giant in stature—insolent, rapacious, filthy; had the gall of a bullock with the heart of an hyena and the brains of a peacock. He died, at length, by dint of his own energies, which exhausted him. Nevertheless, he had his uses, as everything has, however vile, and taught mankind a lesson which to this day it is in no danger of forgetting —never to run directly contrary to the natural analogies. As for Republicanism, no analogy could be found for it upon the face of the earth—unless we except the case of the 'prairie dogs,' an exception which seems to demonstrate, if anything, that democracy is a very admirable form of government—for dogs."[43]

It is not strange, then, that the anti-democratic Poe did not share Jefferson's optimism about the possible worth of the American city. In "Mellonta Tauta" Poe has New York destroyed in 2050 by an earthquake which is so disastrous that by 2848 there is no reliable evidence for constructing an archaeological theory of the natives' customs and manners. The natives, Poe reports in retrospect, were by no means uncivilized. "It is related of them that they were acute in many respects, but were oddly afflicted with a monomania for building what, in the ancient Amriccan, was denominated 'churches' —a kind of pagoda instituted for the worship of two idols that went by the names of Wealth and Fashion. In the end, it is said, the island became, nine-tenths of it, church."[44] In his story "Some Words with a Mummy," Poe changes the perspective of his approach to the nineteenth-century city. After a conversation with an Egyptian mummy, who has been brought back to life by a sort of electric shock treatment and who compares his civilization with America's, Poe utters his famous lament: "I am heartily sick of this life and of the nineteenth century in general. I am convinced that everything is going wrong."[45] Railroads, mechanical forces, artesian wells, Progress, Democracy, and Steam seem flat and unprofitable to him, just as glare, glitter, and gaslight do in his "Philosophy of Furniture." What he seeks is a room of his own where "Repose speaks in all."

In summary it may be said that commerce, crime, crowds, and conventionalism were linked with the city in a horrible alliterative dream by our most important writers of fiction before the Civil War. Though they saw the American city in a light less lurid than that which they turned on London, Liverpool, Paris, and Gomorrah, they feared the future New York. And therefore, those who see wishes in dreams might reasonably see a desire for the destruction of the American city in their more fantastic tales of urban life. "All towns," to repeat Hawthorne's grim advice, "should be made capable of purification by fire, or of decay, within each half-century."

V

THE DISPLACED PATRICIAN

HENRY ADAMS

A WRITER who thought the American city should be purified by fire might have found much more reason to think so in the generation that followed the Civil War, and much more to burn. For this was the generation in which, as Arthur Schlesinger says, "the city took supreme command." Between 1860 and 1900 the urban population quadrupled while the rural population only doubled and, Schlesinger reminds us, "In the century from 1790 to 1890 the total population had grown sixteen-fold, while the urban segment grew one hundred and thirty-nine-fold."[1]

Toward the end of the nineteenth century the great exodus from the countryside was in full force, and New England became the scene of deserted hill villages and farms, while the city's problems became the great social problems of the nation. The city became the home of the elevated railroad, the trolley-car, the cable car, the subway, the apartment house, the telephone, the skyscraper, and the massive railroad station; and it continued to encourage the growth of political machines and the rapid proliferation of slums. The Nature of which Emerson spoke was rapidly disappearing, and the romanticism to which he subscribed was taken less and less seriously by men of letters and philosophers. The farmer's dismay at the expansion of urban power received ideological and political expression in the Populist movement, but it would be hard to find after the Civil War a thinker of Jefferson's stature who would defend similar agrarian views on the nature of the good life and the good society. If hostility to the American city continued, it was not given striking intellectual formulation or moving literary expression by writers in revolt against civilization as such. As we continue our selective study of major writers in American intellectual history, concentrating primarily on figures whose ideas and writings continue to deserve interest on more than antiquarian grounds, we find more of a disposition to criticize the American city out of a concern for civilization than a disposition to attack it in the name of nature. Henry Adams and Henry James are two of the most distinguished of such writers. They lived in what has come to be called the Gilded Age and the gilt they saw was all in the city. They were neither romanticists nor agrarians, and they serve therefore as effective counterexamples to the thesis that all of American anti-urbanism may be explained by a universal romantic preference for the forest over the town.

It is true, of course, that one may find certain elements of romanticism in the writings of Henry Adams. Max Baym[2] has argued that Adams' view of himself as a failure in the *Education* links him with a tradition in romantic French writing; and William Jordy has pointed out how much Adams' view that reason is the degradation of instinct links him with the anti-intellectualism of the Romantics.[3] Also, Adams' treatment of the natives in his book on Tahiti might be cited as evidence of his romantic primitivism, and his passion for the Middle Ages is to some extent reminiscent of Walter Scott. But the one element of romanticism that seems utterly absent from Adams' thought is a distaste for civilization as such, a pastoralism of the kind that one finds in Emerson and Thoreau. Adams presents a critique of contemporary civilization, of course, but it grows out of a perverse idea of a better form of civilization, and not out of a desire to flee from civilization to nature.

Adams, born in 1838, came to maturity at a time when the city was a growing power in America; so, unlike Jefferson, he could not speak of it as a remote future phenomenon or as something existing in Europe alone. For Adams the age of Walden, Concord, and Monticello was over. He was not a farmer, a hermit, a transcendentalist, or a utopian socialist. Adams was a refined, highly civilized, urbane, and urban man, whose animadversions on the American city are all the more interesting and all the more complex because they cannot be subsumed under a literary formula or doctrinaire philosophy. He looked at urbanized, industrialized, immigrant-filled America with fewer preconceptions about nature than Emerson, and fewer political responsibilities than Jefferson. He was not given to calling the city unreal; nor was he given to confronting it in lurid dreams. For Adams the American city was a solid, three-dimensional, menacing thing. He therefore concentrated his attention on its tendency to destroy his most cherished values, to fall short of his conception of civilization at its best.

Henry Adams was not at every stage of his life a sharp critic of urban civilization or its prospects. His most distinguished contribution to scholarship, his *History of the United States during the Administrations of Jefferson and Madison,* makes clear that he was no follower of Jefferson's view of the city as that was expounded in the *Notes on Virginia.* In his *History* Adams contrasted the lofty, humanitarian ideals of Jefferson with the anti-urban views in the *Notes on Virginia,* observing that the latter seemed even narrower than "ordinary provincialism." "Cities, manufactures, mines, shipping and accumulation of capital led, in [Jefferson's] opinion, to corruption and tyranny,"[4] said Adams, as he remarked on the clash between Jefferson's agrarianism and "his intellectual instincts of liberality and innovation."[5] Even Jefferson, he noted, "with all his liberality of ideas, was Virginian enough to discourage the introduction of manufactures and the gathering of masses in the cities, without which no new life could grow."[6] Adams did not disguise his contempt for the Colonial Virginian's axiomatic conviction that Virginia was the "typical society of a future Arcadian America."[7] The height of an ordinary Virginian's ambition, he pointed out sardonically, was to fix upon the national government the stamp of his own idyllic conservatism. Since Virginians were debarred from manufactures, without shipping, and without domestic markets, they knew no other resource than agriculture. And what is more, according to Adams, they lacked church, university, schools, or literature of any kind that would foster intellectual life.

There is no doubt, then, that Henry Adams was not an agrarian, and that when he wrote his *History* he had the greatest respect for the values of urban civilization. Without manufactures and masses in the cities, he thought, the young nation could not grow. But the nation's urban population in 1800 was so small as to be trifling. The combined population of Boston, New York, Philadelphia, and Baltimore was 180,000; they were the only towns containing a white population of more than 10,000; whereas the total population of the country was more than five million. Life in these cities left much to be desired, according to the cultivated, intellectual author of the *History*. Even Boston, the most cosmopolitan part of New England "made no strong claim to intellectual prominence."[8] Its entertainment, its science, its poetry, its philosophy were all without distinction, he said. New York in 1800, Adams reported, had something of an advantage in being capable of innovation, chiefly because it was not restricted by the kind of morality and religion that dominated New England. But it was backward too. And Philadelphia, although it was the "intellectual center of the nation"[9] was to Adams no Athens. As he made light even of Philadelphia's accomplishments, Adams concluded his discussion of intellectual life in New England and the Middle States by declaring: "The labor of the hand had precedence over that of the mind throughout the United States. If this was true in the city of Franklin, Rittenhouse, and West, the traveller who wandered farther toward the south felt still more strongly the want of intellectual variety, and found more cause for complaint."[10]

In concluding his discussion of American ideals, Adams asked a series of testing questions which made it clear that he was not then a romanticist just as he was not an agrarian: "These were in effect the problems that lay before American society: Could it transmute its social power into the higher forms of thought? Could it provide for the moral and intellectual needs of mankind? Could it take permanent political shape? Could it give new life to religion and

57

art? Could it create and maintain in the mass of mankind those habits of mind which had hitherto belonged to men of science alone? Could it physically develop the convolutions of the human brain? Could it produce, or was it compatible with the differentiation of a higher variety of the human race? Nothing less than this was necessary for its complete success."[11] He might have added that nothing less than a flourishing urban civilization could hasten that success.

During the years that followed the completion of his *History* in 1890, Adams gave voice to a change of heart and mind that deeply affected his view of the American city. In 1894, echoing Poe, Adams wrote to his friend, Charles Milnes Gaskell, that the nineteenth century had become rotten and bankrupt. William Jordy has argued persuasively that the spiritual shift from the *History* to the *Education of Henry Adams* and the *Mont-Saint-Michel and Chartres* was one during which Adams abandoned the confident Comtism of the earlier work.[12] For at least in the early years of the *History's* composition, Adams hoped that most of the burning questions he had posed in his chapter on American ideals would be answered affirmatively; that American society *would* transmute its social power into higher forms of thought; that it *could* provide for the moral and intellectual needs of mankind; that it *could* give new life to religion and art; that it *could* create and maintain in the mass of mankind those habits of mind which had hitherto belonged to men of science alone; that it *could* physically develop the convolutions of the human brain; and that American society was likely to produce a higher variety of the human race. But the older Adams was a different man. Gone was his optimism and his nineteenth-century liberalism, his faith in science, and his hope for the mass of mankind. In their place came pessimistic, turgid, philosophico-historical speculation fed by his misunderstanding of physics and biology, and leading to the conviction that the second law of thermodynamics dictated a cold, gray death for all of civilization.

The death that Adams predicted was that of urban civilization as he knew it throughout the western world, and particularly as he knew it in his own country. The crowd, the bankers, and the Jews all became obsessive symbols of the cities he came to despise. In his *History* he was, as we have seen, condescending about the Boston, Philadelphia, New York and Washington of 1800. But in his *Education* he looked at post-Civil War New York—which had followed the urbanizing course he had seemed to admire in his *History*—with all the disturbed feelings of a displaced patrician. Coal, iron, and steam had triumphed over agriculture, handiwork, and learning, and Adams' world, as he put it succinctly, "was dead." "Not a Polish Jew fresh from Warsaw or Cracow," he continued, "not a furtive Yacoob or Ysaac still reeking of the Ghetto, snarling a weird Yiddish to the officers of the customs—but had a keener instinct, an intenser energy, and a freer hand than he [Adams]— American of Americans, with Heaven knew how many Puritans and Patriots behind him, and an education that had cost a civil war."[13]

Although the literary expression of Adams' change of heart about urbanization takes place primarily between the appearance of the first volume of the *History* in 1889 and the *Education,* which was apparently begun around 1902, there were indications of disapproval of city life in his correspondence and writing before the turn of the twentieth century—disapproval that did not fit with the optimistic tone of the *History.* The *Education* itself speaks of such disapproval existing as far back as 1868 when he returned to this country after a stay in England. As reported in the *Education,* Adams' reaction to the New York of 1868 was different only in degree from his reaction to Boston upon coming home from England. The Boston of 1868 seemed simple to the author of the *Education,* just as it seemed simple to the author of the *History,* but in 1868 he said, "Boston meant business" and the Bostonians were also feverishly building railways.[14] And, although the author of the *Education* would have liked to help in building railways, he reported with mock humility that he had no education for such a task. He was "not fit," he complained, and he had been made unfit by the New York and Boston of 1868 precisely in the degree to which they had abandoned their colonial simplicity and adopted lines of development he had recommended by implication in his *History*. There he had scoffed at Jefferson for thinking that cities, manufactures, mines, shipping and accumulation of capital would lead to corruption and tyranny. Now he pitied himself for being buffeted and dislocated by these very urbanizing forces. "The world after 1865," he lamented in the *Education*, "became a banker's world, and no banker would ever trust one who had deserted State Street."[15]

* * *

One of the most illuminating ways in which to observe Adams' development into the irritated anti-urbanist of the *Education* is to read the letters that treat the various places he had known in his life: mainly, Boston, Quincy, London, Paris, and Washington. There one finds mounting anti-urban feeling, beginning in young manhood, increasing after the Civil War, coming to a climax in the nineties, and continuing into the obsessed last years of his life. Although in the *History* he published some of his more favorable hopes for the city in America, even prior to its publication there were indications of what his later view might become once he could formulate his antipathy with the help of a philosophy of history and a formalized prejudice against the Jews. This may be seen by turning first to the development of his views on Boston, and then to his disappointment with Quincy, London, Paris, and his once-beloved Washington. For it was after he had exhausted, or had been exhausted by, all of them that he turned to the civilization of the Middle Ages for solace.

For seven years, from 1870 to 1877, Adams lived in Boston while he taught medieval history at Harvard; but he was not, he said forcibly, a Bostonian: "he felt himself shut out of Boston as though he were an exile; he never thought of himself as a Bostonian; he never looked about him in Boston, as boys commonly do wherever they are, to select the street they like best, the house they want to live in, the profession they mean to practise. Always he felt himself somewhere else."[16] As early as 1858 he had written to his brother,

Charles Francis Adams, from Berlin: "I have never felt quite so glad of being out of Boston as I felt after reading that [his brother's] epistle. There was in it a sort of contented despair, an unfathomable depth of quiet misery that gave me a placid feeling of thankfulness at being where I am . . . For myself, I believe that I can find more interesting women among the very dregs of society here, than Papanti's Hall can turn out."[17] As we shall see, Adams' opinion of Berlin was not high, so that putting Boston's women below Berlin's was as severe a condemnation of them as Adams could issue. In a famous letter of advice to Henry Cabot Lodge, written in 1872, Adams reported that "Boston is running dry of literary authorities."[18] In 1876 he wrote to his friend Charles Milnes Gaskell that in Boston "there is no society worth the name, no wit, no intellectual energy or competition, no clash of minds or schools, no interests, no masculine self-assertion or ambition. Everything is respectable, and nothing amusing. There are no outlaws. There are not only no strong convictions, but no strong wants . . . But when a society has reached this point, it acquires a self-complacency which is wildly exasperating. My fingers itch to puncture it; to do something which will sting it into impropriety."[19]

By 1895, the tone of his attacks on Boston became more strident, in harmony with the theory of history he was developing. He no longer confined himself to protesting against complacency and dullness, but now dragged poor Boston into his philosophical system. He traced for his brother, Brooks, the decline of their ancestry from its palmy days in Normandy to its end in New England. "So we get Boston," was his flat conclusion, as he depicted the decay of his forbears' art, their religion, and their military tastes.[20] In 1896 he was deep in his absurdity about the Jews and so he pined for Boston to get itself some "real Jews. The imitation Pharisee is maddening."[21] No Conservative Christian Anarchist, as he began to call himself, could live in Boston.[22] In 1896 he urged his brother Brooks to clear out of Boston.[23]

And when Henry James published his *William Wetmore Story and His Friends* in 1903, Adams congratulated him for gently stripping Adams' intellectual generation in Boston and putting a surgical knife to their ribs. "The painful truth," Adams confessed, "is that all of my New England generation . . . were in actual fact only one mind and nature; the individual was a facet of Boston. We knew each other to the last nervous center, and feared each other's knowledge. We looked through each other like microscopes. There was absolutely nothing in us that we did not understand merely by looking in the eye. There was hardly a difference even in depth, for Harvard College and Unitarianism kept us all shallow. We knew nothing—no! but really nothing of the world . . . God knows that we knew our want of knowledge! the self-distrust became introspection—nervous self-consciousness—irritable dislike of America, and antipathy to Boston."[24]

In 1907 he despondently associated himself with Boston society and saw in himself a disease that was present in the Cabots too. Upon receipt of the *Letters of Elizabeth Cabot* he writes: "Boston cankers our hearts. I feel it in me. We lived side by side for years, and she seemed a worldly friend of every day. I was of the same loaf. I recognise the strange disease. I'm just like a Cabot. So are we all. Sturgis Bigelow, Brooks, all all all, nothing but Cabots, and run Art Museums, and change our will walking down to State Street! Oh World, Oh Life, Oh Time."[25]

If Boston proved so cankering to Adams' heart, what alternatives were there for a man of his background and temperament in the Gilded Age? There was Quincy, of course, his ancestral Adams home. And he did speak of Quincy nostalgically in the *Education*. In his boyhood, Quincy represented the country as against the town, he said. "Town," he reminisced, "was winter and confinement, school, rule, discipline; straight, gloomy streets, piled with six feet of snow in the middle; frosts that made the snow sing under wheels or runners; thaws when the streets became dangerous to cross; society of uncles, aunts, and cousins who expected children to behave themselves, and who were not always gratified; above all else, winter represented the desire to escape and go free. Town was restraint, law, unity. Country, only seven miles away, was liberty, diversity, out-lawry, the endless delight of mere sense impressions given by nature for nothing, and breathed by boys without knowing it."[26] In his youth, Quincy was only two hours' walk from Beacon Hill and yet it was a different world. Quincy's proximity to Boston produced conflict for the boy who shuttled between them, and thereby intensified what Adams conceived as the great problem of his life—to unite two sets of spiritual opposites: "for two hundred years, every Adams, from father to son, had lived within sight of State Street, and sometimes had lived in it, yet none had ever taken kindly to the town, or been taken kindly by it. The boy inherited his double nature."[27]

The struggle between town and country for his spirit was intensified in young Henry Adams by the fact that his grandfather Brooks was one of the wealthiest Bostonians of the time. Of the two families, Henry "liked the Adams side best, but for no other reason than that it reminded him of the country, the summer, and the absence of restraint." Yet he also felt that Quincy was inferior to Boston, and that Boston looked down on Quincy. The reason, Adams says, "was clear enough even to a five year old child. Quincy had no Boston style. Little enough style had either; a simpler manner of life and thought could hardly exist, short of cave-dwelling. The flint-and-steel with which his grandfather Adams used to light his own fires in the early morning was still on the mantelpiece of his study. The idea of a livery or even a dress for servants, or of an evening toilette, was next to blasphemy. Bathrooms, water-supplies, lighting, heating, and the whole array of domestic comforts, were unknown at Quincy. Boston had already a bathroom, a water-supply, a furnace and gas. The superiority of Boston was evident, but a child liked it no better for that." Quincy, Adams said, "smacked of colonial age, but not of Boston style or plush curtains. To the end of his life he never quite overcame the prejudice thus drawn in with his childish breath. He never could compel himself to care for nineteenth century style. He was never able to adopt it, any more than his father or grandfather or great-grandfather had done. Not that he felt it as particularly hostile, for

63

he reconciled himself to much that was worse; but because, for some reason, he was born an eighteenth century child."[28]

Quincy was not represented by Adams as Emerson represented the Wilderness, although there is a certain similarity in their praise of freedom and simplicity, and their dispraise of State Street. As a boy, Adams "leaned towards the Concord faith,"[29] but "he never reached Concord, and to Concord Church he, like the rest of mankind who accepted a material universe, remained always an insect, or something much lower—a man."[30] In turn, Emerson's philosophical protest was regarded by the Adams clan as "naif."[31] Neither transcendental forest nor Jeffersonian farm provided an alternative to Boston for Adams in his disappointment with the effects of coal, steam, and iron on American society. He had no inclination to walk toward Oregon with Thoreau, since "neither to a politician nor to a businessman nor to any of the learned professions did the West promise any certain advantage, while it offered uncertainties in plenty."[32] When he went West in 1871 and felt the atmosphere of Indians and buffaloes, his unromantic and un-agrarian comment was that "one saw the last vestiges of an old education, worth studying if one would; but it was not that which Adams sought; rather, he came out to spy upon the land of the future."[33] In 1889, when his mother died, he returned to Quincy and sadly observed: "Apparently I am to be the last of the family to occupy this house which has been our retreat in all times of trouble for just one hundred years. I suppose if two Presidents could come back here to eat out their hearts in disappointment and disgust, one of their unknown descendants can bore himself for a single season to close up the family den. None of us want it, or will take it. We have too many houses already, and no love for this."[34] With the abandonment of the Quincy retreat, one more alternative to Boston and New York was closed to Adams.

If he had been Henry James, the cities of Europe might have provided an avenue of escape, but Adams' net judgment of the

cities of Europe was negative. The word "net" should be emphasized since Adams' writings do contain qualified expressions of approval for some of those cities. In 1858 the *Education* reports of
London that "A certain style dignified its grime; heavy, clumsy,
arrogant, purse-proud, but not cheap; insular but large; barely
tolerant of an outside world, and absolutely self-confident."[35] And
Adams intended to praise the unfashionable London of 1864 in a
passage that T. S. Eliot once quoted with approval: "Fashion was
not fashionable in London until the Americans and the Jews were
let loose."[36] In general Adams spoke well of London in his youth
when it accepted him into its high society, and condemned it when
it did not. But as he grew older, he began to look at London with
the distorting eyes of a sort of detached Anglophobe and an anti-
Semite, just as he then looked at every city, whether in America or
abroad. When in the *Education* he looked back at Rome in May
of 1860, he called it "divine." But even then he could not avoid an
invidious comparison between Rome in 1860 and Rome in the
twentieth century: "No doubt other young men, and occasionally
young women, have passed the month of May in Rome since then,
and conceive that the charm continues to exist. Possibly it does—
in them—but in 1860 the lights and shadows were still medieval,
and medieval Rome was still alive; the shadows breathed and
glowed, full of soft forms felt by lost senses. No sand-blast of
science had yet skinned off the epidermis of history, thought, and
feeling. The pictures were uncleaned, the churches unrestored, the
ruins unexcavated. Medieval Rome was sorcery."[37] In 1865,
Adams wrote to Gaskell: "Rome . . . in spite of the cantankerous
men and women in it, is as enjoyable as ever."[38] And Paris, of
course, was also the subject of occasional bits of qualified favorable
comment. In 1901 it was the inevitable place to visit for one in
search of scientific and artistic education; but it was, nevertheless,
like New York, the scene of "chaos"—a symbol for all that was bad
in the later view of Henry Adams. Paris and New York in 1901
were venal, sordid, vulgar but "society nursed there, in the rotten-
ness of its decay, certain anarchistic elements, and thought them

65

proof of art. Perhaps they were."[39] While the *Education* contains expressions of qualified approval for some European cities, others, like Berlin, were completely damned. "In 1858 Berlin was a poor, keen-witted, provincial town, simple, dirty, uncivilized, and in most respects disgusting,"[40] and "The derisive Jew laughter of Heine ran through the university and everything else in Berlin."[41] In 1901, "forty years of varied emotions had not deadened Adams' memories of Berlin" and he refused to visit it with the Lodges while they were all on a European tour together.[42]

If the *Education* contains qualified approval of European cities, Adams' letters are almost totally condemnatory of them. Let us begin with London. In 1861 he writes that London "is a great unpleasant body"[43] in which no one has asked him to dinner, no one looks at him, no one introduces him.[44] In 1863 Adams finds London's fashionable society "intolerably stupid,"[45] its rushing life a bore.[46] And when Lothrop Motley says it is "the perfection of human society," Adams comments: "If his remark applies merely to a few dinners and a few visits to country houses with clever people, I shouldn't quarrel with it. But as for fashionable society here, I say clearly that in my opinion it is a vast social nuisance and evil."[47] No wonder Adams reported in 1863: "I now find myself in London alone, without a house I care to go to, or a face I would ask to see."[48] No wonder he complained in a letter to John Gorham Palfrey in 1864 that London did not allow him any "home-like feelings," that he was struck by "the solemnity, the gloom, the squalor, and the horrible misery and degradation" that brooded over London. Its magnificence he knew and could appreciate, he added, but that "had done its best to make him a socialist and . . . nearly succeeded." As if he had not said enough in condemnation of London, he concluded by saying that he thought the society dull, and the art and literature poor.[49] London was still "dull and oppressive" in 1879 and Adams reported that "Henry James haunts [its] streets gloomily."[50] Once again in 1880, Adams sounds the same theme of isolation from high society: "We are very quiet ourselves, go out little, and as the fashionable people come to town our little tallow-dip disappears in the glare." Once again the same theme of dullness: "There is nothing very much worth seeing."[51]

At the beginning of the nineties there was some semi-ironical relenting in Adams' correspondence on London. In 1892 he speaks of it as restful because "I feel even deader than I did in the South Seas, but here I feel that all the others are as dead as I. Even Harry James, with whom I lunch Sundays, is only a figure in the same old wall-paper, and really pretends to belong to a world which is extinct as Queen Elizabeth. I enjoy it." And his reasons for enjoying London were not unlike those that figure in some of Henry James' reflections. Adams continued: "These preposterous British social conventions; church and state, Prince of Wales, Mr. Gladstone, the Royal Academy and Mr. Ruskin, the London fog and St. James's Street, are all abstractions which I like to accept as I do the sun and the moon, not because they are reasonable but because they are not. They ask me no questions and need no answers."[52] Yet the pleasant and quieting atmosphere of London in 1892 did not continue for long, for by 1895 Adams was deep in his madness about the Jews, in London and everywhere else. In 1895 he writes to his brother, Brooks: "I duly called on your Jew friend, and had a chat with him about your book. He seems to have got it all fixed to suit him, and to suit you as well . . . Your Jew No. 2 I have not heard from."[53] In the same year he writes to John Hay that "London is smothered in gold, and all industry is dying of inanition,"[54] and then once again to John Hay in 1895 he writes one of his most disgraceful anti-Semitic letters on the subject of London: "If New York is mad, London is certainly ten times more so. The Kaffir Circus is the most startling phenomenon since the South Sea Scheme. It is almost wholly in Jew hands, and a new set of rich Jews has inundated May Fair and St. James. Beit is building a palace in Park Lane. Barnato has rented Spencer House. The Christians are furious. They talk of making a new Ghetto. They secretly encourage the Anti-Semite movement. After all, the Jew question is really the most serious of our problems. It is Capitalistic Methods run to their logical result. Let's hope to pull their teeth. Only in this day of

67

dentistry they would have them pulled painlessly, and put in false ones."[55]

Adams' letters on Paris are just as hostile as those on London. As early as 1867 he wrote Gaskell: "you should run over to Paris by all means. Otherwise you will be deprived of the precious privilege of abusing it; a privilege which I value so highly that I have done little to exercise it since I arrived there. I do not hesitate to say that at present it is a God-forsaken hole, and my party unanimously agreed that their greatest pleasure since arriving was in quitting it; and as we are all more or less familiar with the town, our opinion is entitled to weight. I never imagined the city so thoroughly used up, and given over to hordes of low Germans, English, Italians, Spaniards and Americans, who stare and gawk and smell, and crowd every shop and street. I did not detect a single refined-looking being among them, but there may have been one or two who, like ourselves, had drifted there by accident or necessity and were lost in the ocean of humanity that stagnates there in spite of its restlessness."[56] He then goes on to recount an incident in which he finds himself in the middle of a mob of *ouvriers* in blouses, almost beaten up because he had pushed back "a big devil" who had tried to push his way into a crowded railroad car. Adams' distaste for the Parisian mob was formed rather early, and it, along with his hatred for the moral and even artistic shortcomings of Paris, figures in his complaints for the next forty years. "At the best of times," he writes Henry Cabot Lodge in 1880, "Paris is to me a fraud and a snare; I dislike it, protest against it, despise its stage, condemn its literature, and have only a temperate respect for its cooking."[57] By 1899 we find Adams reporting of Paris that it is flat and tired and that "the Jews have won along the whole line."[58] In 1900 he tells Mabel Hooper La Farge that she "can hardly imagine how Paris strains one's nervous resources" and that "Paris is a place for the elderly to prepare for Hell, if there is to be a Hell. For the young, I cannot recommend it."[59] And in 1901 he declares to Elizabeth Cameron: "I feel not the smallest wish or desire to go there any more."[60]

Washington was the only city in the whole world for which Adams could express almost unqualified affection over a considerable period of time. But Washington also fell in the end. Although he oscillated between extended pleasure and occasional disappointment with Washington in the earlier years of his life, when Washington finally fell in his esteem, it fell with a resounding crash along with all the other cities that had become "Jewish" in his warped judgment.

During one of his early visits to Washington in 1869, he was taken with the place; its society was easy, its spring soft, and living there was not too expensive. "One could not stay there a month without loving the shabby town."[61] But Adams could not stay there for much more than a month in the days of Grant, and it was not until the days of Grant were over that he could develop a more favorable opinion of it. In 1877 he moved to it from Boston and began his forty years' residence in the capital. "Home was Washington," he exclaimed with pleasure.[62] Though he had once dreamed during his London period of becoming a political reformer of American society, he did not go to Washington as a politician to enter the rough-and-tumble life of the capital; he went there as a critical observer—to mingle in society, to study the national archives, to write, and hopefully to influence the nation's destiny indirectly, to be a "stable-companion to statesmen, whether they liked it or not."[63] His reactions to the capital city were at first most favorable. He was intensely exhilarated when he exclaimed in a letter: "the fact is I gravitate to a capital by a primary law of nature. This is the only place in America where society amuses me or where life offers variety . . . As I belong to the class of people who have great faith in this country and who believe that in another century it will be saying in its turn the last word of civilization, I enjoy the expectation of the coming day, and try to imagine that I am myself, with my fellow gelehrte here, the first rays of that great light which is to dazzle and set the world on fire hereafter. Our duties are, perhaps, only those of twinkling . . . But twinkle for twinkle I prefer our kind to that of the small politician . . ."[64] Or the small college professor, he might have added, for Adams aspired to be free of the "provincialism of place, and class and culture" which he had feared when he had taught at Harvard. He moved into an elegant Washington house in Lafayette Square in sight of the White House, and "for the first time in his life—felt like a gentleman." Within two years after settling in Washington, he described his social life there as an "unqualified success." But indefinite and ominous doubts about it lurked in his mind for he felt that the capital would become a very great city only "if nothing happens to it."[65]

Some of its limitations and something of what could happen to it he had seen in the days of Grant and expressed in his novel *Democracy,* secretly given to the publishers in the spring of 1879 with instructions to bring it out anonymously. In *Democracy,* a wealthy, high-minded widow, Mrs. Lightfoot Lee, fatigued by the sterile society of Boston and New York, and by philosophy and social work as well, because "they led her nowhere," takes up residence shortly after the Civil War in Washington. The nearby Potomac River is presented in the novel, according to Ernest Samuels, as a "mystic symbol of the developing life of the American democracy." On the Mt. Vernon side of the river in a country setting lie the heroic aspirations of the past, while on the other side is the real capital "city built on the edge of a swamp, a sort of parody of the American dream."[66] On several occasions in the novel, Mrs. Lee with a small, select party of prominent politicians goes for an excursion to Mt. Vernon. "They passed on, wandering across the lawn and into the house. Their eyes, weary of the harsh colors and forms of the city, took pleasure in the worn wainscots and the stained walls . . . There was no uncomfortable sense of repair or newness . . . From the heavy brick porch they looked across the superb river to the raw and incoherent ugliness of the city, idealized into dreamy beauty by the atmosphere and the soft background of purple hills behind." The appearance of Washington in their eyes was only made bearable by distance and the frame of nature. Just as Adams had been partial to the colonial village of Quincy with its aura of bygone political associations, rather than to the growing, commercial city of Boston, so he revealed a preference for rural, eighteenth-century Mt. Vernon rather than for booming Washington after the Civil War. In the *Education,* he wrote that "Mount Vernon was only a Quincy in a Southern setting."[67]

The general effect of physical rawness was bad enough in "the dreadful Capital," but what was worse was Washington's political and social degeneration. Adams makes his heroine, Mrs. Lee, well enough acquainted with Washington high society to realize that Silas P. Ratcliffe, the prototype of the American politician, is no true representative of the people, but a practical, shrewd, uncultivated, and corrupt man whose ultimate goal is power and wealth. The American President, known as Old Granite Face, is perhaps an amalgam of Grant and Hayes; he is caricatured as a political simpleton who apes monarchical forms at his garish receptions while his First Lady is presented by Adams as a small-minded social snob. Around the political inner circle there are swarms of shady office-seekers, who have no vestige of consciousness of high national purposes. Suggesting that Washington merely represents the social climate of American cities in the eighteen-seventies, Adams has a sophisticated foreign diplomat, Baron Jacobi, observe to Mrs. Lee: "You Americans care not for experience . . . I have found no society which has had elements of corruption like the United States. The children in the streets are corrupt, and know how to cheat me. The cities are all corrupt, and also the towns and the counties and the State Legislatures and the Judges." Adams' reservations about Washington in *Democracy* were more than balanced, perhaps, by the years of gaiety and society in the period that Ernest Samuels calls "The Golden Age of Lafayette Square," but by the 1890's those reservations were magnified, supplemented by others, rolled into a philosophy of history and a system of discontent. Something *did* happen to Washington for Henry Adams. Though he continued to live there, he expressed his dislike and bewilderment with it as he did with all of the great cities of his time. The same anti-semitism that permeated Adams' view of London, Paris, and even Boston, appeared in his estimate of Washington in 1914: "The atmosphere

71

really has become a Jew atmosphere. It is curious and evidently good for some people, but it isolates me. I do not know the language, and my friends are as ignorant as I. We are still in power, after a fashion. Our sway over what we call society is undisputed. We keep Jews far away, and the anti-Jew feeling is quite rabid. We are anti-everything and we are wild-uplifters; yet somehow we seem to be more Jewish every day."[68]

And in the *Education* he singled out New York for an attack on the score of its capitalism and barbarity. Like so many tourists returning to this country, he found the approach wonderful and more striking than ever, but it was like nothing he ever cared to see. "The outline of the city became frantic in its effort to explain something that defied meaning. Power seemed to have outgrown its servitude and to have asserted its freedom. The cylinder had exploded, and thrown great masses of stone and steam against the sky. The city had the air and movement of hysteria, and the citizens were crying, in every accent of anger and alarm, that the new forces must at any cost be brought under control. Prosperity never before imagined, power never yet wielded by man, speed never reached by anything but a meteor, had made the world irritable, nervous, querulous, unreasonable and afraid. All New York was demanding new men, and all the new forces, condensed into corporations, were demanding a new type of man—a man with ten times the endurance, energy, will and mind of the old type—for whom they were ready to pay millions at sight. As one jolted over the pavements or read the last week's newspapers, the new man seemed close at hand, for the old one had plainly reached the end of his strength, and his failure had become catastrophic. Every one saw it, and every municipal election shrieked chaos. A traveller in the highways of history looked out of the club window on the turmoil of Fifth Avenue, and felt himself in Rome, under Diocletian, witnessing the anarchy, conscious of the compulsion, eager for the solution, but unable to conceive whence the next impulse was to come or how it was to act."[69]

The chaos of New York and the "Jewishness" of Washington

were all far from the Quincy of Adams' youth. But there was no turning to Quincy, no turning to Paris, Rome, London, Madrid, or Berlin. All that was left for Henry Adams was the past, the past that went well beyond eighteenth-century Quincy and into the Middle Ages. For in his last years, Adams became an admirer of medieval life and a Mariolatrist, worshipping the Virgin in all of her chateaus, palaces, and cathedrals. He expounded his view at greatest length in his *Mont-Saint-Michel and Chartres*. When the American Institute of Architects reprinted that work, Ralph Adams Cram spelled out the significance of Henry Adams' philosophy for at least one student of the American city in 1913. Cram found it "vastly heartening and exhilarating." While it did not flatter American architecture in the twentieth century, Cram thought it established "new goals for attainment," that it opened up "the far prospect of another thirteenth century in the times that are to come," that it urged men "to ardent action towards its attainment."[70]

There was irony in this call for another thirteenth century, for Henry Adams' philosophy of history did not permit this as a possibility. The decline of civilization was logically entailed, he thought, by the second law of thermodynamics. The passage from the unity of the Middle Ages to the multiplicity of the twentieth century was inevitable and irreversible, according to Adams. For that reason, Cram exaggerated the practical significance of *Mont-Saint-Michel and Chartres*. It was not a blueprint of cities that Adams thought could be restored in America, but an unrealizable vision of what civilization should be like. It was the expression of Adams' values and hardly a description of any city that he thought could exist any more. The world of the twentieth century, as Adams saw it, was full of "complexity, multiplicity, variety, and even contradiction."[71] From the time of St. Thomas' *Summa Theologiae* and Beauvais Cathedral, the universe had become "steadily more complex and less reducible to a central control."[72] Adams doubted whether modern art and modern science could possibly encompass this complexity, could possibly produce an organic unity of thought, feeling, and architecture. By the same reasoning, he doubted

73

whether the destruction of the American city would count as a great loss. After the San Francisco earthquake, Adams coolly expressed his lack of enthusiasm for that beleaguered city even though he thought that it had more style than any city in the nation: "San Francisco burned down last week, and I have been searching the reports to learn whether the whole city contained one object that cannot be replaced better in six months. As yet I've heard of nothing."[73] And so San Francisco went the way of Boston, New York, and Washington in Adams' estimation, to say nothing of London, Paris, and Rome.

VI

THE VISITING MIND

HENRY JAMES

Except for Jefferson's concessions to the American city in 1816, our story has been mainly one of adverse metaphysical speculation and bad dreams about urban life, of esthetic and moral recoil from the American city's ugliness, commercialism, and crime. Nevertheless, many writers granted that before the Civil War the American city, for all of its defects, was less iniquitous, less dirty, and less menacing than the European city. But after the Civil War, when industrialization and immigration swelled to previously unknown dimensions, writers no longer illustrated their anxieties by pointing primarily to Europe. Henry James thought the post-bellum American city had succumbed to many of the ills that earlier writers had feared and dreamed about. Like Henry Adams he did not think of New York as purer than the capital cities of Europe. On the contrary, James came to look with horror at New York and found in it remarkably few of the compensations that he saw in the European metropolis. True, he thought London was a place of "rookeries," brutality, gin-shops, and ugliness, but he also thought it was *the* place for an English-speaking man of sensibility. New York, by contrast, was both squalid and gilded, to be fled rather than enjoyed, to be abandoned for Europe, for less bristling towns like Philadelphia, for Washington's slower and more interesting conversation, and, in desperation—with Henry Adams—for the past. The American city that Henry Adams and Henry James saw after the Civil War led Bryce, the successor to de Tocqueville among studious foreign visitors to the United States, to say in 1888 in a much-quoted passage: "There is no denying that the government of cities is the one conspicuous failure of the United States. The deficiencies of the National government tell but little for evil on the welfare of the people. The faults of the State governments are insignificant compared with the extravagance, corruption, and mismanagement which mark the administrations of most of the great cities." The burden of taxes is so great in the cities, Bryce noted, "that there is a strong tendency for rich men to migrate from the city to its suburbs in order to escape the city collector."[1] But while literary men like Henry James also fled the American city, to places more distant than its suburbs, their aim was not so much to escape its tax collectors as its taxpayers.

The estrangement of Henry James from the American city was both more decisive and more complex than Henry Adams' recoil. James' earliest consciousness had been stamped with a European imprint, but he had enjoyed the intimacy of New York, Albany, and Boston with few interruptions up to his twelfth year in 1855, during a period when each of these cities retained a small-town appearance. Then he lived in a succession of places on both sides of the Atlantic: Geneva and Bonn in Europe, and Newport, Boston, and Cambridge in the United States. After another European tour, James finally expatriated himself in 1875 and settled in London for many years before taking up his final English residence at Rye in 1898. Though he returned to the eastern coastal cities of the United States a few times between 1865 and 1900, not until 1904 did he ever make an extended trip around America as far south as Florida and west to California. After that trip he returned with relief to England, but he was forced to come to America briefly in 1910, the year of his brother William's death. Henry James' expatriation expressed more than amply the fact that was understated by William when he said that Henry was never thoroughly reconciled to America.[2] Though he settled in England and remained unreconciled to America, he continued to be a "restless analyst" of American cities.

The numerous years Henry James spent abroad in his youth made "the international scene the land of his particular breeding."[3] But in addition to his having spent much time on the move from America to Western Europe, young Henry, like all the James children, had been subjected to his father's explicit educational theory that he should be trained without attachment to any particular place, religion, political system, ethical code, or set of personal habits: to be, in short, a cosmopolitan. That theory was prompted by his father's profound dislike of the narrowly competitive drives of American life. He hoped his sons would participate in the greatest possible range of spiritual experience before they were obliged to choose careers. He wanted them "just to *be* something, something unconnected with specific doing, something free and uncommitted."[4] This education was not the exclusive explanation of Henry's settling abroad since William with a similar education remained in the United States; but it combined with Henry's temperament and his literary propensities to hasten his search for a place of residence more congenial than the nineteenth-century American city. The history of his attitude toward New York confirms this, since it is a story that progresses from fondness for what he remembered of it in his youth to mature disappointment. In between, the attractions of the European city drew Henry James to a kind of urban civilization that he invidiously contrasted with what he regarded as the alien and commercial Manhattan of the turn of the century.

Henry James was especially endowed with an acute sensibility to his urban surroundings. He could remember back to the age of two when he first saw the Place and Colonne Vendôme in Paris; and when he was quite old, he could even remember the fragrance of Albany, where he had lived in his childhood, for there was a large orchard of peaches in the spacious garden behind his grandmother's house. New York City of 1847 he remembered as "the small, homogeneous, liquor-scented, heated-looking city of no pavements" with little shops, squares, fountains, and the park by City Hall. Pre-Civil War New York was pictured in his only complete novel of that city, *Washington Square,* and a favorable image of it remained with James all his life, when he recalled the square itself rather than other parts of "the long, shrill city." His early impressions of the physical aspects of American cities remained especially vivid when he set them down in his writing, and his experience of the social homogeneity of those cities before the Civil War had left a cherished imprint. They floated, he said, "in such a clean light social order."[5]

By contrast, though Henry James lived for several years in New England as a young man, little about that region strongly attracted his admiration and allegiance. The one exception was the town of Newport with its lovely natural setting. The James family had settled there for several years, and Henry declared that before it became a famous resort it was the place in America they all most cared to live in. He described it as having had a quality of "shy sweetness" and remembered it more fondly than he did any other New England town or city.[6] On the other hand, he saw Boston bifocally as a rural center and as a town of history; a history, however, in which he showed no great interest. He loved neither the gentility of the Brahmins nor the frugality of Concord and could not abide New England's conception of culture as a matter of duty rather than of joy.[7] He described the rural, provincial, solemn life of the independently wealthy New Englanders who lived in the environs of Boston about 1850 in his first short novel, *Watch and Ward,* and later in *The Europeans.* In his novel *The Bostonians,* published in 1886, he summed up his disappointment at the decline of Boston society by subtly satirizing the idealists and reformers surrounding Olive Chancellor, who fails to realize that her interest in Verena Tarrant is more the product of Lesbian passion than of a desire to further the cause of feminism. James concerned himself with the frustrations and deviations of the more comfortable members of Boston society, but he was not exhilarated, as naturalists like Dreiser would have been, by the transformations of Boston brought about by immigration and industrialization after the Civil War. Nor could the meagerly cultivated rural scenes of New England detain him. In America, he said: "Nature herself . . . has the

7 8

peculiarity of seeming rather crude and immature. The very air looks new and young; the light of the sun seems fresh and innocent, as if it knew as yet but few of the secrets of the world and none of the weariness of shining."[8] James' deep feeling for his family and a few friends led him to view Cambridge affectionately, but he came to realize that Boston as a city and a society "is absolutely nothing to me. I don't even dislike it. I like it on the contrary; I only dislike to live there."[9]

Although he disliked living in Boston, when James began exploring Europe by himself after the Civil War, again and again he was enchanted by the "aesthetic presence of the past" in the cities of Italy, France, and England. In Rome he enjoyed and critically took possession of the artistic masterpieces. He was not preoccupied with that city's shadows, nor by a sense of its gloomy wrongs as Hawthorne had been; and he noticed loitering beggars, soldiers, and white-cowled monks only in passing. He was instead filled with admiration for Santa Maria Maggiore with its "gathered memories," and in St. Peter's was exhilarated by the general spacious beauty of the edifice, which revealed to him "the reach of our dreams and the immensity of our resources" above "the highest tide of vulgarity." Travelling on through the chain of cities in Tuscany, he was to declare his unqualified love of "adorable Italy in which, for the constant renewal of interest, of attention, of affection, these refinements of variety, these so harmoniously-grouped and individually-seasoned fruits of the great garden of history, keep presenting themselves!"[10] He profoundly felt that the presence of beautiful surroundings sustained high spirits in spite of severe privations. He explained that Venetians "have little to call their own—little more than the bare privilege of leading their lives in the most beautiful of towns . . . Not their misery, but the way they elude their misery is what pleases the sentimental tourist."[11]

James does not appear ever to have thought seriously of settling in Italy, but he did consider the possibility of taking up a residence in Paris. In May 1876 he wrote to his friend, William Dean Howells, that the great merit of Paris "is that one can arrange one's life . . . exactly as one pleases—that there are facilities for every kind of habit and taste, and that everything is accepted and understood. Paris itself meanwhile is a sort of painted background which keeps shifting and changing, and which is always there, to be looked at when you please, and to be most easily and comfortably ignored when you don't."[12] However, James found that the decorative qualities of the Paris background were being marred by "the deadly monotony that M. Haussmann called into being . . . its huge, blank, pompous, featureless sameness." The Avenue de l'Opéra, he said, smelled of modern asphalt and was lined with great white houses decorated with machine-made arabesques that destroyed individuality and jarred his sense of what the architectural environment should be.[13] What he called the foreground of an urban environment, the opportunity for social life, was at first a delight to him in Paris, but then fell short of his expectations. He was pleasantly stimulated by the socially perceptive and responsive intelligence of the ordinary Frenchman, and he made valuable literary acquaintances. For entertainment he could indulge his taste for the drama, learning the Théâtre Français by heart. But even though social life in Paris was "easy and smooth-flowing," James finally had to confess a feeling of "weariness and satiety" with the French mind, and he became convinced that the circle of literature was too tightly closed to outside influence. Though he spoke French well, he felt too much alone in "glittering, charming, civilized" Paris, having insufficient rapport either with French writers and intellectuals or with American compatriots touring the French capital. In 1876, he moved from a Paris that he found brilliant to a London that he found crude by comparison.[14]

The welcome James received in literary London was of immense importance to him and more than made up for the crudeness he might have seen in the city; it exactly encouraged his deepest need for free-ranging and urbane communication. He had found himself alone on his travels because of the limitations of his American compatriots. "It's the absolute and incredible lack of *culture* that strikes you in common travelling Americans," he exclaimed in a letter to his mother. Then he went on to add that "the English have manners and a language. We lack both, but particularly the latter."[15] So even more than beauty of surroundings he valued England's possession of *the* language in which he wished to mold his artistic expression; and the warmly hospitable attitude of English literary society to an unusual, lonely, young man of letters finally settled his mind about the kind of city he preferred over American cities. As Leon Edel has observed, London assumed a magnificent air and a grandness it was always to have for James, in spite of its slums, squalor, dirt, and darkness.[16] We may recall that neither Melville nor Henry Adams was as captivated as James was by what they too called the magnificence of London. Nor did its language mean as much to them. But to James, London's congenial possibilities for communication meant more than even the rich, visual impressions of continental cities and played a major part in his choice of England as his home.

In London James satisfied his need for communication and also his great penchant for observation. He wrote often of his "pedestrian gaping," and said that "the only form of riot and revel" his temperament would ever know was that of "the visiting mind."[17] He felt that "when one should cease to live in large measure by one's eyes . . . one would have taken the longest step toward not living at all."[18] In 1877, after having taken up his residence in England, James wrote to Grace Norton: "I feel now more at home in London than anywhere else in the world . . . I have taken a great fancy to the place; I won't say to the people and things; and yet these must have a part in it . . . So my interest in London is chiefly that of an observer in a place where there is most in the world to observe."[19] So much was there to observe that very soon after his arrival in London he wrote to his sister Alice: ". . . up to this time I have been crushed under a sense of the mere magnitude of London—its inconceivable immensity—in such a way as to paralyze my mind for any appreciation of details." The overwhelming impact of the city also produced "an extraordinary intellectual depression . . . and an indefinable flatness of mind. The place sits on you, broods on you, stamps on you with the feet of its myriad bipeds and quadrupeds. In fine it is anything but a cheerful or a charming city. Yet it is a very splendid one."[20] He thought that the factory-studded banks of the Thames were hideous, but London had other features that provoked his reflection.

In *The Princess Casamassima*, published in 1886, James made no effort to describe London's rapid industrial development. Instead he elaborated the overwhelming effect of class inequality on fine consciences. He described the symptoms of a "sinister, anarchic underworld," and recorded the deposit of his "visual and . . . constructive sense of London."[21] His hero Hyacinth Robinson constantly communicates awareness of "the great ulcers and sores of London—the sick, eternal misery crying out of the darkness in vain, confronted with granaries and treasure houses and places of delight where shameless satiety kept guard."[22] Though Hyacinth loves the city streets at all times, he takes refuge from the foul air occasionally in a green park, one of the few city breathing-places. He is the disinherited victim of class inequality whose innate sensibility and passionately aroused social conscience involve him in a revolutionary conspiracy. He falls in with a cool-headed, young scientist and a little band of socialist-revolutionaries as well as with the cosmopolitan Princess, who is the daughter of an aristocratic Italian father and an expatriated American mother, and who is obliquely and verbally obsessed with the social question, as it was then called. James selects central characters who are articulate, literate, reflective, and primarily concerned with extending consciousness; the relatively inarticulate, illiterate and unreflective people of the great city are seen only in passing. Hyacinth would seem to be expressing James' own unresolved question when he wonders by what wizardry the horrible populace of London could ever be raised to "high participations" for "there were nights when everyone he met appeared to reek with gin and filth . . . Some of the women and girls in particular were appalling—saturated with alcohol and vice, brutal, bedraggled and obscene. 'What remedy but another deluge, what alchemy but annihilation?' he asked himself as he went his way . . .

If it was the fault of the rich, the selfish, congested rich who allowed such abominations to flourish, that made no difference and only shifted the shame; since the terrestrial globe, a visible failure, produced the cause as well as the effect."[23] As in *The Bostonians* there is in *The Princess Casamassima* a persistently detached tone of satire and resignation about tragic urban predicaments.

At one crisis in the story, James presents Hyacinth with a trip to the country, away from the "mere ravelled fringe of London." He sends him to the cultivated estate of Medley Hall with its ivy, gardens, and ponds. Part of the estate is given a long, continuous description: this was the garden that "took the young man's heart beyond the others; it had high brick walls, on the sunny side of which was a great training of apricots and plums: it had straight walks bordered with old-fashioned homely flowers and enclosing immense squares where other fruit trees stood upright and mint and lavender floated in the air."[24] Henry James, in his youth, had also been enchanted by English gardens and countryside, and he was enjoying a dilation of spirits when he wrote to his family that while trudging to Worcester past elm-scattered meadows and broken-down farms, he felt as if he were pressing all England to his soul.[25] It was not crude or wild country—not the kind of country of much of his native America—that won his admiration, but rather country that had been cultivated for centuries with such continuous devotion and art that land-use could also rank as an achievement of civilization.

After his sojourn at the country estate, Hyacinth Robinson is transported to Paris and comes to appreciate the precious things society had produced—the beauty and power it had created in the splendid French metropolis. As he wanders through the city, "the Boulevard was all alive, brilliant with illuminations, with the variety and gaiety of the crowd, the dazzle of shops and cafés seen through uncovered fronts or immense lucid plates, the flamboyant porches of theatres and the flashing lamps of carriages, the far-spreading murmur of talkers and strollers, the uproar of pleasure and prosperity, the general magnificence of Paris on a perfect evening in

June . . . All Paris struck him as tremendously artistic and decorative." It was a civilization that had no visible rough spots.[26] Although during his Parisian visit Hyacinth remembers excitedly how his ancestors had mounted the barricades in the French Revolution, he becomes less and less concerned with making a revolution. Like James himself on many of his travels, he sought "simply the spectacle, the picture." After his contemplation of "splendid Paris, charming Paris" his socialist convictions begin to relax, and his worship of the Princess and his dedication to the revolution become fatally confused.

Unlike his creation, Hyacinth Robinson, Henry James himself was never even momentarily diverted by revolutionary zeal from appreciating those items of high civilization which he found in Paris and London, and which, he complained, were absent from the texture of American life when he wrote his book on Hawthorne. Even though the London scene and London society could be oppressive, he found many compensations in its atmosphere. In his essay "London" of 1888, he recounted how he was gripped above all else by the city's literary associations. He was reminded of *The Ingoldsby Legends* and of *Henry Esmond* and thrilled by the thought that the very small and dirty statue of Queen Anne had been known to the hero of *Henry Esmond*. "All history appeared to live again, and the continuity of things to vibrate through my mind."[27] For a man of letters, he went on, "who endeavors to cultivate, however modestly, the medium of Shakespeare and Milton, of Hawthorne and Emerson, who cherishes the notion of what it has achieved and what it may even yet achieve, London must ever have a great illustrative and suggestive value, and indeed a kind of sanctity. It is the single place in which most readers, most possible lovers, are gathered together; it is the most inclusive public and the largest social incarnation of the language, of the tradition." James observed that "if the sense of life is greatest there, it is a sense of the life of people of our incomparable English speech."[28] So it is not surprising that he was later disgusted by the wail of New York's Ellis Island, for his London was a more uniformly articulate city than the New York of Stephen Crane or the Chicago of Theodore Dreiser. James' fascination with London as the headquarters of one language and literature was consistent with his admiration of the "whole national consciousness" of the Swiss and the Scot. It was a long way from Dreiser's admiration of polyglot New York.

James was himself aware of the narrowness of his view. He tells us that London is immense and that "one has not the alternative of speaking of London as a whole, for the simple reason that there is no such thing as the whole of it . . . Rather it is a collection of many wholes, and of which of them is it most important to speak? Inevitably there must be a choice, and I know of none more scientific than simply to leave out what we may have to apologize for. The ugliness, the 'rookeries,' the brutalities, the night-aspect of many of the streets, the gin-shops and the hour when they are cleared out before closing—there are many elements of this kind which have to be counted out before a genial summary can be made."[29] "A genial summary"—that is the purpose of his account of London, but not of his later account of New York. Having focused on language in his praise of London, he had to acknowledge, but did not take too much time to criticize, "the terrible way in which the idiom is misused by the populace in general, than whom it has been given to few races to impart to conversation less of the charm of tone."[30] And while he later attacked New York's skyscrapers quite sharply, James here said briefly that "the great misfortune of London, to the eye (it is true that this remark applies much less to the City), is the want of elevation. There is no architectural impression without a certain degree of height, and the London street-vista has none of that sort of pride."[31]

James was aware of London's misery. That he was deeply aware of it appears in *The Princess Casamassima,* and he acknowledged it even in a summary that purported to be genial. Though he explored moral consciousness, his treatment of social misery in his essay on London was indicative of what remained a basically esthetic attitude toward the city. In his remarks on the method of genial summary he writes: "I should not go so far as to say that it

85

is a condition of such geniality to close one's eyes upon the immense misery; on the contrary, I think it is partly because we are irremediably conscious of that dark gulf that the most general appeal of the great city remains exactly what it is, the largest chapter of human accidents. I have no idea of what the future evolution of the strangely mingled monster may be; whether the poor will improve away the rich, or the rich will expropriate the poor, or they will all continue to dwell together on their present imperfect terms of intercourse. Certain it is, at any rate, that the impression of suffering is a part of the general vibration; it is one of the things that mingle with all the others to make the sound that is supremely dear to the consistent London-lover—the rumble of the tremendous human mill. This is the note which, in all its modulations, haunts and fascinates and inspires him. And whether or no he may succeed in keeping the misery out of the picture, he will freely confess that the latter is not spoiled for him by some of its duskiest shades. We are far from liking London well enough till we like its defects: the dense darkness of much of its winter, the soot on the chimney-pots and everywhere else, the early lamplight, the brown blur of the houses, the splashing of hansoms in Oxford Street or the Strand on December afternoons."[32]

While Henry James' attachment to London had been ripening, his dissatisfaction with his birthplace, New York, had gradually increased. As far back as 1865, in a review of Whitman's *Drumtaps,* he had crystallized an antipathetic view of the American metropolis, charging that the millionaire was the city's sole god except when the Union regiments poured through its streets in the first months of the Civil War.[33] Just before taking up residence in London, he registered growing disappointment with the New York of 1874; its activity was not to his liking. He confessed in his *Notebooks* that he had failed to work up an interest in New York in spite of a great effort. He had found that he did not have sufficient privacy to devote himself to his writing for "the interruptions in the *morning* here are intolerable. That period of the day has none of the social sanctity here that it [has] in England . . . People—by which I mean ladies—think nothing of asking you to come and see them before lunch . . . All my time has slipped away in mere movement."[34] He had stored up many impressions for his own later writing, and he had enjoyed intermittently a certain exhilaration. He summed up both pleasure and unsettlement in a letter to his friend, George Du Maurier, in 1883. "Though I am 'New Yorkais d'origine' I never return to this wonderful city without being entertained and impressed afresh. New York is full of types and figures and curious social idiosyncrasies, and I only wish we had someone here, to hold up the mirror, with a 15th part of your talent. It is altogether an extraordinary growing, swarming, glittering, pushing, chattering, good-natured, cosmopolitan place, and perhaps in some ways the best imitation of Paris that can be found (yet with a great originality of its own). But I didn't mean to be so geographical; I only meant to shake hands, and to remind myself again that if my dear old London life is interrupted, it isn't heaven be praised, finished."[35]

When Henry James revisited the land of his birth again in 1904, he reevaluated the scene in ways that gave full expression to his attitude toward urban life in America. Glimpses of hope for an American city came to him, like Henry Adams, during his visit to Washington. There, what he chiefly valued in urban life—historical association and the possibility of communication—were vaguely present, and civilizing opportunities still floated in its air. His chapter on Washington in *The American Scene* was an intricate summary of impressions, memories, and questions about the future of that city. James thought that the natural endowment of climate performed the function in Washington, as in the rest of America, of covering up much of the "impertinence and ugliness" of the manmade parts of the environment, and of disguising "the unsurmounted bourgeois character of the whole." He was able to find some associations of historical significance, though they were few and far between. Mount Vernon under the lovely yellow-green sunlight of spring was situated luckily in a beautiful, natural setting; but its crowning feature for James was that it communicated the heroic image of the first president, and preserved the history of his great public service.

By contrast to Mount Vernon, James felt that within the elaborately arranged capital city the Washington Monument rather wasted itself, "not a little as if some loud monosyllable had been uttered, in a preoccupied company, without a due production of sympathy or sense."[36] James also felt that history was seated with that "most prodigious of all Presidential effigies, Andrew Jackson, as archaic as a Ninevite king, prancing and rocking through the ages." James noted with gratitude and relief that the Library of Congress took on its magnificence not from the fact that money had been lavished on its materials, but rather because money had bought the treasures of knowledge that gave life to the building. He felt that the French statues of Lafayette and Rochambeau were the best of the city's more recent embellishments. He also admired the charming White House in its "fortunate isolation," and both adored and was amused by the nation's Capitol, which played very much the part that St. Peter's played in Roman life since it recorded "half the collective vibrations of a people; their conscious spirit, their public faith, their bewildered taste, their ceaseless curiosity, their arduous and interrupted education." However, the stretches of city surrounding these monuments struck James as an "unfinished cloth . . . marked with the queerness among many queernesses, of looking always the same . . . never emerging from its flatness, after the fashion of other capitals, into the truly, the variously, modelled and rounded state."[37]

What appealed most to James about Washington was its being more intensely than any other capital a City of Conversation. He found that—with the exception of a few isolated buildings which succeeded in communicating historical significance—the world of cosmopolitan conversation in Washington was of paramount importance because it nourished social consciousness. "The spectacle . . . was that of a numerous community in ardent pursuit of some workable conception of its social self, and trying meanwhile intelligently to talk itself . . . into a *subject* for conversation." James thought that Washington was the only American city in which men lived fully by transcending the values of business. What could not fail to impress him was that Washington society, and its male society especially, seemed to have "on its conscience to make one forget for an hour the colossal greed of New York."[38]

When he revisited New York, he was not immediately repelled by its commercialism, but—wanting perhaps to be favorably disposed toward his birthplace—he was momentarily exhilarated by the extent, ease, and energy of New York, and by the way in which "nature and science were joyously romping together."[39] On closer inspection he admired especially the "almost incomparable" Hudson River and its boats, having taken to heart the natural endowment of the great metropolis and its links with Europe.[40]

But the famous New York skyscrapers insulted Henry James' complex sensibilities. Steaming up the river, he saw the city as a "pin-cushion in profile." And he complained of the lack of history and the lack of time for history in a way that takes one back to the complaints in his *Hawthorne*. The buildings "never begin to speak to you, in the manner of the builded majesties of the world . . . towers or temples or fortresses or palaces—with the authority of things of permanence or even of things of long duration." History had given way to commerce. "The great city is projected into its future as, practically, a huge, continuous fifty-floored conspiracy against the very idea of the ancient graces, those that strike us as having flourished just in proportion as the parts of life and the signs of character have *not* been lumped together, not been indistinguishably sunk in the common fund of mere economic convenience." Nor did the skyscrapers as a new discovery in architecture have any more appeal to Henry James' esthetic feelings than did the rapid conversation of New Yorkers. His contempt for both was summarized when he wrote: "If quiet interspaces, always half the architectural battle, exist no more in such a structural scheme than quiet tones, blest breathing-spaces, occur, for the most part, in New York conversation, so the reason is, demonstrably, that the building can't afford them. (It is by very much the same law, one supposes, that New York conversation cannot afford stops.) The building can

89

only afford lights, each light having a superlative value as an aid to the transaction of business and the conclusion of sharp bargains."[41] Besides a more varied and refined architecture James wanted a more measured and varied kind of conversation which he found in the England of his period, where people were not so constantly on the *qui vive* as in America.

What seemed especially to disturb James in his observation of the New York scene was the assault of disordered elements on his perceptions, and the roughness, confusion and perpetual motion of so many elements. He disliked so much "the turbid air . . . the tramp, the whole quality and *allure,* the consummate monotonous commonness, of the pushing male crowd, moving in its dense mass— with the confusion carried to chaos for any intelligence, any perception; a welter of objects and sounds in which relief, detachment, dignity, meaning, perished utterly and lost all rights." He also spoke of "all the signs of the heaped industrial battle-field, all the sounds and silences, grim, pushing, trudging silences too, of the universal will to move—to move, move, move, as an end in itself, an appetite at any price."[42]

Besides the lack of ordered structure, dignity and history in New York, Henry James spoke of the lack of "organic social relations." Hence he felt some soothing relief when he visited Philadelphia, because it didn't "bristle" and because "it went back." In this spirit he warned "let not the unwary . . . visit Ellis Island," as Henry Adams might also have warned in his snobbish way. James was upset by the combination there of the quantity and quality of immigrants, "that loud primary stage of alienism which New York most offers to sight." To recover confidence, he said, to "regain lost ground . . . we, not they, must make the surrender and accept the orientation. We must go . . . *more* than halfway to meet them; which is all the difference, for us, between possession and dispossession." Feeling so dispossessed, as Henry Adams did too, he dreamed again "of the luxury of some such close and sweet and *whole* national consciousness as that of the Switzer and the Scot." His final dour conclusion was "that there was no escape from the ubiquitous alien into the future, or even into the present; there was no escape but into the past."[43]

New York at the beginning of the twentieth century engulfed James, for one feels that like the hero of his story, "A Round of Visits," he had been sated "with meaningless contacts, with the sense of people all about him intensely, though harmlessly animated, yet at the same time indifferent . . . There was nothing like a crowd, this unfortunate knew, for making one feel lonely." The loneliness he experienced in New York, James recaptured more fully in "The Jolly Corner," also written shortly after his American tour. In that story the fifty-six-year-old Spencer Brydon appears to speak for James himself in pondering the quality of New York's transformation. "The great fact all the while however had been the incalculability since he had supposed himself, from decade to decade, to be allowing and in the most liberal manner, for brilliancy of change . . . Proportions and values were upside down; the ugly things of his far-away youth . . . placed him rather under the charm; whereas the 'swagger' things, the modern, the monstrous, the famous things, those he . . . had come over to see, were exactly his sources of dismay . . . It was interesting, doubtless, but it would have been too disconcerting had not a certain finer truth saved the situation." That finer truth was the spiritual discovery of what he had escaped becoming by *not* remaining in New York. For Spencer Brydon is pictured as having just returned to New York for a brief visit to look after his property, the old family residence. The light during the daytime in which he saw everything bathed was "the cynical light of New York"; and at night "the great builded voids, great crowded stillnesses put on, often, in the heart of cities . . . a sort of sinister mask, and it was of this large collective negation that Brydon presently became conscious." The masses of dwellings appalled him with addresses "among the dreadful multiplied numberings which seemed to him to reduce the whole place to some vast ledger-page, overgrown, fantastic, of ruled and criss-crossed lines and figures . . . in the vast wilderness of the wholesale, breaking through the mere gross generalization of wealth and force and success." Spencer Brydon was

91

hoping to save his old home at the Jolly Corner from the tidal wave of real estate development, since this home represented the annals of nearly three generations of his family and not just "beastly rent values." Brydon had lived his life with his back turned to such concerns as business until his return to New York. When, after a suspenseful series of visits to his home, he finally manages to confront his alter ego—the man he would have become if he had remained in New York City—he meets an elegantly dressed millionaire, an utter stranger, "evil, odious, blatant and vulgar." This horrible specter—so briefly sketched in—represents for James the prominent, powerful and disgusting human type that the greatest American metropolis had produced.

Again in his last unfinished novel, *The Ivory Tower,* Henry James portrays the wealthy elite of American society, the tycoons who had made their money in American cities and then deserted them to reside in "vast," "florid," "non-descript excrescences" of architecture in the Newport of 1900. There was "the vulgar rich woman," Mrs. Bradham, who wanted "everyone for something so much more than something for everyone," and her rich husband, not vicious, but "a sponge of saturation in the surrounding medium." There were the millionaires, Mr. Gaw and Mr. Betterman, formerly associates and then bitter enemies, the first a terrible little man who tried to destroy the other and whose one overwhelming curiosity was how much money was going to be left by his rival. Mr. Gaw "was incapable of thought save in the sublimities of arithmetic [for] money was his life." And finally there was the financier's lawyer, dry Mr. Crick, who presided over millions of dollars and "insisted in having no more personal identity than the omnibus conductor stopping before you just long enough to bite into a piece of pasteboard with a pair of small, steel jaws . . . whose mind was so full of perfect nests or bags of other facts, leaving no room in their interstices for mere appreciation to turn around . . . They so covered the ground of his consciousness to the remotest edge that no breath of air either of his own mind or of anyone else's could have pretended to circulate about them."[44] In these sketches New York business people are shown against the background of their leisure retreats since down-town New York and its business were closed to James by upbringing, education, and profession, and he had never penetrated most regions where city dwellers lived and worked. But he summed up in these sketches some distortions in human consciousness and conscience; they are his indictment of the American city atmosphere produced by rampant commercialism.[45]

The central, and approved characters of Henry James' novels can be typed, according to Edmund Wilson, as the cultivated American bourgeois "who lives on an income derived from some form (usually left extremely vague) of American business activity but who has taken no part in the achievements which made the income possible. These men turn their backs on business; they attempt to enrich their experience through the society and art of Europe . . . They wince alike at the brutalities of the aristocracy and at the vulgarities of the working class; they shrink most of all from the 'commonness' of the less cultivated bourgeoisie, who, having acquired their incomes more recently, are not so far advanced in self-improvement."[46] James' final portrayal of this type of hero is Graham Fiedler, the nephew of millionaire Betterman in *The Ivory Tower*. Born of American parents, Fiedler had spent much of his life abroad at the turn of the century, and is sensitive and cultivated. He has been chosen by Betterman as his heir because he has matured into a man beyond the corrupting influences of money, and "shan't become as beastly vulgar as the rest, and shan't *like* all that ugliness and bareness, that poverty of form." If he had completed *The Ivory Tower*, James would probably have had Fiedler return to Europe, where he could fuse the form and the spirit of life by combining European culture and American idealism, and by escaping American materialism. Henry James himself had been able to make an artistic reconciliation only by maintaining most of his life a spiritual distance from the life of American cites.

In the course of painstaking observation and appraisal Henry James had come to feel that American cities at the turn of the century were lacking in so many of the amenities of life as to be for him uninhabitable. He regretted their loss of the pleasant and cultivated vestiges of the country—gardens and orchards. He deplored the social change in cities from homogeneous communities with a common language and discernible customs to polyglot and mannerless metropolises. Boston, of course, had had a literary tradition, which by his period was declining; and to his mind that city had not succeeded in developing the spirit of joy in civilizaton which European cities possessed, while New York was already becoming an architectural wasteland and the locus of the lonely crowd. In James' view the physical appearance of New York, with its prickly, new growth of skyscrapers, only expressed the incessant development of commercial and industrial capitalism in complete disregard of esthetic and historical values. The swarming population of New York also generally depressed him—both the influx of non-English-speaking, ignorant immigrants and the growing dominance of a class of money-obsessed millionaires. Though he had been able to read Walt Whitman's celebration of democracy with rapture to a select gathering of friends at his English retreat, he had not really wished to rub shoulders with crowds of vulgar or foreign-born American citizens. While his writings do reveal a disposition on Henry James' part to believe that Americans were typically less cynical and more democratic than Europeans, he was not concerned with, nor sanguine about, organized movements for social experiment and social betterment, such as were being performed by Jane Addams and eliciting the interest of his brother, William, and his friend, William Dean Howells. Instead Henry James remained all his life the detached, sensitive, ironic, visiting observer of the American city, and within the range of his interests described some manifestations of urban growth with stunning accuracy and intense dismay at its social effects.

VII

THE AMBIVALENT URBANITE

WILLIAM DEAN HOWELLS

THE reaction of Henry Adams and Henry James to the American city was in many ways similar to, but in crucial respects different from, that of their contemporary, William Dean Howells. While James abandoned the American scene for England and Adams retreated to the medieval past, Howells remained steadfastly at home. Although it would be an exaggeration to think of Adams and James as judging American urban life from a detached, purely esthetic point of view—they were too moral and psychological in their condemnations of the American city to be characterized in that way— they certainly did not aspire, like Howells, to be literary chroniclers of life in America's growing centers of commerce and industry. This, Howells did deliberately and explicitly, and for his labors he became "the chief American realist" in the years between 1881 and 1885, dedicated in his criticism to "banging the babes of romance about" and in his fiction to showing how men lived in America's cities.[1]

By the end of the century large American cities housed two new American types, the millionaire and the recently arrived immigrant, and Howells was intrigued by both of them. As he studied the development of America, he saw a change in its popular ideals of greatness which reflected the larger transformation of the nation into a predominantly urban one. He saw the country as having gone through four stages of hero worship, the last of which was the era of the triumphant millionaire. Immediately after the revolution, he maintained, politicians, publicists, and statesmen were idealized and considered models of greatness by the people. And when the country developed an intellectual life of its own, the literary figure came in for his share of adulation before the Civil War. The war brought the soldier to the front, and the ten or fifteen years that followed it were the years of the generals. By 1894, when Howells published these thoughts in *A Traveler from Altruria,* immense fortunes had developed in America, and heroes of an altogether different variety emerged in the popular mind. "I don't think there is any doubt but the millionaire is now the American ideal. It isn't very pleasant to think so, even for the people who have got on, but it can't very hopefully be denied. It is the man with the most money who now takes the prize in our national cakewalk."[2] Had Howells been writing down these thoughts at a slightly later date, he might have added a new stage in the development of national ideals—the era of the successful immigrant. But whether or not this would have been an acceptable appendix to Howells' history of popular ideals, the fact is that by the end of the nineteenth century the immigrant and the millionaire were *the* two new types in American history. Both symbolized the city, and both disturbed the sleep of Henry Adams and Henry James, whose dismay over the immigrant and the millionaire Howells shared in a lesser degree.

Unlike Adams, of course, Howells did not allow his dismay about the immigrant to drive him into bigotry, nor did he flee to London, the headquarters of the English language. But Howells did worry during his early years in Boston about what the urban immigrants might do to American life, and at the time he did not think their growing power was a very pleasant thing to contemplate. In 1875 he was forced to say that "the general character of the population has not gained by the change" brought about by the arrival of the Irish in Boston and the Chinese in California. "What is in the future, let the prophets say," he added characteristically, "anyone can see that something not quite agreeable is in the present; something that takes the wrong side, as by instinct, in politics; something that mainly helps to prop up tottering priestcraft among us; something that one thinks of with dismay as destined to control so largely the civil and religious interests of the country." With typical gentleness, however, Howells disassociated himself from the kind of obsessive prejudice that one finds in Henry Adams, for he added that "this, however, is only the aggregate aspect. Mrs. Clannahan's kitchen, as it may be seen by the desperate philosopher when he goes to engage her for the spring house-cleaning, is a strong argument against his fears. If Mrs. Clannahan, lately of an Irish cabin, can show a kitchen so capably appointed and so neatly kept as that, the country may yet be an inch or two from the brink of ruin, and the race which we trust as little as we love may turn out no more spendthrift than most heirs."[3]

Howells became less nervous on this question of immigration as he became the chief American realist, the dean of American letters, and the literary hero of socialists, social workers, liberals, and reformers who lived in the cities and tried to improve them. His affection for certain aspects of the newcomer's life and his encouragement of writers who were either immigrants or of recent immigrant background, is written all over his later novels and his correspondence.[4] There is no suggestion of the fear of Jews that haunted Henry Adams.[5] Even Howells' early ruminations on the problems of immigration typify a tolerance which lasted all his life, one that was well illustrated by his effort to distinguish between the unpleasant "aggregate aspect" of the problems created by the Boston immigrant and the charms of Mrs. Clannahan's kitchen. The same thing emerged in his treatment of that other disturbing urban type—the millionaire, although here the problem was undoubtedly more complex. Howells was in later life a socialist, but even then his sympathy transcended ideology.

To see this, one need only consider his comparatively gentle treatment of businessmen in *The Rise of Silas Lapham, A Hazard of New Fortunes, A Traveler from Altruria, Through the Eye of the Needle,* and *Letters Home.* Howells had difficulty in communicating deep psychological darkness and was incapable of describing anything like the "evil, odious, blatant and vulgar" alter ego of

Spencer Brydon in Henry James' "The Jolly Corner." And his incapacity to present the urban millionaire in Jamesian terms was parallelled by his amiable tendency to balance the neatness of Mrs. Clannahan's kitchen against the troubling "aggregate aspect" of the Boston Irish in 1875. Even while attacking what Dryfoos, in *A Hazard of New Fortunes,* and Mr. Ralson, in *Letters Home,* stood for, Howells could treat them in a way that prevented him from communicating an unambiguous attitude toward urbanization. Howells could neither penetrate nor arraign the vulgar millionaire with anything like the power of Henry James, and he could not communicate the titanic quality of the financier as Dreiser did in his Cowperwood trilogy. But in addition to his incapacities, we must reckon Howells' blandness and his need to distinguish, out of concern for justice, between the impersonal forces he detested and their individual representatives. Howells' reasonableness, as well as his limitations as a novelist, prevented him from personifying in fiction the objections he felt toward urban life.

A similar set of qualities made it possible for Howells to be, as he said he was, a theoretical socialist and a practical aristocrat.[6] Being a theoretical socialist in 1890 corresponded to being a theoretical worrier about immigration in 1875; being a practical aristocrat corresponded to being an admirer of Mrs. Clannahan's kitchen. Howells could therefore dine with pleasure in Fifth Avenue mansions and ramble with excitement on the lower East Side, even while he had the deepest reservations about New York as a whole. He was a theoretical anti-urbanist and a practical city-dweller, critical of the city's way of life but attached to urban people and places.

For any place in which Howells dwelt he could conceive some kind of affection. And those places were many. "If it be true that the modern author does not really live anywhere, Howells had become in that sense 'modern' perhaps as early as the date of his leaving his Beacon Street house in 1885."[7] He was born in Jefferson, Ohio; lived in every part of the state; held a consular appointment in Venice; lived in Cambridge and Belmont outside of Boston;

moved into Boston itself; left Boston for New York in his most famous move; went back for a short time to Boston; and then returned to New York. He spent a good deal of his remaining time visiting Europe and occupying summer houses in Maine. He therefore knew intimately every form of social life open to an American in his time: rural village, small city, suburb, American and European metropolis. About his "nomadic changes" as he called them, he was highly self-conscious, not only in 1900[8] but also as far back as a sentimental story called "Flitting," in which he also showed his capacity to like something about any place he lived in: "If the reader is of a moving family—and so he is as he is an American— he can recall the zest he found during childhood in the moving which had for his elders—poor victims of a factitious and conventional sentiment — only the salt and bitterness of tears." In this same piece, Howells announced that he "would not willingly repose upon the friendship of a man whose local attachments are weak," and that as proof of sensibility and constancy he would expect his friend to show "a sentiment for the place where one has lived two or three years, the hotel where one has spent a week, the sleeping car in which one has ridden from Albany to Buffalo."[9] For the forty-five years that remained to him after he published these words, Howells fully demonstrated, by his own exacting standards, his capacity for friendship. There are kind words for every form of social life and almost every sort of place in Howells' writings— friendly bouquets for New York, Boston, small towns, big towns, suburbs, and metropolises.

Howells' affection for people and his attachment to places may therefore prevent one from seeing how critical of the American city he could be. So many of his novels about city life are saturated with sympathy for the Dryfooses in New York and the Clannahans of Boston that it is hard to see in his treatment of city people the kind of anti-urbanism that emerged when he treated the city in its "aggregate aspect," as in *A Traveler from Altruria* and *Through the Eye of the Needle*. There are so many moments when Howells demonstrates a desire to understand the city's new inhabitants, the millionaire and the immigrant, that it is hard to think that he came, at one point in his life, to the conclusion that the American city of the early twentieth century should be destroyed. The story of this period, when he became disenchanted with the city as he knew it, is worth telling not only for its own sake but also because it is closely related to similar developments in the lives of younger realistic or naturalistic novelists like Dreiser. Moreover, there is great significance in the fact that Howells, the realist and city-dweller, the youthful rebel against the small town, who called upon southern writers to turn away from Poe,[10] who rejected the romantic view of the West as a place for the development of a national literature in opposition to Hawthorne, Emerson, and James Russell Lowell,[11] finally joined with his literary opponents against the American metropolis. Howells is a striking counterexample to the thesis that a belief in science, social democracy, and pragmatic reform always goes hand in hand with an affection for the city. Not all socialists, especially those in America at the end of the nineteenth century, saw the American city as a scene of virtue, nor did they share Marx's and Engels' scorn for the "idiocy of rural life."

The two main cities in Howells' life were Boston and New York. In *Years of My Youth,* he reported his and his sister's "discontent with the village limit of our lives,"[12] and by the beginning of the Civil War he was off to the East, determined to follow a career as an author. When he compared New York and Boston in the sixties, he much preferred Boston. After his first visit to New England he seems to have been advised by the Boston publisher, James T. Fields, to seek a place on the New York *Post,*[13] but he wrote to Fields soon after his arrival in New York in August 1860 that his regret at not getting a place on the *Post* "was softened by the fact that the more I saw of New York, the more I did not like it . . . The truth is, there is no place quite so good as Boston—God bless it! and I look forward to living there some day—being possibly the linchpin in the hub."[14] A week later he wrote to Lowell: "At New York, I spent four days, and was glad to come away. Indeed, the metropolis disappointed me—which was sad for the metropolis, and annoying to me."[15] Some of its annoyances Howells reported in 1900, as he reminisced about his "First Impressions of Literary New York." He had been disturbed by the literary Bohemians of the day, who made up "a sickly colony, transplanted from the mother asphalt of Paris, and never really striking root in the pavements of New York; it was a colony of ideas, of theories, which had perhaps never had any deep root anywhere." Howells was also annoyed by "those infamous New York streets, then as for long afterwards the squalidest in the world."[16] New York was a little more attractive to Howells upon his return from his stay in Venice, for in 1865 he was offered a position on *The Nation* by E. L. Godkin. Howells did not stay in New York very long, but he found time to record the filth of its streets, the daring of its brigands, and the vileness of its slums.[17] So when Boston beckoned in 1866, Howells bickered but finally accepted the post that would ultimately lead to his becoming a kingpin there and not a mere linchpin.

His first days in the region were spent in suburban Cambridge, and their record is to be found in the *Suburban Sketches* we have already sampled. Happy years in Boston followed, during which he was the editor of the *Atlantic Monthly,* the handpicked successor of the Brahmin writers who laid upon him, as Dr. Holmes said, the hand of apostolic succession. But in the eighties the bloom of Boston was less bright and he entered upon a period of transition which was typified by his novel *A Modern Instance* of 1882, a period which prepared the way for Howells' first cautious steps in the direction of New York.[18] Before choosing New York as a place for which he would abandon Boston, he wrote to Mark Twain, "Why not both of us remove to Washington? W. is running powerfully in my head these days,"[19] but nothing came of the Washington plan. Howells' first tentative interest in New York of the eighties was brought about more by repelling forces in Boston than by the attractions of New York. These forces he analyzed in a series of novels that critics labeled "Boston-Torn-to-Tatters."[20] It included *A*

101

Chance Acquaintance of 1873, *The Lady of the Aroostook* of 1879, *The Rise of Silas Lapham* of 1885 and *The Minister's Charge* of 1886. One of the main purposes of the saga was to indict upper-class Boston for its complicity in the urban evils of the time.[21] In *The Minister's Charge* it was argued that "no man . . . sinned or suffered to himself alone; his error and his pain darkened and afflicted men who never heard of his name. If a community was corrupt, if an age was immoral, it was not because of the vicious, but the virtuous who fancied themselves indifferent spectators."[22] This doctrine of complicity Howells carried with him to New York, where he tried to combine his truth-seeking realism with reformism in *A Hazard of New Fortunes,* continuing his effort to create, as Everett Carter has said, "a realistic literature whose function is to depict society truthfully so that men might reform it."[23]

There was a good deal of wobbling between Boston and New York before Howells finally settled in the latter. "I look forward to the winter in Boston with a feeling of satiety towards the place," he wrote to Henry James, who would be so sympathetic with this feeling in 1890. "I can only console myself by reflecting that it is much too good for me."[24] But then in 1891 Howells wrote his father, "I look forward to a winter in New York with loathing; I would so much rather be in the country; but it will be well for the work I am trying to do, and it seems the only thing for the children. Between the two cities I prefer New York; it is less 'done,' and there is more for one to see and learn there."[25] Howells' feeling of satiety towards Boston and his loathing of New York make it clear that his "feelings about living in Boston, New York, or anywhere else were hopelessly beset by ambivalences,"[26] and these ambivalences were voiced in his best novel, *A Hazard of New Fortunes,* a New York story in which Howells looked back at proper Boston with qualified distaste and at New York with very mixed feelings.

A Hazard of New Fortunes was described by Howells as the first fruit of his life in the commercial metropolis. Several of its characters really enjoyed the life they saw in the gaslit New York of 1889, many of whose avenues were covered with Elevated tracks. "There's only one city that belongs to the whole country and that's New York," one of them exclaims. And another insists that New York is splendidly gay or squalidly gay; but, prince or pauper, it's gay always." The bends in the "L" are admitted to be "perfectly atrocious, of course, but incomparably picturesque," and "the gayest things in the world." Howells' literary men find the cosmopolitanism and the Bohemian parts of the city exhilarating. They explore foreign restaurants and wander about Greenwich Village with zest and curiosity, excited by the city's contrasts and happy to be in a city where "you may do anything." In spite of the poverty of Mulberry Street, Chinatown, and Chatham Square, Basil March was delighted with the city. It was huge, it was ugly, it was noisy—but it was kindly and gay, and that counted for a great deal with him, as it did with Howells himself.

This attitude toward New York did not, of course, coincide with that of Henry James. In a well-known letter to Howells he praised *A Hazard of New Fortunes* ("it has filled me with communicable rapture"; "the Hazard is simply prodigious"), but expressed a reservation about it that was related to his own different view of New York at the turn of the century. James said to Howells: "The novelist is a particular window, absolutely—and of worth in so far as he is one; and it's because you open so well and are hung so close over the street that I could hang out of it all day long. Your very value is that you choose your own street—heaven forbid I should have to choose it for you." Then James added his significant reservation: "If I should say I mortally dislike the people who pass in it, I should seem to be taking on myself that intolerable responsibility of selection which it is exactly such a luxury to be relieved of."[27] But James *did* mortally dislike the people on Howells' New York street, and he was sorry that Howells looked at them so intently. More than fifteen years before James' letter was written, Howells had himself used a window-metaphor in a critique of Thomas Bailey Aldrich's literary sentimentalism. Aldrich, according to Howells, "is apt, if anything, to be over-literary, to see life through a well-selected library window,"[28] and this kind of window Howells did not want to look through or to be. But in his effort to escape library vision, Howells became too much of a tenement-house window to suit Henry James.

James could certainly approve of Howells' abandonment of Boston and of Basil March's conclusion that Boston, with all of its refinement, was "death-in-life," but James did not share Howells' sense of complicity with New York life even though James was able to express sympathy for the suffering of the London populace in *The Princess Casamassima*. When it came to the American metropolis, James, unlike Howells, did not share Basil March's feeling that he "could not release himself from a sense of complicity with [New York], no matter what whimsical, or alien, or critical attitude he took." Nor could James say with March that "a sense of the striving and the suffering deeply possessed him; and this grew the more intense as he gained some knowledge of the forces at work—forces of pity, of destruction, of perdition, of salvation."[29] By living in the great American metropolis and by trying to transcend the attitude of the indifferent spectator, Howells' character, March, personified the kind of experiment that pragmatists associated with all inquiry, and which William James and John Dewey contrasted invidiously with the "spectator theory of knowledge." Unlike Howells' hero, Hawthorne's in *The Blithedale Romance,* one recalls, liked to hover in the air above the city, watching it through the back windows of Boston boardinghouses, and Melville's Pierre failed to make any contact with New York City. But Howells, like some of his characters in *A Hazard of New Fortunes,* tried to penetrate the depths of the American city at the end of the nineteenth century. He knew that the city had its faults, but he was attracted by it. His view of nature was more inclusive and comprehending than that of Emerson and Emerson's contemporaries.

With sociologists and social workers, Howells at one point in his life found the city interesting enough to describe and attractive enough to reform, so he did not feel obliged to disregard its defects. By adopting this attitude he illustrated a lack of symmetry in the literary war between city and country. Romantic partisans of the country rarely view nature as a neutral entity which is capable of producing destruction and ugliness as well as beauty, but realistic admirers of the city are often exceedingly conscious of the city's defects and limitations. The war between romanticism and realism over the city frequently involves battles between a well-organized, completely patriotic party which suppresses all doubt about its rural cause, and an opposing party which is critical enough to have grave doubts about the city. And so in *A Hazard of New Fortunes,* one is candidly shown by a realist how the city looks to characters who are hostile to urban life.

Mrs. March, for example, first looks at New York as a Boston-born lady with intellectual pretensions and unfeeling stuffiness about the more active and more powerful city. From the beginning of the novel, she expresses hesitation about going to New York: "I don't like New York. I don't approve of it. It's so *big,* and *so* hideous! Of course I shouldn't mind that; but I've always lived in Boston and the children were born and have all their friendships and associations here.' "[30] And Mr. Dryfoos, the wealthy backer of the magazine edited by Basil March, is the head of a family which does not share Mrs. March's Bostonian view of New York, but the family dislikes it for other reasons. Mrs. Dryfoos is a simple, pathetic old Pennsylvania Dutchwoman who says to her husband, without being contradicted by him: "I can't see as we've got a bit more comfort of our lives, Jacob, because we've got such piles and piles of money. I wisht to gracious we was back on the farm this minute. I wisht you had held out ag'inst the children about sellin' it; 'twould 'a' bin the best thing fur 'em, I say. I believe in my soul they'll git spoiled here in New York. I kin see a change in 'em a'ready—in the girls."[31] The girls, for their part, are isolated in New York, unable to find love or friends, or to enter society. One is described by Beaton, the artist of the magazine, as "a simple, earthly creature, as common as an oatfield; and the other a sort of sylvan life: fierce, flashing, feline." The oatfield, Mela, detests New York, and the sylvan huntress, Christine, falls in love with Beaton, who does not love her. Neither is at home in New York City.

105

Of the Dryfooses, the son Conrad is treated most sympathetically by Howells. Conrad is a saintly young man who joins one of the Episcopalian "institutional churches" of the time in order to help the poor of the city. He feels a "sense of complicity" with the city in the highest degree, and characteristically remarks to March that he hopes their literary magazine can "do some good." At that point, March, before he is credited as he is later in the novel with seeing the city as a "life" rather than as a "spectacle," expresses his own, different conception of the magazine. "March asked rather absently, 'Some good?' Then he added: 'Oh yes; I think we can. What do you mean by good? Improve the public taste? Elevate the standard of literature? Give young authors and artists a chance?' This was the only good that had ever been in March's mind, except the good that was to come in a material way from his success, to himself and to his family. 'I don't know,' said the young man; and he looked down in a shame-faced fashion. He lifted his head and looked into March's face. 'I suppose I was thinking that some time we might help along. If we were to have those sketches of yours about life in every part of New York—.' " Conrad thinks of the magazine as an instrument of social uplift, while March thinks of it in terms of esthetic effect and circulation. Conrad says: "If you can make the comfortable people understand how the uncomfortable people live, it will be a very good thing, Mr. March. Sometimes it seems to me that the only trouble is that we don't know one another well enough; and that the first thing is to do this." " 'That's true,' said March, from the surface only. 'And then, those phases of low life are immensely picturesque. Of course, we must try to get the contrasts of luxury for the sake of the full effect. That won't be so easy. You can't penetrate to the dinner-party of a millionaire under the wing of a detective as you could to a carouse in Mulberry Street, or to his children's nursery with a philanthropist as you can to a streetboy's lodginghouse.' "[32]

This exchange between March and Conrad symbolizes two distinct types of reflection on the American city. March sees the city's contrasts "from the surface only" as something "picturesque" to be exploited "for the sake of full effect," while Conrad, like Howells, seeks communication and understanding between the city's contrasting elements. In between both views lies the basic doctrine of Howells' realism, the idea that the city is not to be "bracketed" for purposes of phenomenological analysis, not to be disregarded in favor of impressions or appearances, but rather to be regarded as a complex, rich, three-dimensional life and evaluated accordingly. And this kind of interest in the American city prepares the way for the pragmatic phase of reflection about it, when action and reform become paramount. The phenomenologist of the city concentrates on sense-data, a philosopher might say, but the reformer must deal with a full-blown object about which he has sociological knowledge and moral conviction. It was such a concern with urban life that distinguished Howells the sympathetic realistic novelist of the city, especially when he was not writing under the aegis of his unguarded (and unfairly exploited) remark that the novelist should deal with the "smiling aspects" of American life.

Yet somewhere between 1889, the year of his arrival in New York, and 1907, the year in which *Through the Eye of the Needle* appeared, the Howells who saw the city as a real thing wanted to erase all of what he saw, and was not content to tinker with the American city. "Whether or not the sights and scenes of New York were chiefly responsible for his sharpened awareness of the world about him," says Daniel Aaron, "it is apparent by the middle nineties that Howells' loosely thought-out social views had hardened into something resembling a philosophy of society."[33] And part of that philosophy entailed the destruction of the American city as it was known at that time. In *A Hazard of New Fortunes,* Howells had criticized urban ugliness, filth, poverty, and misery, but Howells' utopian works revealed a desire to do away with urban life altogether. In this respect they go beyond anything that one may read in Henry Adams or Henry James. To find equally forceful attacks on the city in this story one must go back to the early Jefferson or to one of Hawthorne's drastic asides in *The Marble Faun.* Howells, who was once prepared to see the post-bellum American city in a

107

favorable light, was overcome with frustration when the city did not measure up to his hopes and expectations. So he recommended radical methods for dealing with it.

Howells' recommendation was influenced by the socialist and utopian literature of the late nineteenth century. He was deeply affected by the writings of Tolstoy, Ruskin, and William Morris among European writers, and by Edward Bellamy, Henry George, and Lawrence Gronlund among Americans. And almost all of them were at that time advancing views of modern society which were profoundly anti-urban in their implications. Tolstoy's *What Shall We Do Then?* is dominated by the idea of escape to the country from wretched Moscow, and Edward Bellamy wrote of urban life that it was a false and unhealthy state of things which bred incalculable disease in politics, society, and religion. Lawrence Gronlund argued: "The present relation of city to country is an abnormal one. Every civilized country, with its overgrown cities, may be fairly compared to a man whose belly is steadily increasing in bulk, out of all proportion to the body, and whose legs are constantly growing thinner. This evolution is as yet perfectly legitimate. Our large cities and towns are the necessary fruits of our industrial system, and are destined to become the needed and inevitable centres for the coming changes; in their hands will chiefly lie the threads of destiny. But," Gronlund continued as he sounded the note of anti-urbanism, "then their purpose will have been fulfilled. Then the evolution will necessarily have to go back in the contrary direction: population will have to take its march back into the country."[34] Henry George was even more outspoken about the evils of urbanism: "This life of great cities is not the natural life of man. He must, under such conditions, deteriorate, physically, mentally, morally. Yet the evil does not end here. This is only one side of it. This unnatural life of the great cities means an equally unnatural life in the country. Just as the wen or tumor, drawing the wholesome juices of the body into its poisonous vortex, impoverishes all other parts of the frame, so does the crowding of human beings into great cities impoverish life in the country."[35]

The most explicit indication of the influence of Morris, Tolstoy, Bellamy, Gronlund, and George is to be found in Howells' *A Traveler from Altruria* and *Through the Eye of the Needle*. These books reveal a profound disappointment with urban life that stands in contrast to some of the more optimistic attitudes expressed in *A Hazard of New Fortunes*. Commenting on that novel in 1909, some twenty years after its original publication, Howells speaks of his early "hopes of truer and better conditions" in New York, and says that these hopes are no less dear in 1909 than they were in 1890, even though their fulfillment had not come as quickly as he had hoped. But any doubt he may have had about the American city's capacity to fulfill those hopes had been magnified in his utopian writings. In trying to understand Howells' later view of the American city, it is of course important to distinguish a distaste for the city as the city happens to be, and a distaste for the city as such. A writer who wishes to improve urban life may recount its faults without rejecting it totally as a social form. Present in the mind of such a moderate critic there may be a distinction between the essence of city life and its accidents, and he may hate the accidents alone. When Marx and Engels spoke of the idiocy of rural life in the *Communist Manifesto* they obviously evinced a preference for the city, but Engels in the *Condition of the Working Class in England in 1844* did not hesitate to describe the horrors of Liverpool just as vividly as Melville did. The interesting fact about Howells' utopian romances is the degree to which they do reject the American city as such, and hence may surprise the reader of *A Hazard of New Fortunes*.

In between the *Hazard* and *A Traveler from Altruria,* one published in 1889 and the other in 1894, Howells wrote a novel which is transitional for the student of his attitudes toward the city, *The World of Chance,* published in 1893. It prepared his readers for the full effect of his blast at New York in his later utopian romances. When the hero of *The World of Chance*, Percy Ray, arrives in Jersey City, he looks at the New York shore "with a sense of the beauty struggling through the grotesqueness of the huge panorama . . . the mean, ugly fronts and roofs of the buildings beyond, and hulking high overhead in the further distance in vast bulks and clumsy towers, the masses of those ten-storied edifices which are the necessity of commerce and the despair of art, all helped to compose the brutal and stupid body of the thing, whose soul was collectively expressed in an incredible picturesqueness. Ray saw nothing amiss in it. This agglomeration of warring forms, feebly typifying the ugliness of the warring interests within them, did not repulse him. He was not afraid."[36]

As the novel progresses, it becomes evident that Howells himself is afraid of the menacing city, afraid of its destructive impact on human beings. He expresses himself through the character, David Hughes, who expounds the utopian doctrine set forth by Howells in *A Traveler from Altruria.* Hughes is at work on a book called "The World Revisited," and chooses to illustrate his dismay about modern civilization by animadversions on the city: "My book is a criticism of modern life in all its aspects, though necessarily as the field is so vast, I can touch on some only in the most cursory fashion. For instance, take this whole architectural nightmare that we call a city. I hold that the average tasteless man has no right to realize his ideas of a house in the presence of a great multitude of his fellow-beings. It is an indecent exposure of his mind, and should not be permitted. All these structural forms about us, which with scarcely an exception are ugly and senseless, I regard as so many immoralities, as deliriums, as imbecilities, which a civilized state would not permit, and I say so in my book. The city should build the city, and provide every citizen with a fit and beautiful habitation to work in and rest in."[37] Hughes does not go as far in his attack on the city as another character in the novel, Denton, whose view is much simpler: "If I had my way," he announces, "there wouldn't be a city, big or little, on the whole continent."[38] Hughes and Denton represent the two positions between which Howells oscillated in the nineties, but his utopian romances concluded with a message far closer to Denton's than to Hughes'. For, as we shall see, although Howells advocated the continuation of social centers that faintly resembled the American city as he knew it, his Altrurian spokesman said flatly to his American audience: "There are now no cities in Altruria, in your meaning."

Howells' radical anti-urbanism emerges most explicitly when the traveler from Altruria tells his American friends about life in his utopian land before the tyrannical power of "The Accumulation" was broken by the people. "The land," the traveler says in terms reminiscent of Gronlund and Henry George, "was filled with cities where the rich flaunted their splendor in palaces, and the poor swarmed in squalid tenements. The country was drained of its life and force, to feed the centers of commerce and industry."[39] And when the Altrurian begins to describe his land as it became after the "Evolution," he says: "I will tell you, as well as I can, what Altruria is like, but, in the first place, you will have to cast out of your minds all images of civilization with which your experience has filled them. For a time the shell of the old Accumulation remained for our social habitation, and we dwelt in the old competitive and monopolistic forms after the life had gone out of them. That is, we continued to live in populous cities, and we toiled to heap up riches for the moth to corrupt, and we slaved on in making utterly useless things, merely because we had the habit of making them to sell."[40] Life in populous cities, then, was part of the shell of the old society which was later replaced.

Before turning to Howells' conception of the new social shell, it is well to read his circumstantial description of what happened to the cities of the old era: "We had, of course, a great many large cities under the old egoistic conditions, which increased and fattened upon the country, and fed their cancerous life with fresh infusions of its blood. We had several cities of half a million, and one of more than a million; we had a score of them with a population of a hundred thousand or more. We were very proud of them, and vaunted them as a proof of our unparalleled prosperity, though really they never were anything but congeries of millionaires and the wretched creatures who served them and supplied them. Of course, there was everywhere the appearance of enterprise and activity, but it meant final loss for the great mass of the businessmen, large and small, and final gain for the millionaires. These, and their parasites dwelt together, the rich starving the poor and the poor plundering and mis-governing the rich; and it was the intolerable suffering in the cities that chiefly hastened the fall of the old Accumulation, and the rise of the Commonwealth.

"Almost from the moment of the Evolution the competitive and monopolistic centers of population began to decline. In the clear light of the new order, it was seen that they were not fit dwelling-places for men, either in the complicated and luxurious palaces where the rich fenced themselves from their kind, or in the vast tenements, towering height upon height, ten and twelve stories up, where the swarming poor festered in vice and sickness and famine. If I were to tell you of the fashion of those cities of our egoistic epoch, how the construction was one error from the first, and every correction of an error bred a new defect, I should make you laugh, I should make you weep. We let them fall to ruin as quickly as they would, and their sites are still so pestilential after the lapse of centuries, that travelers are publicly guarded against them. Ravening beasts and poisonous reptiles lurk in those abodes of the riches and the poverty that are no longer known to our life. A part of one of the less malarial of the old cities, however, is maintained by the commonwealth in the form of its prosperity, and is studied by antiquarians for the instruction, and by moralists for the admonition it affords. A section of a street is exposed, and you see the foundations of the houses; you see the filthy drains that belched into the common sewers, trapped and retrapped to keep the poison gases down; you see the sewers that rolled their loathsome tides under the streets, amidst a tangle of gas pipes, steam pipes, water pipes, telegraph wires, electric lighting wires, electric motor wires and grip-cables; all without a plan, but makeshifts, expedients, devices, to repair and evade the fundamental mistake of having any such cities at all."[41]

After this outburst it is not surprising that the Altrurian traveler should say to his American audience: "There are now no cities in

Altruria, in your meaning." Instead, he tells them, there are capitals, one for each of the regions of the country and one for the whole commonwealth. But these are merely the residences of public officials who are changed every year. Capitals exist merely for the conduct of public affairs, and they are periodically frequented by artists, for the Altrurians considered the arts "the chief of [their] public affairs." The permanent social life of the country was lived in villages and hamlets within easy access of the capitals. Truly, the city "in our meaning" no longer existed for the Altrurians. In effect, the views of Denton in *A World of Chance* had triumphed over those of David Hughes, for Hughes seemed to think that cities would still exist, while if Denton had his way "there wouldn't be a city, big or little, on the whole continent." Obviously Denton had had his way with Howells in Altruria. The novelist who had felt such discontent with the "village limit" in his youth lived long enough to romanticize its ideals of family, neighborliness, and closeness to the earth. His Altrurian spokesman reported: "If it can be said that one occupation is honored above another with us, it is that which we all share, and that is the cultivation of the earth. We believe that this, when not followed slavishly, or for gain, brings man into the closest relations to the deity, through a grateful sense of the divine bounty, and that it not only awakens a natural piety in him, but that it endears to the worker that piece of soil which he tills, and so strengthens his love of home. The home is the very heart of the Altrurian system, and we do not think it very well that people should be away from their homes very long or very often. In the competitive and monopolistic times men spent half their days in racing back and forth across our continent; families were scattered by the chase for fortune, and there was a perpetual paying and repaying of visits. One-half the income of those railroads which we let fall into disuse came from the ceaseless unrest. Now a man is born and lives and dies among his own kindred, and the sweet sense of neighborhood, of brotherhood, which blessed the golden age of the first Christian republic is ours again."[42]

Through the Eye of the Needle continues in the same vein, al-

113

lowing the Altrurian to turn his critical attention to the American city in greater detail. Howells' sequel to *A Traveler from Altruria* begins with a sentence for which the reader who has gone through its predecessor is well prepared: "If I spoke with Altrurian breadth of the way New Yorkers live," writes the Altrurian emissary to a friend, "I should begin by saying that the New Yorkers did not live at all."[43] To document his view of New York as a non-life, the Altrurian launches on an elaborate description of housing in the period. There is a chapter on the evils of the tenement house and another one on the apartment house; there are constant references to the city's filth, of course. The noise of the elevated train comes in for special condemnation; and here, in this apparently trivial detail, one can see a profound difference between the Howells of *A Hazard of New Fortunes* and the Howells of the utopian romances. In the novel Mrs. March was "infatuated" with the elevated. And Basil March said "it was better than the theater, of which it reminded him, to see those people through their windows: a family party of work-folk at a late tea, some of the men in their shirt-sleeves; a woman sewing by a lamp; a mother laying her child in its cradle; a man with his head fallen on his hands upon a table; a girl and her lover leaning over the window-sill together. What suggestion! What drama! What infinite interest!"[44] But Howells' Altrurian emissary has an entirely different picture of life near the "L," a picture to which he responds with an entirely different set of exclamations: "People are born and married, and live and die in the midst of an uproar so frantic that you would think they would go mad of it; and I believe the physicians really attribute something of the growing prevalence of neurotic disorders to the wear and tear of the nerves from the rush of the trains passing almost momently, and the perpetual jarring of the earth and air from their swift transit . . . In health it is bad enough, but in sickness it must be horrible beyond all parallel. Imagine a mother with a dying child in such a place; or a wife bending over the pillow of her husband to catch the last faint whisper of farewell, as a train of five or six cars goes roaring by the open window! What horror! What profanation!"[45]

It has been said many times, of course, that the anti-urbanism of the utopian romances is already present in Howells' earlier work, that he was always dominated by a kind of Jeffersonian admiration for the small town.[46] But it cannot be denied that this feeling for the small town is more muted—if it is present at all—in *A Hazard of New Fortunes* than it is in the utopian romances. In the romances it is much more obvious that Howells hated New York at the turn of the century as much as Henry James did. Unlike Jefferson, a chastened agrarian who lived long enough to say that the city was here to stay, Howells was a disenchanted city-dweller who lived long enough to return nostalgically to the values of the village he knew as a young man. By a village he did not mean deep country, for he appears to have felt keenly the terrors of loneliness away from all sociability. The unhappiness of country loneliness appears in several of his writings, for example in *The Minister's Charge*,[47] and in *A Traveler from Altruria*.[48] He also expressed it in his letters. In 1896, when he was fifty-nine, he explained his purchase of a house at Far Rockaway on a village street in this way: "When Elinor and I came to think seriously of the country we found ourselves too old and timid to face its loneliness, and we have long idealized our home as on a village street."[49] In 1901 he once again reported his fear of living in the country and added a pathetic reason for living in the city: "We discovered not long ago that we were too old for living in the country as we have meant to do, now these many years, and in proportion as we have lost our teeth we feel the need of being near a dentist."[50] And while there are a few remarks in his letters about being homesick for New York while traveling, in 1920, the year of his death, Howells issued a book of travel called *Hither and Thither in Germany*,[51] in which the narrator compared New York's streets invidiously with those of German cities. In spite of his disapproval of a sign reading, "Weinhandlung," on a residential street in Mayence, the narrator and his wife "had to confess once more that any inferior city of Germany [was] of a more proper and dignified presence than the most purse-proud metropolis in America. To be sure, they said, the German towns had generally a thousand years' start; but, all the same, the fact galled them."[52] And so one of our most eminent novelists of urban life ended his career living in New York but looking wistfully at the American village and the German city.

VIII

DISAPPOINTMENT IN NEW YORK

FRANK NORRIS AND THEODORE DREISER

IT IS customary for literary historians to make a distinction between a realist like Howells and writers who continued his tradition of fidelity to life while espousing philosophies or using techniques that make it convenient to call them "naturalists" instead. And so, for example, Theodore Dreiser is called a naturalist because of his materialism and determinism, or because he treated sex, violence, and poverty with more candor than appears in the writings of Howells. Nevertheless, there was an important community of feeling between the "Dean of American Letters," as Howells was called at the turn of the century, and his naturalistic allies in the campaign to portray American life: all of them came to be disappointed with the city of New York. The roots of that disappointment are not the same in each case although they intertwine. Howells criticized the American metropolis on grounds that reflected his preference for the small village; Norris' distaste for New York was partly dictated by a love for the West and for the values of the red-blooded man; while Dreiser's quarrel with New York in the nineties was that of a city-lover who had no alternative ideal of social existence but rather a personal grievance against New York.

The first American city to engage Norris' attention was San Francisco, whose liveliness and complexity attracted him. It was full of drama; it was picturesque; it was exciting. Under the influence of Zola he came to think of life on Polk Street as worthy of serious literary treatment, and the main result was *McTeague,* which appeared in 1899.[1] In *McTeague* Norris gives considerable space to the fascinations of the city scene. For some time after McTeague had opened his dental parlors in San Francisco, the constant pageantry of the small streets offered him a liveliness that his own mind lacked. "The street never failed to interest him. It was one of those cross streets peculiar to Western cities, situated in the heart of the residence quarter . . . There were corner drug stores with huge jars of red, yellow, and green liquids in their windows, very brave and gay; stationers' stores where illustrated weeklies were tacked upon bulletin boards . . . sad-looking plumbers' offices; cheap restaurants, in whose windows one saw piles of unopened oysters weighted down by cubes of ice, and china pigs and cows knee-deep in layers of white beans . . . Occasionally a cable-car passed, trundling heavily, with a strident whirring of jostled glass windows."[2] And although the approaches to San Francisco were drab, and McTeague first kissed his future wife, Trina Sieppe, near a city dump heap, the presence of the city sights and sounds were for the most part a pleasant background accompaniment to the McTeagues' domestic bliss in the early days of their marriage.

Such a view of San Francisco corresponded to Howells' earlier, more favorable, impression of New York and to Dreiser's first excitement in both Chicago and New York. But Howells' effort to portray city life seemed too weak and halting to his successors among the realists and naturalists. They tried with a vengeance to make up for his alleged failings. They were often inquisitive newspapermen in a muck-raking age and they saw themselves cutting through the jungle of city life to urban reality. For them the city was not only a place of lively sights but also a place of violent social struggle in which only a few people rise to positions of enormous power while many others sink to a primitive level and lose their identity. Norris, in particular, became more and more aware of urban horror and of the spread of the commercial spirit across the country. Even lively San Francisco streets were full of tragic contrasts that he exploited, often melodramatically. Mrs. Hooven, in *The Octopus,* comes to one of its crowded downtown sections

118

after her husband's death has delivered their ranch over to the railroad interests, and there she wanders the endless, hilly streets until she drops dead from starvation on an evening when the railroad owners are dining luxuriously in a splendid San Francisco mansion. Industrialization, urban expansion, and the scramble for money in the nineties have deeply disturbing effects on many of Norris' characters. McTeague gradually becomes obsessed with greed, not content with being a modestly successful San Francisco dentist. And in *The Octopus* the manager of the Union Pacific railroad interests and the ranch manager are both motivated only by the desire to accumulate money and power in fierce competition. The ranch falls under the spell of commerce and is connected by wire with San Francisco, Minneapolis, Duluth, Chicago, New York, and Liverpool; fluctuations in the price of the world's crop of wheat thrill straight to its office. Prices are avidly followed on the ticker by rancher-businessmen who, at such moments, no longer feel their individuality. The ranch becomes part of a world-wide organic whole, and experiences in a moment the effects of causes thousands of miles away.

While the ranchers lose their individuality by becoming part of the vast communications network of the wheat market, McTeague's wife loses hers by failure to communicate with anyone in San Francisco. "Often entire days passed when she did not hear the sound of her own voice. She was alone, a solitary, abandoned woman, lost in the lowest eddies of the great city's tide—the tide that always ebbs."[3] Thus, the forces of urbanization can destroy individuals either by absorbing them into the system of communication or by banishing them from it. Norris' generation was given to viewing vast business organizations as overwhelming forces. For this reason, it has been noted frequently that American novelists of the period were peculiarly prone to use titles like *The Octopus, The Titan, The Jungle,* and *The Pit.* Such titles expressed a sense of monstrous power present in business organizations or in the cities that housed them. But Norris and Dreiser, like Howells, were often ambiguous in their feelings about these mammoth organizations and their

119

leaders. Both Norris and Dreiser went through periods of acceptance or even admiration of the energy, the force, the dynamism of powerful business men. A careful interpreter of Norris has remarked that one could not have predicted his attack on the tycoon in *The Octopus,* for up to that time he had admired magnates, despised radicals, reformers, and the *canaille,* and watched the struggle for existence with indifference.[4] But although students of Norris have found it hard to explain his transition, Norris made it, and *The Octopus* was an attack on commercialism and urbanization.

Greed, impersonality, selfishness, and lack of sympathy were attacked in *The Octopus* by a somewhat philosophical entrepreneur, Cedarquist, who decries the indifference of businessmen to public affairs, as well as the lethargy of ordinary men. And Norris, in the name of Cedarquist, called this lack of responsibility the one crying evil of American life. Other characters in *The Octopus* resisted both the spectacle and the evil influences of urban life. Hilma detested the "crude, raw city, with its crowding houses all of wood and tin, its blotting fogs, its uproarious trade winds." In it "there was no outlook for the future," she felt; and it made her homesick for the ranch and the dairy-house.[5] Mrs. Magnus Derrick was troubled by the new order of things invading the country, by a ranch ruled by iron and steam and bullied into a yield of 350,000 bushels. She yearned to escape from the monotony of the industrialized ranch to the Old World cities of Rome and Naples.

The character most out-of-tune with the reverberations of San Francisco's growth and the mechanization of the ranch country is Vanamee, an intelligent, college-trained man who has become a shepherd. He is pictured as a strange, sensitive being, who has kept his personal gifts alive by Thoreauvian contact with nature and by total rejection of all urbanized life. He believes "in a sixth sense, or rather a whole system of other unnamed senses beyond the reach of our understanding," and thinks that "people who live much alone and close to nature experience the sensation of it . . . something fundamental that we share with plants and animals."[6] Vanamee disappears with his flocks into the vast, uncultivated pastures of the Southwest, and Norris leads us inexorably to the conclusion that the rapidly growing cities and their tributary farmlands will destroy people immersed in money-grabbing, and drive out talented and humane people in search of an integrated life of service to humanity.

Like so many writers of his generation, Norris was lured to New York from San Francisco just as Howells had been attracted to Boston in an earlier generation. Norris' biographer remarks that the movement of writers to New York in the nineties was connected with the rise of yellow journalism, the appearance of the Sunday edition, the growth of advertising, the improvement of methods of illustration, and the emergence of cheap magazines with large circulation.[7] Editors looked to the West for literary help in their exciting ventures; it was the age of S. S. McClure, William Randolph Hearst, and Joseph Pulitzer. McClure discovered Norris by reading his contributions to the San Francisco *Wave;* he then offered him a job on *McClure's Magazine* and promised to publish his book *Moran of the Lady Letty.* When Norris arrived in the big city, his first reaction was that "New York is *all* right." He got himself a "nifty little room in a mighty nifty little place just opposite the Waldorf Hotel" and reported in a letter in March 1898 that he thought he was going to "get on." He saw Howells, who treated him well, and he found his San Francisco friends all riding on the crest of the New York literary wave.[8]

In New York Norris found ways of combining his instinctive romanticism with the attractions of the big city. Romanticism as he defined it was concerned with the abnormal, the violent, the deviation from the commonplace; and this could easily be found on Chicago's Michigan Avenue or on the Lower East Side of New York. There was as much romance, he said, in the brownstone and the office building as in the chatelaine's chamber and the dungeon. But it could not be found while taking tea at a neighbor's house, and its discovery was not a task for the sensitive or the delicate who could not enter the slums. It was rather a task for the robust romanticist who could portray the sombre aspects of the city, the squalor of its dives, its distorted lives, and then cry out: "Look! Listen! This, too, is life. These, too, are my children! Look at them, know them, and, knowing, help!"⁹ Yet Norris' interest in the slums of New York did not last long. In principle they could provide drama, color, and romance, but in fact they did not for Norris.

After a trip to Cuba during the Spanish-American War, he returned to New York but soon tired of the "New Bohemia" that had settled in Washington Square. The West was calling him back, and he wrote home in March of 1899: "New York is not California nor New York City San Francisco, and I am afraid that because of the difference I shall never be reconciled to the East . . . There is not much color here and very little of the picturesque . . . I have almost forgotten how a mountain looks and I never can quite persuade myself that the Atlantic is an ocean—in the same sense as the Pacific. I miss the out-of-doorness of the West more and more and the sea fogs and the Trade Wind, and I don't suppose I shall ever feel at home away from there. Indeed I have come to look forward to the time when I shall come back to San Francisco to live for good and all." This same letter continues with a report of a conversation with Howells which is quite understandable after one has read that author's *A Traveler from Altruria* and *Through the Eye of the Needle*. "I was talking to Mr. Howells about this and he rather encouraged me to do my work wherever the surroundings were most congenial, and told me that as soon as I had 'once established my connection' in New York there was no reason why I could not 'go home' and that a 'literary' man could do his work anywhere."¹⁰

New York was not a literary centre, Norris insisted in his ironically entitled essay "New York as a Literary Centre." He protested against the notion of some Western writers that New York was the only place they could "stand on and holler." Once upon a time, he recalled, Boston had the distinction that he was now denying to New York. New England writers rightly crowded into Boston, where they could dine with each other and talk with each other profitably. But this, he said, was before "the reactionary movement of populations from the cities toward the country had set in" (*pace*

Gronlund), at a time when "a constant residence winter and summer in the country was not dreamed of by those who had the leisure and the money to afford it." Moreover, the writer needs no city office; he is not forced to be in touch with the business life of Broadway. Poems may be and are written in Dakota, criticism is done in Kansas, novels composed in Wyoming, and essays are written in Utah. Literary centres and groups exist everywhere even though the publishers and the commercial machinery are in New York. New York is merely a distribution centre for literature much as Chicago is a distribution centre for wheat in his novel *The Pit*.

Norris then hit New York literature another blow where it really hurt. Unlike Paris, London, and Boston, New York "can claim ridiculously few of the men of larger [literary] calibre as her own" natives. Indiana claims James Whitcomb Riley, Hamlin Garland was a westerner, Bret Harte a Californian, Mark Twain a middle westerner, and "Harold Frederic and Henry James found England more congenial than the greatest cities of their native land." The writer not only does not *need* New York, but it is positively hostile and inimical to good work. Its literary clubs "stultify ambition, warp original talent, and definably and irretrievably stamp out the last spark of productive ability." The best writers never come to the meetings of the clubs, whose discussions are puerile, commonplace, conventional, and unoriginal. As in his story *Dying Fires,* Norris concluded his argument by saying: "The best thought is not in New York; and even if it were, the best thought of other men is not so good for you as your own thought, dug out of your own vitals by your own unaided efforts, be it ever so inadequate. You do not have to go to New York for that. Your own ideas, your own work will flourish best if left alone untrammeled and uninfluenced. And believe this to be true, that wherever there is a table, a sheet of paper and a pot of ink, there is a Literary Centre if you will."[11]

In *Salt and Sincerity,* a series of essays that appeared in the last year of his life, Norris continued the attack on the city as a literary centre by advising the writer who had fears for his productive powers to thrust himself out of the grooves and cogs of other men's

123

lives, out of "the life of the city and comfortable stay-at-home, hour-to-hour humdrum." And the further afield the better. "The Master-note will not be heard within 'commuting distance of the city.' The whir of civilization smothers it. The click of the telegraph, the hiss of steam and the clatter of the printing-press drowns it out."[12] Only in mountains, canyons, plunging streams, swirling rivers, deserts, plains, and wildernesses will it be heard. And so, after he completed *The Pit,* Norris left New York for good, returning to California to what he thought were the sources of his creativity. He was, unlike most critics of the city after the Civil War, a romantic admirer of the wilderness who was also fascinated by the slums.

Norris' fellow-naturalist, Theodore Dreiser, was born in 1871, a year after him. And although Dreiser's background was very different from that of Norris, he, too, became disenchanted with New York in the nineties. He had no clear preference, it would appear, for a different kind of life, as Howells and Norris had, for he was not an admirer of either small towns or mountains. His reaction to New York was more personal. The city acted on him as a pretty girl once did: "Her whole manner was at once an invitation and repulsion—the two carefully balanced so as to produce a static and yet an irritating state. I half liked and disliked her. If she had been especially friendly, no doubt I should have liked her very much. Since she was so wholly evasive, I fancied that I could dislike her quite as much."[13]

One need not be a speculative psychoanalyst to say that Dreiser often sees the American city as he saw this girl. When the city smiles at him, he likes it; when it turns him down, he doesn't. Those who capture the city he admires, those who don't, he despises or feels sorry for. But the city is always a living thing for Dreiser. The city is a part of nature for him, so we find very little disparaging talk about urban artificiality in his writings. This is not unqualified praise, as it would have been if Dreiser had viewed nature in the manner of more traditional American writers. Although Dreiser puts the city back in nature, his nature is not as uniformly beneficent as that of Jefferson or Emerson. Most often Dreiser sees it as blind, dark, indifferent, and meaningless; and when the city is located in a nature so conceived, it too seems cold, gray, and alien to Dreiser. He then sees himself and his characters as threatened by it, and in this mood Dreiser can be the most anti-urban of American novelists. Then he is the unrequited lover, the disappointed suitor, the man on the make, as Kenneth Lynn[14] sees him, who loathes the city that denies him.

Dreiser's earliest visions of the city have been compared with those of Whitman and the painter John Sloan. For all of them, David Brion Davis says, the city is an awing spectacle and an object of sympathy. In Dreiser's earliest years, as Davis also points out, his sympathy for the city's victims was not accompanied by an urge to reform the world.[15] This emerges with great clarity and explicitness in Dreiser's account of his life from earliest childhood to his arrival in New York in the early nineties. His story was a pilgrim's progress from a tiny town to the metropolis of America, from the middle west to the east, through small cities to the largest of them all; from Evansville, Indiana, to Chicago and finally to New York, with stops at St. Louis, Pittsburgh, Cleveland, and lesser cities along the way. He approached New York just as he had approached Chicago, with anticipation, wonder and awe, but once there he was shocked into antipathy by the poverty, the squalor, and above all by the frustration he experienced. At this time he was not advancing views as to how the city might be changed for the better. He was too much of a fatalist to think that man could control or deflect the titanic "chemical" forces of life and nature. The result was despair and disgust, a feeling of hopelessness while he was in the American city.

In earliest childhood Dreiser was entranced by the stories of Chicago told by his adventurous and shiftless brother, Rome. When Dreiser was about nine, in 1880, Rome came home and exclaimed: "You never saw such a place! . . . That's the place for a family,

125

where they can do something and get along! Not stuck off in a little hole like this! Why, say, there must be four or five hundred thousand people there! And the shops! And the high buildings!"[16] Rome had been watching America grow, Dreiser recalled; Rome was electrified and astonished by it, filled with the wine of this new life in the Middle West. So, before Dreiser himself saw the great midwestern metropolis, he was stirred by his brother's pictures of city life and by reading that led him to hope that he could see New York, Paris, Rome, and St. Petersburg.[17] Even life in a tiny city like Evansville, Indiana, could bring forth his typical cascade of exclamation points: "Those poor scum back in Sullivan, I thought! What could they know of a place like this? A city! And such a city!"[18]

In 1883, when Dreiser was twelve, his mother was persuaded by some of her older children to move to Chicago and once there Dreiser thought it was a dream city: "The city of which I am now about to write never was on land or sea; or if it appears to have the outlines of reality, they are but shadow to the glory that was in my own mind." He saluted this city of his dreams: "Hail, Chicago! First of the daughters of the new world! . . . Here came the children of the new world and the old, avid for life and love, seeking a patrimony."[19]

This was the Chicago to which his character Cowperwood came after his defeat in Philadelphia; it was the Chicago of *Sister Carrie;* it was the dynamic, bustling Chicago of the late seventies and the early eighties. In *The Titan* Dreiser described it in the same exclamatory terms. Chicago was "this Florence of the West . . . this singing flame of a city, this all America, this poet in chaps and buckskin, this rude, raw Titan, this Burns of a city . . . Take Athens, oh, Greece! Italy, do you keep Rome! This was the Babylon, the Troy, the Nineveh of a younger day." To it the gaping westerner and the hopeful easterner came; the dreamy southern gentleman who had been robbed of his patrimony; the hopeful alumnus of Yale, Harvard, or Princeton; the California miner; the Pole, the Swede, the German, the Russian, the negro, the prostitute, the gambler, the adventurer. It was a city with only a handful of native born, according to Dreiser, packed to the doors with riff-raff. He saw the lights of the bagnio flaring and heard the gin-mill's banjos, zithers and mandolins tinkling. "All the dreams and the brutality of the day seemed gathered to rejoice (and rejoice they did) in this new-found wonder of a metropolitan life in the West."[20]

When Dreiser described his first days in Chicago, he spoke of the constant and varying panorama before his windows, of the girls and women making endless toilets near their open windows, of clerks bustling in at five-thirty to dress, to lounge, or to rush to an evening engagement. These scenes were possessed of life, and the spirit of Chicago flowed into him and made him ecstatic. Its personality was different from anything he had ever known. "It was a compound of hope and joy in existence, intense hope and intense joy." Cities, like individuals, he said, can flare up with hope, and Chicago did just that in the eighties. Throughout Dreiser's early writing there is this excitement about growing cities, coming cities, cities on the make. In *Dawn* he wrote that even though he had seen the furious growth of New York and Los Angeles, his impression of the rapid growth of Chicago in the eighteen-eighties had never been equaled.[21] In *A Hoosier Holiday* he recalled that in the nineties "America was in the furnace stage of its existence. Everything was in the making—fortunes, art, its social and commercial life, everything."[22]

This was the period in Dreiser's life when he viewed the American city primarily as a spectacle. It was like a scene in a play, like a view in the Arabian nights.[23] It was a mystery when thought of as a whole. For Dreiser in those days, a streetcar strike "was little more than an odd spectacle of persons, ordinarily accustomed to ride in streetcars, now seated on chairs in wagons and hauled to and fro. In short, placed before a given series of facts which, had I been in the least economically or society or individually-minded, must have given rise to at least some modest social speculation, I saw only the surface scene, and other than artistically my mind was a blank. I had no gift for organic sociology. Trade and all that related to it was interesting as a strange, at times even lovely, spectacle, but as a problem or compulsion, at once, under certain conditions desperate and terrifying, I was not able to register it. Rather, my one gift, and one only, appeared to be to stare about and admire this world so wide . . . As a writer and thinker, it profited me, for this picture stuck, and in time I was able to identify its true economic and social significance, and so my own personal relationship thereto. But not then. Rather, it was only the exterior of America, its surface forms, not its internal nature, that registered."[24] Dreiser recollected that Cleveland in the nineties was a great spectacle, and that he was something of a recluse, fonder of spectacles than he was of people.[25]

So Dreiser at the end of the nineteenth century adopted an attitude toward the city that was similar to the one that Howells' character Basil March was trying to escape at almost the same time. But Dreiser did not contrast seeing the city as a spectacle and seeing it as a life. Even when Dreiser called the city a spectacle, he never thought of it as anything but a living, moving, throbbing thing. What Dreiser meant to contrast with seeing the city as a spectacle became a little clearer when he said that he was not interested in organic sociology. He was not interested in the scientific analysis and explanation of the life he was viewing as a spectacle, but he did not deny that he was viewing a life. And he was caught up in that life when he moved to Chicago. Chicago was an organism for him even though he did not examine it with the sociological techniques taught at the University of Chicago and applied at Hull House in the nineties. Chicago had a personality for him, a personality that he could love and hate. He could sympathize with its poor and envy its rich. He himself was a poor boy in the city, not a rubber-necking literary man from Boston, as March was; and he could identify himself with the ordinary people of Chicago in a way that neither Howells nor Basil March could do in New York. For this reason Dreiser could complain that even Howells, with every desire to do so, didn't see American life as it was lived.[26]

Shortly after Dreiser's mother took the family to Chicago, she was forced to leave the city and go to Warsaw, Indiana. But Dreiser was captivated by Chicago and he returned there on his own at the age of 16. Upon reentering it, he reported feelings which are very different from those of Howells' Lemuel Barker in *The Minister's Charge*. "Neither fear nor loneliness possessed me; rather, if anything, there was something determined and even aggressive in my attitude, why I cannot say. Also I knew then and there that I loved Chicago. It was so strong, so rough, so shabby, and yet so vital and determined. It seemed more like a young giant afraid of nothing, and that it was that appealed to me."[27] Of all the writers we have examined, and of all we shall examine, Dreiser was the most romantic about the American city. He conceived of his romanticism as compatible with his realism, just as Frank Norris did. In *Newspaper Days* Dreiser recalled that in 1890, "Chicago . . . seethed with a peculiarly human or realistic atmosphere. It is given to some cities, as to some lands, to suggest romance, and to me Chicago did that hourly. It sang, I thought, and in spite of what I deemed my various troubles—small enough as I now see them—I was singing with it."[28] And when he came to list the things he liked about Chicago then, they virtually coincided with the things that most of the earlier literary tradition had deplored: the grinding wheels of trucks and cars, the heavy smoke, the bustle of the people, the prostitutes, the factories, the stockyards, the steel works, the Pullman yards, the unpainted, tumble-down shanties, the can-strewn yards, the lecherous slatterns and brawlers. "I liked the life. I was crazy about it. Chicago was like a great orchestra in a tumult of noble harmonies. I was like a guest at a feast, eating and drinking in a delirium of ecstasy."[29] The romantic Dreiser was the excited spectator of urban life, the Dreiser who talked in terms of abstractions: of Nature, Nature, Nature, and Life, Life, Life, and Cities, Cities, Cities, and Crowds, Crowds, Crowds, and Money, Money, Money, and Sex, Sex, Sex, always triadically named. This was the Dreiser who dreamed of success in the city, who talked in chaotic terms about determinism and the contrasts and forces that moved men about in wildly excited cities.

Through all of this period in Dreiser's life there was the incessant note of sympathy for the defeated people of these growing cities. "I was filled with an intense sympathy for the woes of others; life, in all its helpless degradation and poverty, the unsatisfied dreams of people, their sweaty labors, the things they were compelled to endure—nameless impositions, curses, brutalities— the things they would never have, their hungers, thirsts, half-formed dreams of pleasure, their gibbering insanities and beaten resignations at the end. I have sobbed dry sobs looking into what I deemed to be broken faces and the eyes of human failures. A shabby tumbledown district or doorway, a drunken woman being arraigned before a magistrate, a child dying in a hospital, a man or woman injured in an accident—the times unbidden tears have leaped in my eyes and my throat has become parched and painful over scenes of the streets, the hospitals, the jails!"[30] Dreiser did not limit his sympathy to others. With laudable candor he reported: "The sad state of the poor workingman was a constant thought with me, but nearly always I was the greatest and poorest and most deserving of all workingmen."[31] In short, he felt sympathy for himself too, particularly when the city thwarted him and prevented the fulfillment of his dreams. His resentment of the city is best illustrated in his encounter with New York in the nineties, an encounter that began with something like the excitement generated by Chicago, but which ended in disillusion and disgust. Dreiser's New York experience at that time revealed a pattern which is different from any considered so far, precisely because Dreiser approached the great American city with hope and expectation, with uncontrolled joy of a kind that excelled even the joy of William James, as we shall see. For James was a visiting professor in New York, not an ambitious young man from the provinces seeking his fortune there.

When, before he went to New York, some of Dreiser's newspaper friends called Chicago a way-station by comparison with New York, Dreiser was incredulous. "Ah, you're crazy," he replied, "You're like all New Yorkers: you think you know it all."[32] Later, he said he wanted to apologize to these friends after seeing New York. In *Sister Carrie* he fully acknowledged the differences between the two cities, remarking that millionaires in Chicago were not numerous at the time; that the rich there had not become so rich as to "drown all moderate incomes in obscurity"; that while in Chicago the only two roads to distinction were politics and trade, in New York there were fifty such roads. New York was full of celebrities; there "the sea was full of whales. A common fish must needs disappear wholly from view—remain unseen." For this reason his character Hurstwood was nothing in New York after having been something in Chicago. And Dreiser himself began to feel like nothing in New York after his first flush of excitement over it.

That flush of excitement was considerable. His brother Paul, the song-writer, had been telling him of New York's virtues in the nineties just as his brother, Rome, had introduced him to the virtues of Chicago in the eighties: "there was only one place where one might live in a keen and vigorous way, and that was New York. It was *the* city, the only cosmopolitan city, a wonder-world in itself. It was great, wonderful, marvelous, the size, the color, the tang, the beauty."[33] And when Dreiser finally came to it, he saw the beauty, the hope, and the possibilities that were there. New York was not, he granted, a handsome city. But it was full of the contrasts that stimulated him so much. Life, zest, security, and ease existed side by side with poverty, longing, and sacrifice, giving a keen edge to things. New York had none of the clattering snap, as he put it, of western cities, a snap that arrested one at first and then palled. But it was grossly and blissfully self-indulgent; it communicated a sense of ease, gluttony, and power. "Here, as one could feel, were huge dreams and lusts and vanities being gratified hourly. I wanted to know the worst and the best of it."[34]

Unfortunately for Dreiser, he came to know the worst very soon. He was sharply rebuffed by New York, and in the mood of a disappointed suitor closed his *Newspaper Days* with a denunciation of it that went as far as any considered in this book. It was a denunciation, however, by someone who had been lured into New York, and had been pained by it in a way that neither its pre-Civil War critics nor those who visited it just after the Civil War could have known. Jefferson, Emerson, Thoreau, Poe, Hawthorne, and Melville could not have experienced such pain because such a city had not yet existed in their time; Henry James and Henry Adams could not have known it because they had never immersed themselves in New York as Dreiser had. James and Adams were repelled by the sight of New York but Dreiser, in the familiar anti-urban metaphor, was the moth drawn into the flame. "Drawn" is the word that Dreiser would have applied to himself, since at that moment he was discovering Balzac and the determinism of Spencer, Huxley, and Tyndall. After his first bedazzled entrance into New York, Dreiser went back to Pittsburgh for a few months, saved up two hundred and forty dollars and then returned to the big city, challenged by his first contact with it and influenced by his recent reading of Balzac, especially by *A Great Man of the Provinces in Paris.* But Dreiser also tells us that he returned to New York in a dismal and brooding spirit, mainly because of his reading in Spencer, Tyndall, and Huxley. Lingering elements of his childhood Catholicism were destroyed by this reading. And more important was the destruction of the feeling that one could "get somewhere." "Now in its place was the definite conviction that spiritually one got nowhere, that there was no hereafter, that one lived and had his being because one had to, and that it was of no importance."[35] The net effect of this was a sad submission to fate.

The influence of Herbert Spencer on Dreiser was not unlike the influence on others of Josiah Royce, who at the time was a leader of the opposite party in the Anglo-American philosophical world. While Spencer destroyed religious hope, Royce adopted a theodicy according to which "all things work together for good." And yet both Spencer and Royce encouraged human submission to vast forces beyond human control. Dreiser shows no signs of having read the absolute idealists but he was in a common spiritual predicament at the turn of the century: that of having to choose between a view of the world according to which one could "get nowhere" and a view which asserted, in spite of all evidence to the contrary, that the universe was intrinsically good. This was the dilemma to which William James later addressed himself in his *Pragmatism,* the dilemma he thought his optimistic meliorism would solve. But Dreiser was enthralled by deterministic metaphysics at the time and so entered New York in a Spencerian frame of mind that did not help him absorb the shocks he was about to receive.

As an aspiring young newspaperman Dreiser visited the offices of all the great papers of the day, only to be shown the door. He couldn't get in to see the city editor at the *Sun,* the *Tribune,* or the *World.* And so he walked across the street to City Hall Park, sat down on a bench with the bums, loafers, idlers and tramps, and began to think of the city's cruelty and its hugeness. It was then, he says, that Hurstwood, the character in *Sister Carrie,* was born— Hurstwood who complains so much of the "walled city" that keeps him out. Having been told by Dreiser that the idea of Hurstwood was born on the cold, cruel, benches of City Hall Park, we can better understand his attitude toward urban contrasts in *Sister Carrie,* which appeared in 1900. Dreiser is preoccupied with them throughout the novel. The Chicago to which Carrie came in 1889 "possessed a high and mighty air calculated to overawe and abash the common applicant, and to make the gulf between poverty and success seem both wide and deep." These contrasts were magnified in New York and there Hurstwood developed his image of the walled city within the city: "You could not get in. Those inside did not care to come out to see who you are. They were so merry inside there that all those outside were forgotten, and he was on the outside." But Carrie, who is inside this walled city, feels no great happiness either. Applause and publicity, once far off, are now hers, but they are trivial and unimportant to her. She is as lonely in the walled city as Hurstwood is outside of it.

The idea that the successful are as driven as the defeated also appears in Dreiser's autobiographical writings about his early days. After he managed to push his way into a job at the *World,* he got a glimpse of its owner, Joseph Pulitzer, whom he saw as an urban type, "undoubtedly semi-neurasthenic, a disease-demonized soul, who

133

could scarcely control himself in anything, a man who was fighting an almost insane battle with life itself, trying to be omnipotent and what not else and never to die."[36] Lesser people on the *World* were in constant fear of losing jobs and "every man was for himself." The *World's* city room was in a Hobbesian state of nature, and Dreiser thought that the city itself was too. It was so vast, so rich, so hard. "How was one to make one's way here? I had so little to offer, merely a gift of scribbling."[37] The city was overawing and Dreiser was made to feel "more than ordinarily incompetent" by the city's hugeness, its force and heartlessness, "its startling contrasts of wealth and poverty," its ruthlessness, its indifference, and the disillusion that prevailed everywhere in it.[38] He did not look then for the underlying causes of the city's defects. He had loved the city, it had hurt him, and he came to regard it as a bad place. He rejected it then in a total and unqualified way.

The great contrasts that Dreiser could sometimes treat with admiration as part of the drama and the color of the city now made him feel incompetent. "How was a sniveling scribbler to make his way in such a world?" he asked. "A crushing sense of incompetence and general inefficiency seemed to settle on me, and I could not shake it off." His conclusion was that "New York was difficult and revolting. The police and politicians were a menace; vice was rampant; wealth was shamelessly showy, cold and brutal. In New York the outsider or beginner had scarcely any chance at all, save as a servant. The city was overrun with hungry, loafing men of all descriptions, newspaper writers included."[39] The materialistic metaphysics he had brought with him from Pittsburgh he now thought of as confirmed. His awe of the city was now "awe of the grinding and almost disgusting forces of life itself which I found in Spencer and Huxley and Balzac and which now persistently haunted me and, due possibly to a depressed physical condition at this time, made it impossible for me to work with any of the zest that had characterized my work in the West." Then he said something which made clear how his attitude toward urban contrast would fluctuate with his own relation to that contrast: "There was that astounding contrast between wealth and poverty, here more sharply emphasized than anywhere else in America, which gave the great city a gross and cruel and mechanical look; and this was emphasized not only by the papers themselves, with their various summaries of investigations and exposures, but also by my own hourly contact with it—a look so harsh and indifferent at times as to leave me a little numb."[40] Dreiser had become a hopeless failure as a newspaperman and in that state he was crushed by the urban forces he admired so much in other states and moods.

The fact that Dreiser thought the philosophy of Spencer explained the overwhelming effect of the city is worth remarking, if only because it shows how hard it is to establish a unique correlation between a view of the city and metaphysical doctrine. While Emerson used the metaphysics of romantic idealism in his attack on the city, Dreiser made anti-urban use of its nineteenth-century antithesis—materialism. Once again we confront a salient feature of anti-urbanism in America: the fact that it is not the special property of any philosophical party. Dislike of the city can go hand-in-hand with acceptance of virtually any world view; it can be felt by those who accept the deism of Jefferson, the transcendentalism of Emerson, or the evolutionism of Herbert Spencer.

It is also worth remembering that Dreiser's negative reaction to New York in *Newspaper Days* is different in one respect from any reaction we have considered so far. It is, to underscore the point, *not* the reaction of a writer who dislikes the surface of the city, who is repelled by the very sight of it. Nor does Dreiser, like Poe, Hawthorne, or Melville, have bad dreams of what the American city *might* become, stimulated by experiences of London or Liverpool. On the contrary, Dreiser comes to the American city with pleasant anticipatory dreams of it, but once he lives in it, he is repelled by it. And then he finds more reason to dislike it than did most of his literary predecessors. He sees it and likes it, he comes to it and is conquered by it. He has no bad dreams about its contrasts on the night before he enters the city, but he does on the night after.

The urban contrasts that attracted Dreiser and then repelled him,

135

attracted him once again after the grim nineties receded. In later life he could resume his more detached and more esthetic view of the city's grinding forces. For example, in recording his reactions to New York between 1900 and 1914 in *The Color of A Great City,* he said that the thing that made New York attractive was its sharp and immense contrasts. He preferred "the astounding areas of poverty and beggary" on the lower east side and the Bowery at the turn of the century to the "beschooled and beserviced east side" of 1923, the year in which *The Color of A Great City* appeared.[41] The newer New York he thought duller precisely in the degree to which its social contrasts had diminished, the very contrasts he cursed as he sat in City Hall Park and shook his fist at the *World.* The city was duller because it was less differentiated: "The glory of the city is its variety. The drama of it lies in its extremes."[42] And this is not unlike Henry James' observation that "the impression of suffering is part of the general vibration; it is one of the things that mingle with all the others to make the sound that is supremely dear to the consistent London-lover—the rumble of the tremendous human mill." When Dreiser sees pitiable snow-shovelers pay a rake-off for their shovels, he also follows Henry James: "These men are a bit of dramatic color in the city's life, whatever their sufferings."[43] And such a view is similar to that of Leibniz and Royce, both of whom were criticized by William James in his own reflections on the woes of the city, as we shall see.

Dreiser continued his sentimentality about suffering in New York when he told of the poor, half-demented seamstress who lived in a hall-bedroom the size of a closet and who preferred that hall-bed-room to any fifteen-room house in the country. "The color and noise and splendor of the city as a spectacle was sufficient to pay for all her ills." And Dreiser added: "Have I not felt the glamour of it myself? And do I not still?"[44] In the same sentimental spirit, at the end of *A Traveler at Forty,* after he tells of his wonderful time in most of the great cities of Europe, he comes to the conclusion that New York's atmosphere was the most comforting of any: "The subway is like my library table—it is so much of an intimate.

Broadway is the one idling show place. Neither the Strand nor the Boulevard des Capucines can replace it. Fifth Avenue is all that it should be—the one really perfect show street of the world. All in all, the Atlantic metropolis is the first city in the world to me,—first in force, unrivaled in individuality, richer and freer in its spirit than London or Paris, though so often more gauche, more tawdry, more shamblingly inexperienced."[45]

And yet in this very book Dreiser also says: "I may be mistaken, but London did not seem either so hard or foreign to me as New York. I have lived in New York for years and years and yet I do not feel that it is My city. One always feels in New York, for some reason, as though he might be put out, or even thrown out."[46] Dreiser is, then, extremely ambivalent about the American city, especially about New York. In a curious combination of prose and poetry entitled *My City*—by 1928 he apparently could call it that—Dreiser reveals his double attitude toward New York in comparatively clear terms. There's nothing like it, he says. No city he has seen is as strong and as immense. Paris isn't; London isn't; Moscow isn't. It has lilt and power. It is impressive and he concedes that neither hunger nor loneliness have ever destroyed its impressiveness for him. Of course, it can be cruel and brutal. It can be callous and unsentimental. But it is lyric too, and it casts a spell. It is grand; it is thrilling; it is mysterious. But one may cry aloud in it for help and not be heard. One may seek recognition in it and fail to get it. It is a town of towers and pinnacles, but in it the inevitable winds sap your strength, the inevitable cold bites and eats into you. And the unbroken dust will one day bed all of its inhabitants. This dour ending of *My City* foreshadowed a harsher statement a few years later when Dreiser came to think of New York as sinister, a "handsome woman with a cruel mouth," and as a place that was much worse than it had been when he was a young man in New York creating the character Hurstwood.[47] The difference between the younger and the older city was a measure of Dreiser's disappointment with the American city of his dreams. One was a tantalizing girl, the other a cruel, unsatisfying woman.

So Howells, Norris, and Dreiser all came to hate New York. And they were not physiocrats, transcendentalists, Enlightenment philosophers, or followers of Jean-Jacques Rousseau. They were the founders of literary realism and naturalism, the authors of three of the most influential "urban" novels of our literary history: *A Hazard of New Fortunes, McTeague, and Sister Carrie.* But to know the largest American city at the turn of the century was not to love it.

IX

PRAGMATISM AND SOCIAL WORK

WILLIAM JAMES AND JANE ADDAMS

IN THE nineties Howells wanted to destroy the American metropolis and both Norris and Dreiser were appalled by it, but their attitudes were not shared by all intellectuals of standing at the turn of the century. Notable among those who seemed to take pleasure in the American metropolis was William James. And he became the inspiration of a movement to study the great city carefully and to transform it. James spurred on a reforming generation which was effectively represented by Robert Park, his most devoted pupil among sociologists; by Jane Addams, his worshipper; and by John Dewey, his disciple.

Dewey was born in 1859, Jane Addams in 1860, and Park in 1864, and therefore they were all one critical generation removed from Henry Adams, born in 1838, William James in 1842, and Henry James in 1843. Norris and Dreiser were about ten years younger than Dewey, Addams, and Park, but the novelists had expressed themselves on the city a little earlier, as Park once pointed out. Dewey, Jane Addams, and Park came to maturity in the eighties, a turbulent decade in the history of the American city. They began their intellectual careers in a social and political atmosphere filled by the speeches, writings, and doings of populists, muckrakers, socialists, single-taxers, and all of the others who helped anticipate the "Age of Reform." They were all eager to study and to revamp the body and the mind of the city, to go beyond a passive, complaining attitude toward the surface of city life. They spent their early adult years in Chicago, the great new metropolis of the Middle West, the home of a great university founded in 1893 and the center of the liveliest, city-oriented reflection the nation had seen up to that time. One can understand why William James looked westward to some of these Chicagoans as his friends and disciples, and why they regarded him as a spiritual leader. They were developing the organic sociology which Dreiser ignored in the nineties.

William James' philosophy was notoriously one of hope and possibility. In a notebook of 1873 he was already looking at the past with attitudes that were very different from those his brother came to express in *Hawthorne* and in *The American Scene:* "I am sure," William said, "that an age will come when our present devotion to history, and scrupulous care for what men have done before us merely as fact, will seem incomprehensible; when acquaintance with books will be no duty, but a pleasure for odd individuals; when Emerson's philosophy will be in our bones, not our dramatic imaginations."[1] It was this unwillingness to escape into the past, this desire to transcend it, that permitted William James to look at the American city with more hope and affection than Henry could muster. William, one might say, extended Emerson's exuberant optimism to the American city in spite of Emerson's own doubts about urban life.

William James had often found his sensibilities disturbed by the appearance and spirit of Western European cities, those great repositories of the past. He was delighted by the treasures of architecture and painting, and particularly impressed by Rome's splendor and antiquity; but as his biographer tells us, he also felt a strong moral revulsion against its decay, its paganism, and its traditionalism.[2] For ten days after his arrival in Florence in 1873, he said he "was so disgusted with the swarming and reeking blackness of the streets and the age of everything, that enjoyment took place under protest, as it were."[3] As for London, during William's visit of 1889—one year after the appearance of Henry's admiring essay on that city—he wrote his sister that he was "thoroughly sated" of it, and "never care[d] to see its yellow-brownness and stale spaciousness again."[4] But William had a more enthusiastic opinion of the American city and its environs. In 1865 he spoke warmly of his "native slosh and ice and cast-iron stoves, magazines, theater, friends and everything."[5] In 1873 he reported his difference from his brother, whose temperament was "so exclusively artistic that the vacuous, simple atmosphere of America ends by tiring him to death."[6] In 1889 William preferred Cambridge "to any place in the known world," his ultimate reason being that "where a man's work is best done seems and ought to seem the place of places to him."[7]

In praising Cambridge, James did not dwell on its appearance, and he did have some misgivings about some of its people. While on a Brazilian expedition in 1865, he wrote that at a distance he was amazed by Cambridge's intellectual activity, by people "killing themselves with thinking about things that have no connection with their merely external circumstances, studying themselves into fevers, going mad about religion, philosophy, love . . . breathing perpetual heated gas and excitement, turning night into day."[8] His misgivings sprang from his deep attachment to nature. His disappointment with the hyperintellectuality of some of his Cambridge friends, and his displeasure with prudence and slyness were all part of his undaunted love of natural existence. This love had become articulate when in Germany in the eighteen-seventies he took Goethe's *Gedichte* with him on walks in the woods of pine and laurel, and reflectively wondered how people can pass years without a week of life in the country in which cares, responsibilities, and thoughts for the morrow become a far-off dream; and you are "boarded you don't know how, by what Providence—washed clean, without and within, by the light and the tender air."[9] He felt that the liking and need of this rural, elemental life has deep roots in our natures, "for taking mankind as a whole the open-air existence, from day to day, has been the normal life."[10] This revelling in a simplified life in the country, however, was only one side of the many-sided William James. His love of nature was tempered by a fondness for sociability and he was unable to subscribe either to an extreme primitivism like Thoreau's or to the ultracivilized sentiments of his brother.

The operative word for James was "possibility" so far as the American city was concerned, for he was never completely satisfied with the unformed quality of the American scene, neither with country nor city landscape as it presented itself to his observant eye. He pointed out that America was "a thousand years behindhand in so many things; and the *attained* social character of European civilizations generally is more *erfreulich* than those mere suggestions and possibilities of good that are perhaps more abundant here. After five months spent mainly in rural England," he continued to write a friend, "both my wife and I were sickened by the shock of the scurviness and *decay* which the face of things presented when we landed [in America]. In 500 years we may hope for polish, but hardly in less, with the West wide-open to drain off every rise of the water level of civilization in the older parts of the country. *Tight fit* is what shapes things definitely; with a loose fit you get no results, and America is redolent of loose fits everywhere."[11] Unconsciously, perhaps, James reversed a metaphor of his anti-urban predecessors. While they thought of the city as a drain on the country, he thought of the country as a drain on the city.

Many of William James' reactions to the loose, buzzing, growing New York of 1880 to 1900 had been antipathetic because of "the clangor, disorder and permanent earthquake conditions" he experienced on his customary day-long visits. But in 1907 he spent a longer time there and "caught the pulse of the machine, took up the rhythm, and vibrated *mit,* and found it simply magnificent." He spoke of it as an *"entirely* new New York, in soul as well as in body, from the old one which looks like a village in retrospect. The courage, the heaven-scaling audacity of it all, and the *lightness* withal, as if there was nothing that was not easy, and the great pulses and bounds of progress, so many in directions all simultaneous that the coordination is indefinitely future, give a kind of *drumming back-*

ground of life that I never felt before. I'm sure that once *in* that movement, and at home, all other places would seem insipid." This was written to his brother after the publication of the latter's *American Scene,* for he says: "I observe that your book—'The American Scene'—dear H., is just out. I must get it and devour again the chapters relative to New York." He might not have liked them upon rereading them, and one can imagine how Henry must have winced when William exclaimed, "I'm surprised at you, Henry, not having been more enthusiastic, but perhaps that superbly powerful subway was not opened when you were there."[12] William James is the philosopher of the American city as Walt Whitman is its poet, and for a similar reason: both of them *like* it as Henry James did not. They do not root, as chamber of commerce executives do, for a city; but they view the city joyfully in a spirit that is very different from Jefferson's grudging acceptance of it. Jefferson merely came to terms with the American city, but both William James and Whitman took pleasure in it.

William James showed that he could rise above the battle between town and country in his influential essay, "On a Certain Blindness in Human Beings." "Wherever a process of life communicates an eagerness to him who lives it," he says, "there the life becomes genuinely significant."[13] In the essay James expressed his admiration not only for Whitman's poem, "Crossing Brooklyn Ferry," but also for parts of Emerson's *Nature.* Of Whitman, James says: "He felt the human crowd as rapturously as Wordsworth felt the mountains, felt it as an over-poweringly significant presence, simply to absorb one's mind in which should be business sufficient and worthy to fill the days of a serious man."[14] Part of a letter of Whitman's which James quotes with approval is worth requoting, not only for its own sake but also as something to be contrasted with the responses of Henry Adams and Henry James to New York.

In 1868, the very year in which Henry Adams was feeling so displaced in New York, Whitman wrote to a car-conductor friend: "Shall I tell you about [my life] just to fill up? I generally spend the forenoon in my room writing, etc., then take a bath, fix up and go out about twelve and loaf somewhere or call on someone down town or on business, or perhaps if it is very pleasant and I feel like it ride a trip with some driver friend on Broadway from 23rd Street to Bowling Green, three miles each way. (Every day I find I have plenty to do, every hour is occupied with something.) You know it is a never-ending amusement and study and recreation for me to ride a couple of hours on a pleasant afternoon on a Broadway stage in this way. You see everything as you pass, a sort of living, endless panorama—shops and splendid buildings and great windows: on the broad sidewalks crowds of women richly dressed continually passing, altogether different, superior in style and looks from any to be seen anywhere else—in fact a perfect stream of people—men too dressed in high style, and plenty of foreigners—and then in the streets the thick crowd of carriages, stages, carts, hotel and private coaches, and in fact all sorts of vehicles and many first-class teams, mile after mile, and the splendor of such a great street and so many tall, ornamental, noble buildings many of them of white marble, and the gayety and motion on every side: you will not wonder how much attraction all this is on a fine day, to a great loafer like me, who enjoys so much seeing the busy world move by him, and exhibiting itself for his amusement, while he takes it easy and just looks on and observes."[15]

It took William James a while to see such qualities in New York immediately after the Civil War, but toward the end of his life he fell in love with it. The year of his discovery of the "new New York"—in 1907—was when he delivered his most famous set of lectures, entitled *Pragmatism,* at Columbia University. James thought of the philosophy he expounded there as one which could mediate between the views of the "tender-foot Bostonians" and the "Rocky Mountain toughs" in philosophy. The imagery is significant. James used it as a device for summarizing his famous contrast between two fundamental types of philosophical temperament, the tender-minded (who were, generally speaking, rationalistic, intellectualistic, idealistic, optimistic, religious, free-willist, monistic, and dogmatical) and the tough-minded (empiricist, sensationalistic, pluralistic, sceptical). James thought that pragmatism avoided the tender insipidity of Boston literary teas and the craggy toughness of the Rockies. This is suggested by his dramatic juxtaposition of a statement by (the tender) Leibniz, who says that "the evil will appear as almost nothing in comparison with the good, if we once consider the real magnitude of the City of God,"[16] and another statement by a tough anarchist who attacks Leibnizian optimism by citing a number of newspaper items on suicides and deaths from starvation in the city of Manhattan.

James spends almost three pages quoting from this exposure of the American city's wounds, and then says in a passage which is of utmost interest to us: "It is at this point that my own solution begins to appear. I offer the oddly-named thing pragmatism as a philosophy that can satisfy both kinds of demand. It can remain religious like the rationalisms, but at the same time, like the empiricisms, it can preserve the richest intimacy with facts."[17] A livable city on earth, one is therefore tempted to say, is the social manifestation of James' pragmatism, and that is why he is one of the first great American philosophers to associate himself with the effort to accept what is good and to root out what is bad in the life of the American city. The City of Man was to mediate between Leibniz's theological dream city and the world described by James' anarchist, much as pragmatism was to mediate between rationalism and empiricism. James does not escape to the country or to the past. He revives the later wisdom of Jefferson, after almost a hundred years of transcendentalism, Brook-farming, bad dreams and expatriation. And at the end of the nineteenth century such an attitude heralded a more open-minded and a more practical approach to a new form of life in America.

When Frank Norris urged intellectuals to look at the people of the slums, to know them, and to help them, he summarized what might be called three moments in the development of urban re-

145

formism. Some, like Jane Addams and Dewey, looked, knew and helped; others like Park looked and devoted themselves to discovering as much as they could about the "city wilderness," as it was called even by those who viewed it with sympathy and who were part of what has been called a "Back to the People" movement in American thought.[18] Social workers, sociologists, and social philosophers turned their attention to the problems of urbanization, following the naturalistic novelists who had already conveyed the magnitude of the change which was coming over America.

Sympathy for and interest in the twentieth-century city were no longer lacking among the more practical of our intellectuals. The city was recognized as real and natural by Jane Addams, Robert Park, and John Dewey; they did not wish to destroy it. But they approached it in a manner which was affected by other varieties of anti-urban doctrine. Like so many thinkers of the Progressive period, they were worried by its sheer magnitude. Their patron, William James, might have been thrilled by the new New York, but in 1899 he wrote to a friend: "I am against bigness and greatness in all their forms, and with the invisible molecular moral forces that work from individual to individual, stealing in through the crannies of the world like so many soft rootlets, or like the capillary oozing of water, and yet rending the hardest monuments of man's pride, if you give them time. The bigger the unit you deal with, the hollower, the more brutal, the more mendacious is the life displayed. So I am against all big organizations as such, national ones first and foremost; against all big successes and big results."[19]

James' idea that the big unit was hollow and brutal was applied with ease to the city itself by reformers like Jane Addams and John Dewey. As Richard Hofstadter has pointed out, progressive reformers continued to espouse the ideals of an earlier period in American history in their attack on big organizations. Jane Addams and Dewey could easily recall their own rural backgrounds, and Park could supplement his personal experience by reading German sociologists like Toennies and American sociologists like Cooley, who glorified the face-to-face relationships of so-called primary

146

PRAGMATISM AND SOCIAL WORK

groups like the family, the village, and the church, in which people saw each other frequently and continuously over the years. If the city had become hollow, that was primarily an expression of the breakdown of communication and the cessation of this continuous contact. It had become "over-differentiated" in Jane Addams' evolutionary phrase, and one task of her Hull House Settlement was to counteract this tendency, to remove hollowness by reconstructing localism, by building within the big city little centers of neighborly communication to take up part of the void created by urban expansion. The basic strategy of this movement of urban thought was therefore not to destroy the city but to recreate within it something like the spirit of life as it was lived in an earlier time. This meant using the settlement house and the school as urban versions of villages that the reformers had known in their youth. And so the age of reform was not without its nostalgia, its preference for certain features of a pre-urban way of life that was receding further and further into the American past.

Jane Addams, America's most distinguished social worker, could appreciate and admire the urban immigrant's pre-industrial environment partly because she came from the country. She could use her knowledge of its life and ways on behalf of the European peasant who had moved into America's booming, industrial cities. She was brought up in a country town in Illinois and was attracted by the human appeal of the immigrant quarters in Chicago. That "primary stage of alienism" which had appalled Henry Adams and Henry James when they saw and heard the immigrants of American cities, struck Jane Addams as attractive, thought-provoking, and challenging. She held the firm conviction, directly inspired by Abraham Lincoln, with whom her father had served in the Illinois legislature, that the basic likenesses of men are better and finer than what keeps men apart and—if properly accented—transcend differences of race, language, creed, and tradition.[20] And so she was more sympathetic to the first generation of immigrants than she was to their children. She preferred the natural manners and gay customs of the first generation to the sophistication and money-

147

grabbing of the second. The children she liked when they were quite young, and she was taken by the "alertness and bonhommie" of their voices in tenement houses, for the voices of the city always sounded more pleasantly in her ears than they had in Henry Adams' and Henry James'. But the qualities of the newcomers she admired most were the qualities that romantic social theorists had praised in pre-industrial life: their naturalness, their neighborhood feeling, their generosity, and their spirit of self-sacrifice. She was directly in touch with the whole range of immigrant experience which Oscar Handlin has so vividly recreated in *The Uprooted.*[21]

Her sympathy with peasant newcomers in the city made Jane Addams all the more aware of their frustrations under urban stress. She was quite ready to admit with Henry James that the American city of their time was ugly in most of its aspects, dingy, sordid, formless, and unsubdued.[22] And there was no doubt in her mind that the pliable human nature of city-dwellers was being relentlessly pressed upon and made apathetic by the physical environment. She constantly pointed out that industrialization was an entirely different achievement from civilization in the city, and therefore she fully agreed with an English visitor who could not understand the enthusiasm of American city boosters, since as far as he could see American cities seemed "essentially alike and all equally the results of an industry totally unregulated by well-considered legislation."[23] Jane Addams therefore warned: "It will certainly be embarrassing to have our age written down triumphant in the matter of inventions, in that our factories were filled with intricate machines, the result of advancing mathematical and mechanical knowledge in relation to manufacturing processes, but defeated in that it lost its head over the achievement and forgot the men."[24] The men it was in danger of forgetting were very much like the natural men, the whole men— of Emerson, of the early Karl Marx, of romantic German sociologists, of Tolstoy and Rousseau—as they were supposed to have been before the Industrial Revolution cast its shadow over them. Much of what Jane Addams did for real men in the slums, she did with this image before her, and in this spirit she admired Lincoln because "he never forgot how the plain people in Sangamon County thought and felt when he himself had moved to town."[25]

Jane Addams founded Hull House in a poor district of Chicago in 1889, the year in which Dreiser's Sister Carrie came to Chicago. In that year the settlement house had been in the suburbs, but by 1893 the city's factories had engulfed it. Its physical surroundings were miserably inferior to what had prevailed in the pre-industrial Philadelphia of 1800. Jane Addams' reasons for founding a settlement house might well have been compelling to an earnest, young American of her background who valued the democratic pattern of an earlier day. Echoing some of Lord Bryce's remarks on the state of municipal government in America, she pointed out in 1892 that self-government had broken down in her Chicago ward, where politicians didn't act without a push, and where there was no initiative among the citizens. There were dingy streets, inadequate schools, and bad lighting and paving; law was unenforced; there was little sanitation; sweat shops filled low-rent hovels; there was an extraordinary amount of child labor. For a population of 50,000 there were 7,072 voters and 255 saloons.[26] She had observed similar conditions often enough to conclude in terms of the standard sociopolitical metaphor of the day that the social organism had broken down in large districts of America's great industrial cities. Community spirit, as that was conceived by certain nineteenth-century sociologists, was disappearing. There were countless poor without leisure and energy for participation in social life. Clubs, libraries, and galleries were blocks away, and the saloon, often presided over by its local demagogue, was the only place for sociability. Cultivated people avoided these districts, and Jane Addams felt that they had much to lose by doing so. By not helping the poor of the slums, they suffered from a sense of divorce between democratic theory and practice; their inaction was debilitating, like disease, poverty, and a sense of guilt.[27]

In the background of Jane Addams' thinking, one can find the passion of the Brook Farmers for cooperative living and the Christian humanitarianism of Tolstoy, without their desire to escape the

149

city. Also unlike Tolstoy, who in *What Shall We Do Then?* sharply attacked "organic" philosophy, Jane Addams said that residents of Hull House "are bound to regard the entire life of their city as organic, to make an effort to unify it, and to protest against its over-differentiation."[28] Hull House was designed to be an antidote against social ignorance, inaction, and apathy, an experiment to aid in the solution of the social and industrial problems produced by modern conditions of life in a great city.[29] Its residents were constantly sustained by the conviction that "certain social sentiments . . . like all higher aims live only by communion and fellowship, [and] are cultivated most easily in the fostering soil of a community life."[30] The metaphorical reference to the soil was not altogether accidental, for Hull House was part of an effort to recapture some of the natural, almost biological features of rural community living. And Jane Addams' idea of the city as an organism even extended to the point where she said that the aim of the residents of Hull House was "to be swallowed and digested, to disappear into the bulk of the people."[31]

Most of the programs initiated at Hull House illustrated Jane Addams' desire to recapture a sense of community and communication, and to stimulate the exercise of natural powers which had been dammed up by life under conditions of urban poverty. Instead of participating in the building of a community from scratch, she felt that she was trying to *re*-build a community, to re-unify the scattered, chaotic thing that city life had become by the eighteen-eighties. It was this that linked her with more theoretically sophisticated philosophers and sociologists who spoke throughout the nineteenth century of alienation and estrangement, of the breakdown of some original and happier community. Jane Addams was far from subscribing to the more blood-thirsty and martial of their doctrines since she was one of the great pacifists of her time. But many of her practical efforts were directed at reinstating the more peaceable pre-industrial qualities that she valued. To this end, she started workers' discussion groups on economic and political problems, an art gallery, a nursery, recreation clubs, industrial and health surveys, exhibitions of the evolution of the textile industry, dances and concerts, series of public lectures, and adult extension courses.

Although Jane Addams' thinking was related to that of certain romantic theorists, her proposals were obviously not dominated by any Thoreauvian or Rousseauian antipathy to civilization as such. And although she spoke of the value of organic social relationships, she did not go to the extreme of recommending a total immersion of the individual in society. While she emphasized the need for making the neighborhood settlement a center for group discussion and communication, she was not a partisan of romantic *together-ness*. For example, she recognized that an important mode of communication takes place during reading, and therefore a library was included within the precincts of Hull House. The value of a library in a social center was justified for her when a young workman gratefully explained that Hull House was the first home he had ever been in where books and magazines just lay around as if there were lots of them in the world. The discovery that some people regarded reading as a reasonable occupation changed his whole outlook on life and gave him confidence in what he could do.[32]

If Jane Addams was influenced to some extent by an image of pre-urban man, that image did not lead her to prescribe in any monolithic manner the kind of lives her people should lead. The effort to create a center for a higher civic and social life invited the participation of all varieties of people—people of different races, nationalities, classes, and temperaments—whether extrovert, introvert, conformist or nonconformist. There was no commitment to an established social type as such; instead there was the inspiration of a broad social purpose "to institute and maintain educational and philanthropic enterprises; to investigate and improve the industrial districts of Chicago." Most of Jane Addams' energy was spent trying to show why her neighbors accepted standards that diverged from those of the middle class. In this spirit she observed the psychological upheavals of immigrants who had given up the satisfactions of skilled craftsmanship for the monotonous duties of the factory, and she saw in this metamorphosis a contributing cause of alcoholism.[33]

Jane Addams' most basic concern was to detect and channelize natural impulses that were being frustrated or misdirected in the city. A striking example of this appears in her discussion of juvenile delinquency. Juvenile delinquents who steal should not be viewed as altogether malevolent, she said. For example, their habit of pilfering from pushcarts was to some extent a carry-over from the rural custom of picking up surplus food and faggots in the open country where this was not frowned upon. She believed that some of the enterprises of city hoodlums entailed activities that squads of country children could indulge in without danger to people and property when they were hunting rabbits and coons. The modern city, she wrote in *The Spirit of Youth and the City Streets,* failed to provide for the insatiable desire for play, whereas the classical city had promoted play with careful solicitude and the medieval city held tourneys, pageants, dances, and festivals. The failure of the modern city to provide for public recreation was all the more serious because of the unprecedented monotony and division of urban industrial labor, and because young people were now released from the protection of the home and allowed to wander unattended through the city streets. The young, susceptible, uneducated person was also earning money independently of family life, and therefore became an especially easy victim of vice masquerading as pleasure.[34]

Although Jane Addams shared a good deal of the nostalgia of romantic theorists who celebrated the virtues of a closely knit group like the family, the village, and the church, she did not reject industrialization as such. But she emphatically reacted against the machine's being used in ways that would crush the individual worker's individuality and rob him of what Veblen called his "instinct of workmanship," which she believed to be central to a sense of well-being.[35] To protect the working population she supported many bills for radical social legislation, and constantly pressed for an educational revolution along with her good friend, John Dewey.

Jane Addams' educational programs at Hull House were based on a belief that the natural man needed to be freshly educated in the modern urban environment. She criticized the standard educational programs of her time as giving exclusive emphasis to skills which only developed a tentative attitude toward life instead of illuminating it, which were divorced from concrete and important life problems, or which trained a person in narrowly conceived vocational programs to become good, cheap labor. Instead she urged that education should be based on the needs of the "whole person" and offer training in manual, intellectual, emotional, and social skills in such a way that the individual could more freely participate in the life of the community. Education, properly conceived, could help remove the stigma of manual labor. Instead of repressing the emotions, the task of education was to lead the individual to express his feelings in imaginative and open communication through the arts and in energetic debates on social questions. Intellectual training could include the history and values of industrialization, for the machine is really a social possession and "represents the 'seasoned life of man' preserved and treasured up within itself, quite as much as an ancient building,"[36] a symphony, or a poem. Jane Addams saw the arts as a universal language, as a bridge between the different language groups and classes of the city, and felt that the arts should not only be used to facilitate emotional expression but also to develop distinguished skills.

Jane Addams viewed the city environment as itself an opportunity for extending social intelligence because it could offer varied possibilities for communication, varied opportunities for removing misunderstanding. And yet her own special way of dealing with the problem of communication in the city was to build a settlement house, a smaller unit within the city that was an effort to revive the localism of an earlier day. In this respect her approach to the problems of urbanization were typical of the Progressive generation, which was so eager to counteract and combat the forces of urban expansion. William James was an inspiration to urban reformers because he liked the city, disliked bigness and thought of his pragmatism as melioristic and individualistic. "You inhabit reality," he once wrote Jane Addams,[37] and she, more than any of his Progressive admirers, took seriously some of his warnings against the dangers of "big organizations as such." She became the founder of a center of direct communication in Chicago, dedicated to filling certain gaps in the urban void.

X

THE PLEA FOR COMMUNITY

ROBERT PARK AND JOHN DEWEY

THE WORK of Jane Addams and her associates at Hull House was primarily practical; but it prepared the way for the more theoretical urban sociology of Robert Park, who acknowledged the exploratory value of the social workers' labors, of studies like *Hull House Maps and Papers*, which appeared in 1895, and Robert Woods' *The City Wilderness* (1898) and *Americans in Process* (1902).[1] Park in turn stimulated the efforts of a group of urban sociologists who operated out of Chicago, one of the first great American centers for such investigation;[2] and they confirmed the prevalent conviction that community feeling and communication were breaking down in the twentieth-century American city. John Dewey shared this conviction and he too came to worry about the effects of industrialization on urban life. The sociologists' preoccupation with the decline of the so-called primary group, Dewey's anxiety about the disappearance of neighborly feeling in the city, and Jane Addams' idea that the settlement house should counteract the erosion of community sentiment—all of these evinced nostalgia for a cozier, warmer form of human association than the city was providing at the beginning of the twentieth century. Their critique of urbanization was not that of a group of literary romanticists, nor was it an expression of philosophical transcendentalism. The untranscendental pragmatist, Dewey, and the empirical sociologist, Park, both shared to some degree the American intellectual's traditional distrust of the city.

155

One might hesitate to apply the term "anti-urbanist" to them because of its suggestion of thorough disapproval of city life, but both Dewey and Park had deep reservations and feelings of uneasiness about the city of the twentieth century, reservations and feelings that arose in part from their favorable estimate of a mode of life they associated with the pre-industrial past. Since they lived in the twentieth century, they could hardly speak seriously of a literal return to that past, but there are unmistakable signs in their writings of a preference for it, inclinations to use its social life as a model for the improvement of city life as they knew it in the twentieth century. Dewey lived most of his adult life in Chicago and New York, and was active in movements to improve both cities; but his nostalgic affection for the small community must be borne in mind when one is trying to understand his attitude toward the American city. In his *Public and its Problems,* which appeared in 1927, he gave full expression to his distaste for certain aspects. of big city life. He made an invidious distinction between a live community and a merely mechanical society which was not unlike Toennies' contrast between *gemeinschaft* and *gesellschaft;* and, of course, as a one-time follower of Hegel, Dewey was familiar with that philosopher's similar distinction between "Family Society" and "Civil Society." There was more direct connection between Dewey's reflections and those of Robert Park.

* * *

Park's career is the story of a sociologist who first saw society at close range as a newspaperman, then developed broad philosophical and sociological interests, and finally became an influential teacher of sociology at the University of Chicago. He traced his interest in sociology to his reading of Goethe's *Faust,* especially to Faust's fatigue with books and his desire to see the world. Starting his world-seeing as a reporter in Minneapolis, Park later moved on to New York, "the mecca of every ambitious newspaperman"; but like Dreiser he too became disenchanted with that city because, as Park put it, the newspaperman of those days usually lasted only about eight years and then was considered obsolete. During his newspaper work, Park came to realize that "a reporter with the facts was a more effective reformer than an editorial writer thundering from the pulpit." Without abandoning his passion for concrete information, he developed an interest in the philosophy of the newspaper that sent him back to the University of Michigan, where he met John Dewey. He also had a crucial encounter with a certain Franklin Ford, who had reported Wall Street, who had become interested in the function of the press and who had influenced Dewey's thinking too. After graduating from the University of Michigan, Park entered Harvard where, he says, he "studied philosophy because [he] hoped to gain insight into the nature and function of the kind of knowledge we call news. Besides, [he] wanted to gain a fundamental point of view from which [he] could describe the behavior of society under the influence of news in the precise and universal language of science."[3]

Like Jane Addams and John Dewey, Park had come under the spell of William James. While Park was at Harvard, he had heard James deliver his famous talk "On A Certain Blindness in Human Beings," in which James decried the blindness we are all afflicted with when it comes to understanding the feelings of people different from ourselves.[4] James urged his audience not to regard as meaningless forms of existence other than their own and to tolerate, to respect, and to indulge those who harmlessly pursue their own ways, however unintelligible these might be. In a thrust at absolutism, James issued a command of toleration: "Hands off: neither the whole of truth nor the whole of good is revealed to any single observer, although each observer gains a partial superiority of insight from the peculiar position in which he stands." This was the kind of advice that could inspire both social workers and sociologists in the city. "Even prisons and sickrooms have their special revelations," said James. "It is enough to ask of each of us that he should be faithful to his own opportunities and make the most of his own blessings, without presuming to regulate the rest of the vast field."[5] James' essay, Park recalled, had a steadily increasing significance for his own thinking. "The 'blindness' of which James spoke," as Park saw it, "is the blindness each of us is likely to have for the meaning of other people's lives." Park came to think that "what sociologists most need to know is what goes on behind the faces of men, what it is that makes life for each of us either dull or thrilling. For 'if you lose the joy you lose all.' But the thing that gives zest to life or makes life dull is, however, as James says, 'a personal secret' which has, in every single case, to be discovered. Otherwise we do not know the world in which we actually live."[6]

After his work at Harvard, Park went abroad to Germany. While in Berlin he studied with Georg Simmel, whose view of the city as a state of mind rather than as merely a physical environment, profoundly affected Park's own conception of city life. Looking back on this period when his interest in sociology crystallized, Park wrote that he first thought of the sociologist as "a super-reporter" of the "Big News," of long-term trends, of what actually is going on rather than what seems to be going on.[7] James had stimulated him to find out what went on behind the faces of individual men, while Simmel had encouraged him to study what the German sociologist called the "mental life" of the city as a whole.[8] While Park acknowledged that Americans at that time were mainly indebted to novelists for their more intimate awareness of modern life, he wanted to go beyond what might be found in their writings with the help of objective, scientific techniques.

Like Jane Addams, Park threw in his lot with Chicago in the early twentieth century, and remained for much of his life interested in its ebullient growth and kaleidoscopic transformations. He concentrated his attention on it and based his generalizations on it during the first three decades of this century, when it was growing at the rate of half a million new inhabitants every decade.[9] He had spent his early years in a small town, but like so many of his generation, he was personally attracted to the city as a social milieu where—as he put it—"everyone is more or less on his own."[10] In more theoretical terms he explained the attraction of the metropolis for masses of people as partly due to the fact that there they found, more than in a small community, the moral climate to stimulate their innate qualities and bring them to full expression. The big city uniquely rewarded eccentricity, according to Park: even the criminal, the defective, and the genius found more opportunities to develop their dispositions in a great city than in a small town. Among other enticements of the city, as compared with small town and country, Park noted the heightened element of chance; and he speculated further that the lure of great cities arises perhaps from stimulation which directly affects the reflexes, "like the attraction of the flame for the moth, as a sort of 'tropism.' "[11]

Park's use of the figure of the moth drawn into the flame is one indication of his view of the city as both attractive and destructive. He observed that the city was full of what he termed plenty of "human junk," who "have fallen out of line in the march of industrial progress."[12] He admitted that the vast, nondescript, deteriorated areas which had become the American city slums were not places of "unity and charm," but the slums seemed to Park unusually interesting because they were in social transition.[13]

For Park, the city is not simply a legal entity; it is, in his much-used phrase, primarily a state of mind. It is not merely a collection of people, of social conveniences, or of administrative arrangements. It is "a body of customs and traditions, and of the organized attitudes and sentiments that inhere in these customs and are transmitted with this tradition. The city is not, in other words, merely a physical mechanism and an artificial construction. It is involved in the vital processes of the people who compose it; it is a product of nature and particularly of human nature."[14] As a human ecologist, he viewed the unplanned concentration of a large population in a small locality as comparable to the natural formation of plant and animal colonies. However, in cities, Park observed, a collection of people is further organized by human "tools" like communication, transportation, political institutions, and economic devices such as factories. Tools, people and place are all woven into one "psycho-physical mechanism."[15] A human society is distinguished from a physical collection of individuals by communication result-

159

ing in corporate action, action directed toward a common end which, Park and his collaborator Burgess held, "is perhaps all that can be legitimately included in the conception of 'organic' as applied to society."[16]

Like Dewey and Jane Addams, Park thought that society exists only in and through communication, and he linked this theoretical conclusion with his own personal interest in the newspaper. The newspaper, Park held, was the great medium of communication within the city. He looked upon the newspaper as an organ for mobilizing public opinion in the city, taking the place of the village gossip, the town-meeting orator, and the local preacher.[17] And because he believed that the newspaper played such a key role in the city, Park thought that the distribution of newspaper circulation might be used as a measure of metropolitan influence. Park and his associate, Charles Newcomb, pointed out that "communication is fundamental to the existence of every form and type of society, and one form of communication, namely the newspaper, has been found to circulate over the natural areas within which society is organized. Thus it may not seem unreasonable that the newspaper should be used as an index in outlining a number of metropolitan regions of the United States."[18] Park thought of a region as a social unit to the extent to which its inhabitants read one group of newspapers.

On the assumption that cities can cohere only so long as their residents communicate with each other, Park tried to discover various social processes in Chicago which encouraged or discouraged human understanding and communication. And his general conclusion was that understanding and communication are more fragmentary in the city than in the town and the village. Though some developments in Chicago around the turn of the century, particularly the cohesion of isolated ethnic groups and the formation of neighborhood associations in the slums, protected people from social dislocation in the new environment and preserved mutual understanding, the more powerful process of division of labor ultimately substituted organization based on occupation and vocational interests for one based on family ties, culture, caste, and status. The result was the gradual dissolution of "the moral order" resting on the latter kind of connection. According to Park, "a very large part of the population of great cities, including those who make their homes in tenements and apartment houses, live much as people do in some great hotel, meeting, but not knowing, one another. The effect of this is to substitute fortuitous and casual relationship for the more intimate and permanent association of the smaller community."[19] Park used the circulation of newspapers as a measure of metropolitan spread, but he agreed with Walter Lippmann that the newspaper was not an altogether effective device for mobilizing public opinion.[20] Dewey also came to this conclusion, as we shall see, and this was partly responsible for Dewey's conviction that the so-called face-to-face group would have to be restored and revitalized if democracy was to remain workable in the industrial age.

The industrial age, on Park's view, is characterized not only by social mobility but also by increased physical mobility brought about by various types of mechanized transportation, as Howells had also observed. In a famous essay on the city which he first published in 1916, Park argued, as Dewey would later, that "it is probably the breaking down of local attachments and the weakening of the restraints and inhibitions of the primary group, under the influence of the urban environment, which are largely responsible for the increase of vice and crime in great cities."[21] And by the primary group he meant what Charles Horton Cooley meant by it —a group in which "face-to-face association and cooperation" predominated. Park reiterated in his essay, "Community Organization and Juvenile Delinquency," that division of labor, social mobility, and the multiplication of the means of transportation and communication had undermined the influence of older forms of social control like the family, the neighborhood, and the local community. "It is probable," he warned, "that the most deadly and the most demoralizing single instrumentality of present-day civilization is the automobile . . . The connection of the automobile with vice is

161

notorious."[22] The newspaper and the movies, he added, were not as deadly but almost as demoralizing. The urban home, Park lamented, had become little more than a sleeping-place, a dormitory, under conditions of modern life.[23] In his essay, "Community Organization and the Romantic Temper," he argued that twentieth-century leisure had created a restless search for excitement in the city, a "romantic impulse . . . to escape the dull routine of life at home and *in the local community.*" Park went on: "This romantic quest which finds its most outrageous expression in the dance halls and the jazz parlors is characteristic of almost every other expression of modern life. Political revolution and social reform are themselves often merely expressions of this . . . We are seeking to escape from a dull world instead of turning back upon it to transform it."[24] By contrast, Park thought, recent immigrants, who maintained their simple village habits in religious and mutual aid organizations, had been best able to withstand the shock of the new environment. And he revealed the extent to which he was impressed by pre-industrial society when he reflected that, "in some sense these communities in which our immigrants live their smaller lives may be regarded as models for our own. We are seeking to do, through the medium of our local community organizations, such things as will get action and interest for the little world of the locality. We are encouraging a new parochialism, seeking to initiate a movement that will run counter to the current romanticism with its eye always on the horizon, one which will recognize limits and work within them. Our problem is to encourage men to seek God in their own villages and to see the social problem in their own neighborhood."[25]

There was no implication here that the modern city should be destroyed or abandoned. But throughout Park's writing there are suggestions of disappointment over the fact that a return to the rural past was impossible. Although he spoke favorably of the city as an expression of man's effort to remake the natural environment after his own desires, he remarked that "if the city is the world which man created, it is the world in which he is henceforth condemned to live."[26] No brief passage can do better than the following to summarize his view that the reform of the city should be seriously influenced by a model of the pre-industrial past: "The social problem is fundamentally a city problem. It is the problem of achieving in the freedom of the city a social order and a social control equivalent to that which grew up naturally in the family, the clan, and the tribe."[27] Although it has been rightly said that "Park's choice lay with the city" because in it "every man is on his own,"[28] it is worth quoting a passage in which Park made that observation about the city in order to see how qualified his admiration was for being on one's own: "The peasant who comes to the city to work and live is, to be sure, emancipated from the control of ancestral custom, but at the same time, he is no longer backed by the collective wisdom of the peasant community. He is on his own. The case of the peasant is typical. Every one is more or less on his own in a city. The consequence is that man, translated to the city, has become a problem to himself and to society in a way and to an extent that he never was before."[29] And in 1931, Park observed that "everything in our modern world, under the pressure of changing conditions, has begun to crumble. This is even true, as one gathers from Oswald Spengler's *The Decline of the West,* of the western world's conviction of its own superiority; the one indomitable idea on which its faith in its future is finally based, has also begun to crack."[30]

One might say in this connection that Park accepted this city-made problem as a challenge, and that he regarded the city as an arena of struggle in which he wished to live and study for just this reason.[31] But acknowledging this should not obscure two things of great importance in understanding Park's place in the development of American thought on the city: that he was not a city-booster, and that he looked back from the metropolis to the days of the family, the tribe and the clan with some sense of nostalgia. He did not admire without qualification the anonymity and impersonality of the city as Dreiser did at times—certainly he did not romanticize the life of the Bohemian. And, when he summed up the contributions of cities to civilization, he said explicitly that they had made

163

no contribution to morals as we ordinarily understand that term. "Quite the contrary. Cities have been proverbially and very properly described as 'wicked.' "[32] And this remark was not ironical or jocose in intention. When Park came to list the contributions of the city, he did so in a matter-of-fact manner. Cities had been melting-pots; they had brought together people of different classes; they had broken what Bagehot called the "cake of custom"; they had diffused inventions by providing market-places; they were the homes of rationality and science.[33]

Although Park challenged the Emersonian view of the city as a mere artifact, he occasionally lapsed into romantic language about the city's defects. In such a milieu, he thought, the detached, anonymous individual was often deprived of natural outlets for expression of interest and energy. Instead the city dweller built up a "world of means" between impulse and distant future ends and values; and he concentrated on such conventional signs as fashion, front, and manners to establish his status. Moreover, as the isolated individual shifted his attachments from primary to secondary contacts, from more continuous association with kin and neighbors to discontinuous associations at distant jobs in the wider world of the city, social control had to be transformed from the *mores* to new legal instruments of discipline that Park describes as necessarily formal and for the most part crude and inefficient. Because of the loosening of social ties in the city, the standing of the individual and the family became uncertain and subject to abrupt changes upward or downward in the social scale. Not only was the individual detached in the urban world, but he lost what Veblen called his instinct for workmanship, as Jane Addams also observed, in monotonous employment in the modern, standardized, industrial system; and in other activities of his life, he ceased to be an actor and became a spectator instead. This whole sum of adaptations to urban life, in the view of Park, Simmel, and many other students of the city, put a premium on rationality and impersonality, for the individual was forced to develop an urbane, emotional reserve and use his intelligence more energetically under city conditions.[34]

164

For Park, however, urbanity was not a virtue. It is developed in the urban world, and not in what he calls the "little worlds" of the family, the tribe, the local community. Since the latter encourage intimate relations and mutual responsiveness, they help nurture definite personalities rather than etiquette, urbanity, sophistication, and finish. "Urbanity is a charming quality, but it is not a virtue. We don't ever really get to know the urbane person, and hence never know when to trust him. It is more or less fundamental traits of personality which arise in the intimate group which enable us to act with definiteness and assurance toward others. Manners are of secondary importance."[35]

In his disparagement of urban etiquette, sophistication, manners, and finish, Park agreed with Thorstein Veblen. Veblen held that conspicuous leisure and conspicuous consumption are the two main ways of achieving social reputation by way of displaying wealth, and went on to say that "the choice between them is a question of advertising expediency simply." So long as a community is small, one method is as good as the other. But in an urban community, where the individual is exposed to so many people who can only judge his eminence by the goods he displays, conspicuous consumption comes to be the typical mode of self-advertisement. Since, according to Veblen, the industrial system does not encourage more than mechanical neighborliness or mere physical proximity in the city, one's mechanical neighbors are not one's social neighbors, nor even one's acquaintances. In the city, social relations are primarily external. The individual is exposed mainly to the gaze of "transient observers" in churches, theatres, hotels, shops, and parks; and therefore "the signature of one's pecuniary strength should be written in characters which he who runs may read."[36]

Park's reflections are also related to those of Hegel and Marx. Though Park usually refrained from explicit moralizing about industrialized, booming Chicago, one cannot help noting that something like Hegel's and Marx's concept of alienation was a prominent theme in his descriptions of it, and that Park, along with several German theorists of the nineteenth century, as we have seen, believed that the life of pre-modern man was more spontaneous, autonomous, and secure than that of the city-dweller. Park looked about him in Chicago and saw that it was attractive and interesting, but that beneath its attractions it generated a maze of social problems as industrialization and mobility increased. His misgivings about the size and complexity of Chicago, as compared to the smaller, simpler community, were summed up by Park and Burgess as follows: "The very existence of a great city creates problems of health, of family life, and social control which did not exist when men lived in the open or in villages. Just as the human body generates the poisons that eventually destroy it, so the communal life, in the very process of growth and as a result of its efforts to meet the changes that its growth involves, creates diseases and vices which tend to destroy the community . . . Communities may and do grow old and die, but new communities profiting by the experience of their predecessors are enabled to create social organizations more adequate and better able to resist social diseases and corrupting vices. But in order to do this, succeeding communities have had to accumulate more experience, exercise more forethought, employ more special knowledge and a greater division of labor. In the meantime, life is becoming constantly more complex. In place of the simple spontaneous modes of behavior which enable the lower animals to live without education and without anxiety, men are compelled to supplement original nature with special training and with more and more elaborate machinery, until life, losing its spontaneity, seems in danger of losing all its joy."[37] The pattern of social development on this view proceeded from poison to scientific antidote to joylessness.

Park and Burgess added no argument to show that urban life merely *seemed* to be in danger of losing all its joy. The implication was that the scientific techniques, which on Park's view were characteristic of the city, really did lead to the destruction of spontaneity and joy. And it must be remembered that Park believed, with his teacher William James, that if one loses the joy of life, one loses all. So the urban sociologist who studied the American

166

city as few had studied it up to his time, continued the intellectual tradition of grave doubt about its future. He thought of the city as a part of nature, but he also thought that it would naturally become corrupt, that the body politic, in the traditional anti-urban metaphor, would succumb to internally generated poisons which would destroy the joy of social existence. Park may have been excited by the city as a challenge to social scientists, as a laboratory for the study of social problems, but he had serious doubts about its moral qualities when he compared it to the pre-urban communities and modes of social organization that had preceded it in America and elsewhere. He may have been excited by the city because it provided him with problems in social science, just as Hawthorne found the decaying city stimulating when viewed as the subject matter of literature. But it is one thing to admire a state of affairs for its own attractive qualities, and another to admire it because its very corruptness challenges one's theoretical, practical, or artistic powers. The physician who works on cancer is challenged by that human scourge without being pleased by it. In the same way, the student of what Jefferson called the cancer on the body politic might be challenged by it without being pleased by it. One is tempted to say that Park's published statements on the city reveal more the admiration of the scientist investigating a fascinating phenomenon than the delight of a person who finds that phenomenon intrinsically pleasing.

The ideas and experiences of some of the Chicago social workers and sociologists were never very far from the thinking of John Dewey about the city. In his writing we find the same preoccupation with communication as the heart of social life, the same preference for the small, neighborly group as over against the overwhelming urban agglomeration. He was a friend of Jane Addams and of Robert Park; and when he wrote on the problems of education and politics, his words made it evident that he was part of a similar intellectual environment. Dewey was born in Burlington, Vermont, in 1859; moved to the Middle West to begin his academic career; and then went to Columbia University in 1905 after a decade of teaching as a philosopher, psychologist, and theorist of education at the University of Chicago.[38] And while Dewey became in his long lifetime the country's symbol of an engaged urban intellectual, his thinking was deeply affected by a love for pre-industrial human relations, by growing anxiety about modern man's loss of respect for the values that the small community supported and nourished, and by a growing fear that this loss of respect would undermine democracy. Dewey's attitude toward the problems created by urbanization is conveyed most clearly in two of his books, his *School and Society*, which first appeared in 1899, and his *Public and its Problems*, published in 1927. They reveal not only his preoccupation with the nature of life in the cities, but also his increasing concern about the impact of increasing industrialization.

In *School and Society* Dewey gave popular expression to the cluster of educational ideas that has been labeled "progressive." In saying there that education should be progressive, Dewey meant that it should transform itself as thoroughly and radically as social life had been transformed in the nineteenth century. Social life had been changed by the application of science to manufacture, by the development of a world market, by the creation of a system of rapid and cheap means of transportation and communication. One consequence of this industrial revolution was the obliteration and shifting of political boundaries, another was the gathering of "population . . . into cities from the ends of the earth."[39] The revolution had also brought about a radical alteration of moral and religious ideas, and Dewey found it inconceivable that it should not affect education in more than a formal or superficial way. Two years after *School and Society* appeared, Charles Beard concluded his little book *The Industrial Revolution* on a similar note. The idea of education progressing in step with "the wonderful nineteenth century" was very much in the air.

Dewey formulated the problem of education with nostalgic attention to the way of life that preceded the Industrial Revolution in

168

America, presenting an affectionate description of the household and neighborhood systems that lay behind the new factory system. He reminded his Chicago lecture audience of the nineties that persons in it could, by going back one, two, or at the most three generations, find the time when the household was the center of industry, when the clothing worn was made at home, when members of the family could shear sheep, card and spin wool, and ply the loom. "Instead of pressing a button and flooding the house with electric light, the whole process of getting illumination was followed in its toilsome length from the killing of the animal and the trying of the fat to the making of wicks and dipping of candles." Flour, lumber, foods, building materials, household furniture, and even hardware were produced in the household's immediate neighborhood by a process open to everyone's inspection. The whole industrial process stood revealed, from raw material to finished product.[40]

Most important for understanding Dewey, however, was his recitation of the psychological benefits of all this to the child. Every member of the household, he recalled, had his share in the work. Children were initiated into its mysteries. Production was a matter of immediate and personal concern in which they participated. Consequently, they were trained in habits of order and industry, in the idea of responsibility, of obligation to do something and to produce something in the world. Something always needed to be done and it was necessary that one should do his part faithfully and in cooperation with others. Nature was seen at first hand, and "there was continual training of observation, of ingenuity, constructive imagination, of logical thought, and of the sense of reality acquired through first-hand contact with actualities."[41]

Dewey was deeply attached to the kind of life he described, a life that had been virtually eliminated by urban concentration of industry and division of labor. But with a wisdom that reminds us of the older Jefferson making peace with the city, Dewey added: "It is useless to bemoan the departure of the good old days of children's modesty, reverence and implicit obedience, if we expect merely by bemoaning and by exhortation to bring them back."

Conditions had changed, and only an equally radical change in education would suffice under the circumstances. Moreover, the picture was not all black. The world of 1899 could boast of an increase of toleration, of greater breadth of judgment, of larger acquaintance with human nature, of sharpened alertness in reading character and interpreting social situations, of greater accuracy of adaptation to different personalities, of contact with greater commercial activities. All of these modern achievements meant much to the "city-bred child" of 1899. But Dewey's formulation of *the* problem of education was completely parallel to Park's formulation of the problem of the modern city, namely: how can we retain these qualities of the new society and yet create schools that would represent the virtues of pre-industrial, pre-urban America?[42]

We cannot read *School and Society,* therefore, without thinking that a good part of Dewey's program was devoted to the perpetuation of values that he had explicitly associated with an earlier period in American life. Thus he conceived of manual training, shopwork and household arts, as devices for bringing home to the child some of "the primal necessities of human life"; and by their means, he thought, "the school itself shall be made a genuine form of active community life." Society, he agreed with Jane Addams and Robert Park, "is a number of people held together because they are working along common lines, in a common spirit, and with reference to common aims. The common needs and aims demand a growing interchange of thought and growing unity of sympathetic feeling."[43] Dewey used his definition of society as a basis for criticizing the school of 1899 because it did not communicate a sense of common and productive activity. On the other hand, he saw such a common effort in the household of an earlier American generation and on the playgrounds of schools whose classroom spirit was deficient by his standards. For on the playground, in game and sport, social organization took place spontaneously: "There is something to do, some activity to be carried on, requiring natural divisions of labor, selection of leaders and followers, mutual cooperation and emulation."[44] In selecting the rural household and the playground as

170

model communities, Dewey reasserted an older conception of the ideal mode of human association, just as Park did. Cooperative activity, spontaneity, closeness to nature, intimate communication, sympathy—these Dewey saw as the values of an earlier time that had to be preserved in some way by the progressive school.

Although progressive education was defined as an education in keeping with the Industrial Revolution, the progressive school was not to be a pure miniature of industrial Chicago in 1899. Dewey spoke of the progressive school as a small community which would "saturate" the student with the spirit of service, a spirit which certainly did not saturate Theodore Dreiser's Chicago in the eighties and nineties. Dewey spoke of his progressive school at times as if it were simply a microcosmic counterpart of the roaring, brassy cities of the late nineteenth century; but in constructing his model school he filtered out aspects of city life that were not compatible with the basic values he saw in his idyllic picture of the household system. Dewey's progressive school was to combine the benefits of the industrial age with the sweetness and light of the farming community.

In 1899 Dewey could be relatively optimistic about the possibility of forming a school which would combine the achievements of a scientific age with the virtues of an older era. The idea that industrial society might be able to foster spontaneity, sympathy, and cooperative activity, and that the worker might cease to be a "mere appendage" to his machine—these seemed to Dewey to be closer to realization in 1899 than they did in later years. Powerful forces were at work which would soon lead beyond the nineteenth-century city to the supercity, so clearly described by Patrick Geddes in 1915 and anticipated in an earlier literature by Emerson and others. "The present Greater New York, now linked up, on both sides, by colossal systems of communications above and below its dividing waters, is also rapidly increasing its links with Philadelphia—itself no mean city—and with minor ones without number in every direction. For many years past it has paid to have tramways continuously along the roads all the way from New York to Boston, so that, taking these growths altogether, the expectation is not absurd that

171

the not very distant future will see practically one vast city-line along the Atlantic Coast for five hundred miles, and stretching back at many points, with a total of, it may be, well nigh as many millions of population."[45] Geddes' prediction might have fazed not only Dewey, but also Jane Addams, whom Geddes affectionately called "that true abbess of Chicago, in whom America possesses such a rare combination of social experience, generous feeling, intellectual grasp and insight, and driving force."[46] Even Jane Addams might have found it hard to regard such a collection of disjected urban members as organically united by community spirit. And Dewey would find it equally hard to think of the super-city as capable of restoring the pre-industrial values he had sketched in *School and Society*.

A growing discrepancy between Dewey's ideals and urban realities forced him to reformulate his view of the promise of urban life. He ceased to give the impression that the forces of history were inevitably tending in the direction of greater communication and greater dispersion of intelligence. When he gave up his Hegelian view of history, he freed himself from the idea that interpersonal communication and thorough social organization were bound to be realized in time. In 1927, he explicitly made a distinction between *society* and *community*, according to which a group of people could make up a society and fail to be a community. He made clear his attachment to the ideals of a small community, which were closely related to those he had described when he reminisced about farm life in *The School and Society*, but the generation that separated that book and *The Public and its Problems* had created forces which raised doubts in Dewey's mind about America's capacity to restore the older way of life.

The older way of life Dewey now characterized with the help of the sociologist Charles Horton Cooley's concept of a primary group. Cooley, as we have seen, defined primary groups as "those characterized by intimate face-to-face association and cooperation." They are primary, Cooley continued, in forming the social nature and the ideals of the individual. Intimate association in such a group fuses individuals into a whole, "so that one's very self, for many purposes at least, is the common life and purpose of the group. Perhaps the simplest way of describing this wholeness is by saying that it is a 'we'; it involves the sort of sympathy and mutual identification for which 'we' is the natural expression. One lives in the feeling of the whole and finds the chief aims of his will in that feeling."[47] For Cooley, the chief examples of the primary group were the family, the play-group of children and the neighborhood—all of which, it will be recalled, came in for praise in *The School and Society*. But Cooley remarked in 1909, "The intimacy of the neighborhood has been broken up by the growth of an intricate mesh of wider contacts which leaves us strangers to people who live in the same house . . . In our own cities the crowded tenements and the general economic and social confusion have sorely wounded the family and the neighborhood, but it is remarkable in view of these conditions, what vitality they show; and there is nothing upon which the conscience of the time is more determined than upon restoring them to health."[48]

In 1927 Dewey was still concerned with the break-up of the primary group, but was more doubtful about its continuing vitality than Cooley had been. Dewey repeated that the new technology applied in production and commerce had resulted in a social revolution. But now he was more definite about the adverse impact of the new technology on the kind of community he had extolled in 1899. "The local communities without intent or forecast found their affairs conditioned by remote and invisible organizations. The scope of the latter's activities was so vast and their impact upon face-to-face associations so pervasive and unremitting that it is no exaggeration to speak of 'a new age of human relations,' " as Woodrow Wilson had in his book, *The New Freedom*. In a reference to Graham Wallas' book, *The Great Society*, Dewey now made explicit his own contrast between society and community: "The Great Society created by steam and electricity may be a society, but it is no community. The invasion of the community by the new and relatively impersonal and mechanical modes of combined human behavior is

173

the outstanding fact of modern life."[49] Ironically, an age which had expanded the physical means of communication had failed to use them properly. The revolution that had brought Bangkok and Chicago closer together had turned Chicago itself into a vast hotel in which neighbors did not communicate with each other in spite of having telephones in each room. And so *the* problem of America in 1927, said Dewey, was that of converting the Great Society into a Great Community.

How this was to be done Dewey did not describe in detail. He argued that a Great Community would not be established unless inquiry was absolutely free and its results widely disseminated. "A subtle, delicate, vivid and responsive art of communication must take possession of the physical machinery of transmission and circulation and breathe life into it."[50] Thus spoke the Dewey who had from earliest manhood been interested in the press as a means of spreading democracy. When he spoke in this vein, he gave the impression that the new society might restore its sense of community by improving its reading matter, that in place of the face-to-face contact of the primary group, we might now communicate with each other in ways that would turn this vast country into a Great Community; that the press might do for the nation what direct contact had done for an earlier age.

However, Dewey could not refrain from adding, as Park had, that "in its deepest and richest sense a community must always remain a matter of face-to-face intercourse . . . The Great Community, in the sense of free and full inter-communication, is conceivable. But it can never possess all the qualities which mark a local community. It will do its final work in ordering the relations and enriching the experience of local associations."[51] There is no substitute, Dewey continued, for direct intercourse and attachment. Love and understanding can only come from the attachment of "near-by union." "No one knows," he said with Park in the midst of the roaring twenties, "how much of the frothy excitement of life, of mania for motion, of fretful discontent, of need for artificial stimulation, is the expression of frantic search for something to fill the

174

void caused by the loosening of the bonds which hold persons together in immediate community of experience."[52] And finally, he made clear that his plea for greater communication and his praise of the immediate community were not unconnected. "The problem of securing diffused and seminal intelligence can be solved only in the degree in which local communal life becomes a reality."[53] So strongly did Dewey feel about the importance of reestablishing "immediate community" that he appealed to a variety of philosophical considerations in order to support his point. "The wingèd words of conversation in immediate intercourse," he argued, "have a vital import lacking in the fixed and frozen words of written speech."[54] Logic is ultimately dialogue; the ear is more closely connected with vital, outgoing thought and emotion than the eye. Vision is a spectator, whereas hearing is a participator. Publication is partial until the meaning communicated passes from "mouth to mouth," he said in a rather extraordinary extension of the metaphor of face-to-face association.[55]

It should not surprise us, therefore, to find in *The Public and its Problems* that Dewey quotes a familiar figure in our story: "We lie, as Emerson said, in the lap of an immense intelligence. But that intelligence is dormant and its communications are broken, inarticulate and faint until it possesses the local community as its medium."[56] Nor should it surprise us to hear that Dewey published in 1940, at the age of eighty-one, an exposition of Jefferson's views which seemed closely connected with Dewey's own admiration for the "immediate community." He pointed out that Jefferson not only feared a centralized government in Washington and believed that state governments "are the true barriers of our liberty," but that he attached great importance to self-governing communities of much smaller size than the state or even the county. Impressed as Jefferson was by the New England township, he wanted to divide the counties into wards. The wards were to have as their first aim the establishment and care of popular elementary schools, but they went far beyond that in Jefferson's mind. Each ward was to be a "little republic," responsible for the "care of the poor, roads, police, elections, nomination of jurors, administration of justice in small cases, elementary exercise of militia." And, Dewey points out, Jefferson thought that when any important wider matter came up for decision, every ward would be called into meeting on the same day in order to determine the collective sense of the people as a whole. This plan was not adopted, but Dewey was insistent on the fact that it was an essential part of Jefferson's political philosophy which, when omitted from expositions of that philosophy, result in a wrong impression of his doctrine of states' rights. In Jefferson's words, "The elementary republics of the wards, the county republics, the State republics and the Republic of the Union would form a gradation of authorities."[57] Dewey himself did not take the occasion to evaluate this plan, but his anxiety to defend Jefferson was evidence of Dewey's own sympathy with a similar localism. Jefferson said that he concluded every speech with the imperative, "divide the counties into wards." In a similar spirit, Dewey might have concluded every one of his with, "divide the city into immediate communities"; Jane Addams with, "divide the city into settlement houses"; and Park with, "divide the city into primary groups." All of them were reacting to what they regarded as the curse of urban bigness in the twentieth century. Their patron, William James, may have been exhilarated by New York's activity, but his vividly expressed hatred of bigness was even more significant for his admirers, Dewey, Park, and Jane Addams. Like so many intellectuals in the Age of Reform, they were part of the new parochialism, a movement to counteract the overwhelming effect of all big organizations, and the big city was not excepted.

✳ ✳ ✳

The practical impact of this new parochialism may be seen in the writings of Frederick C. Howe, one of the most ardent spokesmen for the city in the Progressive era. His evolution from urban reformer to emigré from the city may be recorded as an illuminating footnote to the plea for community just described. In 1905 Howe was already advocating a variety of parochialism that would con-

176

tribute not to the up-building of the American city, but to its decay. In that year, he published a book joyfully entitled *The City: The Hope of Democracy* in which many pro-urban arguments were advanced, but in which another note was sounded. "The open fields about the city are inviting occupancy," Howe announced, "and there the homes of the future will surely be. The city proper will not remain the permanent home of the people. Population must be dispersed. The great cities of Australia are spread out into the suburbs in a splendid way. For miles about are broad roads, with small houses, gardens, and an opportunity for touch with the freer, sweeter life which the country offers."[58]

Howe called *the city* the hope of democracy, but at times he seemed more like a suburban booster than a city-lover. Indeed his later writings made clear that his heart lay even further from the city; for in 1925 he published an interesting document which increases our understanding of the Progressive Era. In *The Confessions of a Reformer,* he reported a discovery which he made about himself with the help of a Johns Hopkins "diagnostician of minds": "He told me that the mind had a way of asserting itself as one fell asleep, and as one came to consciousness in the morning. One had reveries of the things one liked, daydreams of what one wanted to do and wanted to be. I knew very well what my reveries were about. They rested me when I was tired. They gave me peace when I was harassed. They were always of an old fishing village on the far end of Nantucket Island, where I had spent many summers; of simple fisher-folk with whom I felt at ease; of a rambling cottage on the edge of the moors into which the sun, rising from the sea, pushed its way in the morning, brighter and gayer and sweeter than sunlight anywhere else in the world . . . I wanted to live on the Nantucket moors, to be quit of conflict; to live content with simple, friendly contacts, with horses and dogs, with a fire on the hearth. I wanted to build something with my hands; to plant things and see them grow. These reveries were warmer than any other desire. They had something to do with my deeper self. Perhaps they were a throwback to my forebears, to generations of blacksmiths, car-

177

penters and farmers, men who lived close to the soil—my people had been peasants in England, Scotland and Ireland. It may have been the lure of the Scotch moors that called me to Nantucket."[59]

For such a mind the message of Josiah Royce might have been more congenial than the message of John Dewey, Robert Park, or Jane Addams, since in 1902 Royce was calling the province the only hope for democracy and "the self-estranged mind."

XI

PROVINCIALISM AND ALIENATION

AN ASIDE ON JOSIAH ROYCE
AND GEORGE SANTAYANA

WHILE the reforming disciples of William James worked hard in the cities, doing their pragmatic best to restore in them feelings of local neighborliness, two of James' philosophical colleagues reacted differently to the problems of the American city. Josiah Royce, the California-born idealist, advocated what he called a "higher provincialism," and Santayana, the Spanish-born materialist, left Boston for Europe at the first opportunity. Royce was a devotee of the idea of provincial community and had been nourished on the texts of romantic idealism, whereas Santayana was a superb example of the detached individual whom Royce, following St. Paul, thought was an essentially lost being. While Jane Addams and John Dewey acted out James' distrust of bigness in their plea for neighborliness, Royce had come to his provincialism by way of a different philosophical route. Royce had also become anxious about tendencies toward overcentralization, and he too issued a plea for the smaller community. But while Dewey and Jane Addams were primarily worried about the overwhelming city and worked mainly for the cause of localism within it, Royce urged the advantages of a return to the province. However, when Royce came to stating the grounds for his provincialism, he expressed fears that were very similar to the fears of those who hoped to

179

humanize the city by way of Park's "new parochialism." And when Royce came to making recommendations, he outlined a point of view that had obvious kinship with the later idea of a regional city, as Christopher Tunnard and Henry Hope Reed have pointed out,[1] as well as with Howells' idea of regional capitals. Moreover, Royce's ideas on this subject were put forth before Dewey's *Public and its Problems,* and Dewey's words on the subject were probably influenced by Royce's and also by the idealist tradition to which Dewey himself had subscribed before becoming a pragmatist.

Royce outlined three main evils of American life at the turn of the century which he hoped would be reduced or eliminated by what he called a wise provincialism. First of all, he said, the excessive physical mobility of modern life had led to an excess of wandering strangers. Possibly he was thinking of his pioneer childhood in California, but he attributed the evil primarily to the presence of a considerable number of not yet assimilated newcomers in urbanized communities. "The newcomers themselves are often a boon and welcome indeed. But their failure to be assimilated constitutes, so long as it endures, a source of social danger, because the community needs well-knit organization."[2] The second evil of which Royce spoke was what he called the levelling tendency of urban civilization. In calling attention to this after complaining of the failure to assimilate the new immigrants, he unconsciously revealed a tension within the movement he represented. He and his fellow critics of the city wanted it to be in one sense uniform but in another the scene of variety. Because of the consolidation and centralization of industries and social authorities, Royce complained, "we tend all over the nation, and, in some degree, even throughout the civilized world, to read the same daily news, to share the same general ideas, to submit to the same overmastering social forces, to live in the same external fashions, to discourage individuality, and to approach a dead level of harassed mediocrity."[3] The result, Royce continued, is a tendency to crush the individual. And the third evil tendency, according to Royce, was the spirit of the "mob" as it had been described by Gustave

Le Bon in his then popular book, *The Crowd*.[4] Although Royce did not say so explicitly, it is clear that he must have thought that all three of these evil tendencies of American life existed primarily in cities at the turn of the century.

In his book *The Philosophy of Loyalty*, which appeared in 1908, Royce described the malaise of the time in more general terms with the help of Hegel's concept of alienation or estrangement, much as Karl Marx had in the nineteenth century, but with a very different political goal in mind. Hegel, Royce recalled sympathetically, had pointed out that in certain periods of European history the social mind or spirit had become "estranged from itself," notably during the decline and fall of the Roman Empire and during the period of political absolutism in Europe in the seventeenth and early eighteenth centuries. A social mind, spirit, or consciousness could be provincial and not self-estranged, he explained, when for example it was the mind of small commonwealths or provinces like our original thirteen colonies. But "on the other hand, the social life can be that of the great nation, which is so vast that the individuals concerned no longer recognize their social unity in ways which seem to them homelike. In the province the social mind is naturally aware of itself as at home with its own."[5] The government in vast societies like ours presents the individual with a law that he finds alien. It seems to him like a great force of nature rather than his own self writ large. It is the world of imperialism in which the individual sees himself confronted with powers that he cannot understand, and he submits without love or loyalty to them.

Royce, in spite of making a remark to the effect that "such a formula as the one which Hegel suggests is always inadequate to the wealth of life," held that "we are able to understand our national position better when we see that our nation has entered in these days into the realm of the 'self-estranged spirit.' " The distant and irresistible national government, however much we may welcome its authority and regard it as a force guaranteeing our safety, does not provide us with the opportunity "for such loyalty as our distinctly provincial fathers used to feel and express in their early utterances

181

of the national spirit."[6] The overcentralized national government, great industrial forces, aggregations of capital, combinations of enormous physical power were like forces of nature to Royce in 1908. "They excite our loyalty as little as do the trade-winds or the blizzard. They leave our patriotic sentiments cold. The smoke of our civilization hides the very heavens that used to be so near, and the stars to which we were once so loyal."[7]

But what was Royce's recommendation to this world that he described in terms so reminiscent of Marx's sixty-five years earlier?[8] Not revolutionary. "I am not planning any social reform which would wholly do away with these conditions of the world of the self-estranged spirit."[9] Instead he recommended that Americans try to see how, under conditions as they were, they could overcome self-estrangement. "The problem of the training of our American people as a whole to a larger and richer social loyalty is *the problem of educating the self-estranged spirit of our nation to know itself better.*"[10] This was almost the language of Dewey when he later urged that the task of the American public was to find itself. Behind both of these bits of advice stood the Hegelian view according to which the Spirit becomes free only as it develops self-consciousness. And also behind the advice in Royce's case was a Pauline doctrine. "The detached individual is an essentially lost being," Royce said in a manner reminiscent of Howells' equally Pauline doctrine of complicity.[11] Royce hoped to found a Great Community, just as Dewey did after him; and for Royce, the way to achieve this, to lessen the detachment of individuals, and to reduce the self-estrangement of the spirit, was to establish loyalties like those of "our distinctly provincial fathers."

Concerned as he was with the evils of excessive physical mobility, the decline of individuality, the tendency toward levelling, and the increased self-estrangement of the American spirit, Royce said that he could not, in the manner described in Schiller's "Greeting to the New Century," flee to a world of dreams. "In certain respects," one of Royce's commentators has rightly pointed out, "Royce was an inheritor of Emerson and carried on, in an age when Idealism

182

had become unpopular, a campaign for the Over-Soul and the Absolute against the pragmatists."[12] But in spite of this, Royce was aware of the impossibility of romanticism in 1902, when he delivered his paper, "Provincialism." "Schiller spoke in the romantic period," observed Royce, "but we no longer intend to flee from our social ills to any realm of dreams."[13] Rather, Royce held, we must flee to the province. "There must we flee from the stress of the now too vast and problematic life of the nation as a whole. There we must flee, I mean, not in the sense of a cowardly and permanent retirement, but in the sense of a search for renewed strength, for a social inspiration, for the salvation of the individual from the overwhelming forces of consolidation. Freedom, I should say, dwells now in the small social group, and has its securest home in the provincial life. The nation by itself, apart from the influence of the province, is in danger of becoming an incomprehensible monster, in whose presence the individual loses his right, his self-consciousness, and his dignity. The province must save the individual."[14] If, in place of the word "nation," we read the word "city," and in place of the word "province," we read either the word "village" or the words "Regional City," we have a recommendation very close to, if not identical with, that of Lewis Mumford and other contemporaries.[15]

George Santayana might have been one of those mobile strangers of whom Royce spoke in a charitable but critical tone when he outlined the three great evils of his day. Born in Spain, Santayana was brought to America in childhood and then returned to Europe in middle age. He lived in or near Boston while in this country and always found himself a stranger there. He was a Spaniard and a Catholic who was hardly at home with the Protestantism of nineteenth-century New England; he looked down on the commercial path to success that was characteristic of Boston in his youth; he felt out of place spiritually at Harvard; and he was detached in his feelings, as he says and reveals in many ways.[16]

183

Although an alien himself, Santayana did not admire certain other aliens in America,[17] and this affected his view of New York. It was stranger to him than Boston, and in at least one comment on it, as we shall see, he linked New York's defects as he conceived them with his own attitude toward Jews. His anti-Semitism was more refined than Henry Adams', but it existed. "The Jews," he says, as he contrasts them with the Greeks, "and even Spinoza with them, fell into both littleness and arrogance: into the littleness of being content with anything, with small gains and private safety; and into arrogance in proclaiming that, in their littleness they possessed the highest good, heard the voice of absolute truth, and were the favorites of heaven. Undoubtedly if you renounce everything, you are master of everything in an ideal sense, since nothing can disturb you: but the Jews never renounced anything that was within reach; and it was rather the Greek hero who renounced half of what he might have possessed, in order that the other half should be perfect."[18] Santayana did not limit himself to criticizing the Jews of antiquity, for he held that "the modern Jew recognizes verbal intelligence, but not simple spirit. He doesn't admit anything deeper or freer than literature, science, and commerce."[19] Santayana's disapproval of Judaism, positivism, pragmatism and liberalism was not likely to make it easy for him to admire New York intellectual life of the twentieth century, and it is doubtful whether he was altogether happy with the interest shown in his work by some New York philosophers.

On one occasion, he explicitly associated some of their criticisms of him with life in New York: "My critics . . . live in modern New York, where everything is miscellaneous, urgent, and on an overwhelming scale, and where nothing counts but realization. They naturally despise any ideal that is not a living purpose. Living purposes confront them on every side in conservative phalanxes and in revolutionary hordes; and reason for them can mean only to find means for realizing those purposes, or to devise some compromise for realizing as much of them as can be realized together. This is exactly how the principle of moral rationality works when the premises have been accepted; but reason is also competent to criticise those premises, appealing to the voice of nature, to the aroused and clarified conscience, in each individual. This is what Socrates compelled his interlocutors to do, who in the bevy of sophisticated Athens hankered for all sorts of unrewarding things. Have my critics ever questioned the purposes of their environment? Have they ever questioned their own standards? If I had been born by chance among the Israelites in Babylon when Cyrus permitted them to return from exile, probably I should have abandoned that advanced civilization in order to return to the arid solitude of home and to the studious chants of the temple. Would my critics have done so? Or would they have remained with the majority to help carry on the important and varied business of the age? Would they not naturally have supposed, though mistakenly, that it was on that important business that the future of mankind depended?"[20] On this same occasion Santayana speculated about the possibility that his New York critics, who had once published appreciative studies of his work, had now succumbed to extra-philosophical zeal: "Perhaps the times have brought on a fresh wave of zeal in political and racial matters that sweeps aside superficial sympathies and exposes the hidden lines of cleavage in the depths."[21] It was this remark that led John Dewey to reveal his own very different outlook on matters affecting race, politics, and the city. At the age of eighty-one Dewey scolded Santayana, his junior by four years. "It is to be regretted," Dewey said, "that in his reply [to his New York critics] Santayana for once abandons the urbanity which otherwise marks even his most ironical comments. It was unnecessary to the point of gratuitousness to attribute their attitude to 'political and racial zeal.' "[22]

The tendency to speak of Santayana's "urbanity," and Santayana's vehement philosophical attacks on romanticism, have perhaps obscured his attitude toward city life. His rationalism, his materialism, his naturalism and maybe even his Catholicism have led some people to think that he could not possibly be hostile to the modern city in a general way. His attitude toward New York, it might be thought, was merely a lapse, a sign of strong feelings about particular persons in a particular place at a particular time, yet nothing that could be conceived as evidence of full-scale antipathy toward urban life. The fact is, however, that Santayana did speak in general terms about modern city life, and he said quite explicitly that he did not like the great commercial cities of his time: "Civilizations and towns created by commerce may grow indefinitely, since they feed on a toll levied on everything transportable; yet they are secondary. However much they may collect and exhibit the riches of the world they will not breed anything original."[23] Not even Henry James' London, which Santayana remembered as "leisurely" and "gently mocking" rather than "miscellaneously eager and hurried, like New York, [or] false, cynical and covetous, like Paris"[24] could hold him as a young man. The intellectual world of London in the 1880's he found a "Babel of false principles and blind cravings," and the most he wished to be there was a visitor, like Henry James in New York.[25]

The same cliché view of Santayana as "urbane" (and hence urban) might also prevent one from observing in him a strong streak of what might be called ruralism. He said that he loved the earth while he hated the world, adopting a variant of an old anti-urban saw when he said that God made the first, while man, with his needs and his jealousies made the second.[26] He shared Emerson's view that "from the country each city still draws its wealth and sustenance, as well as the fresh hands required for its multiplying trades, the servants for its great houses, and the young soldiers to be enlisted, by force or by bribes, in its feuds and conquests."[27] And he also espoused the view that the modern Jew was anti-rural. Speaking of a trip which he and his college friend, Charles Loeser, were taking in Europe, he reports: "At La Vernia we found the Franciscan community making a procession in their half-open cloister. The monks were evidently peasants, some of them young yokels fresh from the plough, no doubt ignorant and stupid; and Loeser's modern Jewish standards betrayed themselves in his utter scorn of those mere beasts, as he called them. I wondered if St. John the Baptist or Elijah might not also have seemed mere beasts;

but I didn't say so. Being at once a beast and a spirit doesn't seem to me a contradiction. On the contrary, it is necessary to be a beast if one is ever to be a spirit."[28] And at this point he adds his previously quoted statement that the modern Jew recognizes verbal intelligence but not simple spirit.

In his description of his boyhood town, Avila in Spain, Santayana expressed his admiration of situations that he described by the phrases *rus in urbe, oppidum in agris,* or *urbs ruri,* some combination of city and country.[29] And in his last dour comments on life in the twentieth century, he delivered a critique of the modern world from the point of view of one who saw ideal society as housed neither in the romantic wilderness nor in the megalopolitan city, but rather in a rural center. The natural state of mankind, he said, is that of an animal economy, in which men live by agriculture, and the hunting or breeding of animals. "They are materially and morally rooted in the earth, bred in one land or city. *They are civilized,"* he concluded with emphasis.[30] It was the barbarian, the proletariat of antiquity, who disturbed this happy state of civilized agriculture, according to Santayana. And the great problem of the modern world has been the fact that the body of mankind has fallen into the status of a proletariat, this being "an unhappy effect of the monstrous growth of cities, made possible by the concentration of trade and the multiplication of industries, mechanized, and swelling into monopolies."[31]

In the end Santayana could agree with Royce, his philosophical antithesis at Harvard, that the modern urban world had become monstrous in certain of its aspects, that a levelling tendency was abroad in the world, and even perhaps that the world was suffering from an excess of strangers and Hegelian alienation. Being so estranged himself from the modern world, and so lacking in Royce's reforming zeal, Santayana did not advocate a return to the province in Royce's official manner, but his views on the ideal city were not very far from Royce's. Just as Santayana's moral philosophy required that ideals be anchored in natural impulses, and that one must be a beast in order to be a spirit, so his view of the ideal city

187

required that it be rooted in the earth. Once again we find a meeting of the extremes against the city—for Royce and Santayana were certainly extremes—an occasion for the provincialist and the stranger to compose their differences, far from the madding urban crowd.

XII

ARCHITECTURE AGAINST THE CITY

FRANK LLOYD WRIGHT

THE YEARS that came after Dewey's *Public and its Problems* certainly did not bear out his hope for a revival of intra-urban localism, nor Royce's hope for a great community of provinces. In the next three decades the supercity took sprawling possession of a good part of the eastern seaboard, and soon the growth of the suburbs surpassed the growth of the cities in many parts of the country. By the first World War, urban areas had multiplied nine times as fast as rural areas, and by 1920 the nation had become more urban than rural in population. Dewey had hoped that city growth would afford greater opportunities for civilized communication, but the encouraging signs he thought he saw in 1927 were sharply checked by massive metropolitan expansion and signs of decay in the central city. On all sides one heard lamentations about the growth of impersonality, the decline of individuality and the eclipse of community; and these tendencies encouraged another philosophy of urban life, one which preferred to ride the gloomy wave of history rather than to hold it back. Why not, its partisans asked, anticipate what history itself is about to do? Why not dismantle the city and build a new form of life?

The architect, Frank Lloyd Wright, was a strong supporter of this dismantling operation. A powerful artist, a dramatic personality and lively writer, he dominates twentieth-century American

189

architecture in a way that makes him an inevitable representative of his discipline in a study like the present one. He stands out among American architects as the irrascible, bombastic critic of the American city. Even city-lovers who are irritated by his ideas must pay him the compliment of admitting that he saw and concerned himself with many of the problems of today's exploding metropolis. But his inclination to demolish the city was stronger than his desire to rebuild it in anything like its present form. Wright deserves to be included in this story, not because his ideas were particularly deep, cogent, or commonly held in architectural circles, but because Wright occupies a position in his art comparable to that of Dewey in philosophy, Jane Addams in social work, and Robert Park in urban sociology. He is, in short, a famous representative of American architecture and architectural criticism whose views fall squarely into the current of anti-urbanism we are trying to delineate. He was a Wisconsin farm boy who seems never to have changed his mind about cities from the day he first came to "dazzling," "brutal" Chicago in 1887, when he reacted much as Dreiser's Carrie did: "Chicago. Wells Street Station: Six o'clock in late spring, 1887. Drizzling. Sputtering white arc-light in the station and in the streets, dazzling and ugly. I had never seen electric lights before. Crowds. Impersonal. Intent on seeing nothing. Somehow I didn't like to ask anyone anything. Followed the crowd . . . Wondered where to go for the night. But again if I thought to ask anyone, there was only the brutal, hurrying crowd trying hard not to see."[1]

Wright's anti-urbanism, like his architectural theory and his philosophy of life, was closely related to similar ideas expressed by the man he called "Dear Master"—Louis Henri Sullivan, also an articulate architect. Wright has said that he did not need to study his master's writings because Sullivan in his presence and person had been an open book to him for years; and there is enough similarity in their attitudes toward the American city to justify, before turning to Wright, some preliminary comment on Sullivan. According to Richard P. Adams, Sullivan was certainly influenced by romantic literature; and probably he was affected by romantic architectural doctrines through his connection with Frank Furness, who in turn was affected by Horatio Greenough, who received some of his views from Coleridge, the prime source in so many matters affecting romanticism in America.[2] Sullivan's *Kindergarten Chats* overflow with romantic instructions like the following: "I have sought with all due insistence to impress upon you, as a maxim, the simple truth that the heart is greater, worthier, nobler, finer than the head: that the heart is the sanctuary of the Temple of Man, the head its portal. That from the heart comes forth Sympathy into the open: the subtlest, the tenderest, the most human of emotions; and that of Sympathy is born that child of delight which illuminates our pathway, and which we call imagination."[3] Sullivan passed the message of his romantic teachers on to his own student: "The world is filled with Knowledge; it is almost empty of Understanding. For, let me tell you, Knowledge is of the head, Understanding of the heart. Knowledge is of the intellect, Understanding is of instinct."[4]

Having absorbed and transmitted this much of conventional romantic doctrine, Sullivan does not surprise us when he appears as a most outspoken critic of urban life. At the age of eight, in 1864, he was brought to Boston, after a childhood spent in towns like South Reading and Newburyport. In his *Autobiography of an Idea,* Sullivan describes his childhood reaction to Boston of the eighteen-sixties in a passage that is reminiscent of Henry Adams' reaction to the earlier constraints of the same city: "Boston City swallowed him up. The effect was immediately disastrous. As one might move a flourishing plant from the open to a dark cellar, and imprison it there, so the miasma of the big city poisoned a small boy acutely sensitive to his surroundings. He mildewed; and the leaves and buds of ambition fell from him. In those about him, already city-poisoned, even in his own kin, he found no solace, and ceased openly to lament. Against the big city his heart swelled in impatient, impotent rebellion. Its many crooked streets, its filthy streets, lined with stupid houses crowded together shoulder-to-shoulder, like

191

selfish hogs upon these trough-like lanes, irritated him, suffocated him; the crowds of people, and wagons, hurrying here and there so aimlessly—as it appeared to him—confused and overwhelmed him, arousing amazement, nausea and dismay. As he thought of the color, the open beauty of his beloved South Reading, and the great grand doings of Newburyport, where men did things; where there was obvious, purposeful action; an exhibit of sublime power; the city of Boston seemed a thing already in decay. He was so saddened, so bewildered, so grieved, that his sorrow, his bitter disappointment, could find no adequate utterance and relief. Hence he kept it all within himself, and became drugged to the point of lassitude and despair. The prospect of a whole winter to be spent within these confines, shut out from the open world that had been growing so large and splendid for him, filled him at times with a sudden frantic desire to escape. Had not his father at once taken up again the rigorous training of cold baths and outdoor exercise, had he not taken him on long walks to Roxbury, to Dorchester, even to Brookline, where the boy might see a bit of green and an opening-up of things, the boy would surely have carried out his resolution to run away. To run where? Anywhere to liberty and freedom!"[5]

This childhood feeling about the city never left Sullivan in spite of a brief sense of elation when he first came to Chicago as a young man in 1873 and exclaimed, "This is the place for me!" In his *Kindergarten Chats,* he showed hostility toward both New York and Chicago. "Accepting, therefore, New York and Chicago as representing certain miscarriages of democracy, . . . expressible of certain phases of degeneracy afflicting our land and people, we have but to turn, to regain our balance of view, to the country at large and the people at large. In passing, let me say that I am not disposed to ignore or minimize the sane moral and mental and emotional forces, within those cities, which make for righteousness. Far from it, I gladly recognize them and hope that some day they may prevail. But I do say that they are not characteristic of those cities, and the balance of forces at present is heavily against them."[6]

Like Sullivan's imaginary pupil in *Kindergarten Chats,* his real pupil, Wright, must have absorbed some of the master's feelings about American cities. Indeed Wright spoke as though he had breathed all the winds of all the anti-urban doctrine we have been examining. And he exhaled what he breathed in a strikingly exaggerated way. First of all, he asserted with Jefferson that the city is a cancerous growth and the home of the mobocracy. "Once upon a time the Jeffersonian democratic ideal of these United States was, 'that government best governs that governs least.' But in order to keep the peace and some show of equity between the lower passions so busily begotten in begetting, the complicated forms of super-money-increase-money-making are legitimatized by government. Government, too, thus becomes monstrosity. Again enormous armies of white-collarites arise."[7] And thus, according to Wright, "bureaucratic mobocracy is the corruption that would destroy the fruit of every democratic instinct we have developed."[8] Where, asked Wright, does mobocracy flourish if not in the city? The task of the "organic" architect was therefore "to take away all urban stricture and depravity . . . and then—as is the case with all inadvertent health—absorb and regenerate the tissue poisoned by cancerous overgrowth (Urbanism)."[9] In earlier times, Wright argued, the city served human needs as they were. Such a city grew as an organism, the natural result of proper feeding. "Acceleration of tissue by circulation and chemical activity such as characterize a malignant tumor did not then manifest itself. The city then was not malignant."[10] But now things are different, said Wright, as he linked himself not only with Jefferson but also with Howells and Henry George in his image of the city as poisoned, as a wen, a cancer. "To look at the cross-section of any plan of a big city," Wright reported, "is to look at something like the section of a fibrous tumor."[11]

Wright was thoroughly in sympathy with Emerson about the need for a natural, organic life. He spoke warmly of his mother's interest in the transcendentalism of Concord, in the books of Channing, Emerson, Theodore Parker, and Thoreau;[12] and he tells us that his farming family of aunts and uncles in Wisconsin could be brought to tears by readings from the transcendental classics.[13] With his characteristic flare for dramatic expression, Wright included in his last book, *The Living City* (1958), an appendix which was a long excerpt from Emerson's essay "Farming," printed in red for emphasis. Its last paragraph contains that familiar line of the Concord sage: "Cities force growth and make men talkative and entertaining, but they make them artificial." It is highly appropriate that Wright's last printed words should have been taken from one of Emerson's attacks on the city, for it has been shown that many of Wright's ideas are lineally descended from the romantic esthetic which Emerson absorbed from Coleridge, and which distinguished sharply between a mechanical form that is impressed on material *ab extra* and an organic form that develops from within.[14] The amount of turgid prose that Wright devoted to the praise of organic living and organic building, plasticity and continuity, natural versus artificial arrangements, rivals what may be found in the most romantic of German idealists of the nineteenth century. Houses, he insisted, must be continuous with their natural settings, and ornamentation was not to be stuck on the building in an external way, but rather to appear as if it were growing out of it. In the same way, a city, if livable, must be rooted in the ground. In a sense this involved some abandonment of the more extreme romantic tradition, according to which a city was *per se* unnatural, for it permitted Wright to distinguish between good (organic and natural) and bad (non-organic and non-natural) cities, and hence to give a show of being pro-urban. But when he described his city of the future, it was like Howells' regional capital in Altruria, not a city at all "in our meaning." Such a city might be organic and natural but only by becoming a non-city on most current conceptions.[15]

Wright would have thundered agreement with Henry James' description of New York as a fifty-floored conspiracy against the very idea of the ancient graces, as he would have with many of James' other observations about the metropolis. "The skyscraper is no longer sane unless in free green space," Wright declared.[16] In the city it was a fine example of conspicuous waste and a monstrosity.[17] And something called "The Broadway Creed" was a constant source of agitation for him. Just as Howells once worried about the Chinese and the Irish marching across the continent at each other, Union Pacific style, to forge an alliance against true Americans, so Wright complained that "the Broadway Creed has covered the country pretty much until it has Hollywood for its other end." Belittlement, Wright complained, was the business of the Broadway Creed. "Selfishly bred, children of pleasure herding on hard, crowded pavements in congested urban areas, the breed naturally gets the worm's-eye view suited to the Cashandcarry mentality,"[18] Wright observed with Henry Adams. "In spite of the Immigration laws," Wright went on, "it has grown up among us as the natural product of the melting pot."[19]

Wright did not go to the extreme of Henry Adams on the subject of Jews,[20] but he certainly had his philosophical differences with what he took to be elements of the Jewish tradition. "Mosaic roots of human misery" he calls two of the most objectionable features in human character from his point of view, the spirit of revenge and the dictum "spare the rod and spoil the child."[21] And one of the three great "unnatural economic features" of the present-day city, rent, he traces back to "the ancient Mosaic invention of 'interest.' "[22] So Wright shared Henry Adams' antipathy to bankers. They, along with lawyers and insurance companies, rarely escaped Wright's wrath. Apparently bankers would not finance his houses with enough enthusiasm, because they were, he contended, hostile to ideas everywhere.[23] And lawyers, he held, made "the poorest builders in the world. They are narrow-minded dealers in and for and with the strictures of the law,"[24] and their devices "are more useful to the unscrupulous than they are to the conscientious."[25]

Given his kinship with so many figures in our story and his exaggerated repetition of most of the charges that have been directed against the American city, it is not surprising that Wright should have become the active leader of a campaign to destroy it as he knew it. When he came to articulating his argument, he diverged

195

conspicuously and crucially from earlier critics of urban life who stressed the values of community. As Lewis Mumford has remarked, it never appears to have entered Wright's mind "that one might need or profit by the presence of other men within an area compact enough for spontaneous encounters, durable enough for the realization of long-range plans, and attractive enough to stimulate social intercourse. Save for the family, he scarcely recognizes the need for social groups or associations; for him cooperation is a kind of self-betrayal."[26] Wright rarely spoke with anything like the feeling that Dewey, Park, and Jane Addams shared for neighborly contact, or with anything like Henry James' admiration for urban conversation. On the contrary, Wright seemed to think that modern technology was sweeping away the need for the face-to-face relations that had characterized the earlier city. And once that need was swept away, the city would be swept away with it. "The ancient city," according to Wright, "naturally grew and existed as the great aid and abettor of human intercourse. A city became the immediate source of wealth and power by way of such human intercourse as was essential to social, industrial and financial growth. Only by congregating thus in aggregations, the vaster the aggregation the better, could the fruits of human living then best be had. In that day the real life of the city lay in the stress of individual ties, the contacts of super-individuals encountering upon other individualities. The electric spark of curiosity and surprise was alive in the streets, in public meetings. In the home it was found only occasionally as people congregated there. All was excitingly gregarious and gregarious in order to be exciting."[27] But now that the automobile, the airplane and electrified means of communication are available, Wright seems to say, the city is no longer necessary as a way of bringing men together, simply because they don't have to be together. This, of course, is the direct antithesis of Dewey's view, for Dewey, as we have seen, explicitly rejected the idea that mechanical forms of communication could in fact replace face-to-face contact as a basis for a happy, democratic existence. But Wright, one feels, has the idea that when, say, two-way private television is

196

available to us, we shall no longer want to see and talk to each other in the flesh. Once this happens, cities as we now conceive them will no longer be wanted. And when they are no longer wanted, they too will disappear.

Wright holds that the city will *inevitably* decay and disappear because he imagines electrification and physical mobility as *the* dynamic factors in contemporary history, sweeping and carrying all before them. There is something quasi-Marxist about Wright's theory of history in this respect as there is in others. For example, Wright believes about the city, as Marx did about capitalism, that precisely because the city is in decay, we must hasten that process and mercifully turn the moribund city into a corpse. "To put a new outside upon any existing city is simply impossible now. The carcass of the city is far too old, too far gone. It is too *fundamentally* wrong for the future we now foresee. Hopelessly, helplessly, inorganic it lies there."[28] And elsewhere he asks in a Marxist vein: "Why not be intelligently directed by the inevitable?" Why not accept the fact that the "more natural city," that is, Wright's Broadacre City, is being forced upon us all?[29] The present city is not merely useless but harmful. The forces which are molding modern life, he says, are making the city's "concentrations not only useless but deadly or poisonous by force of circumstances being driven inward, meantime relentlessly preparing within, to explode."[30] And this, of course, is the counterpart of Marx's view that capitalist social relations serve as "fetters" on the productive process, fetters which must be broken sooner or later for the good of all mankind. One may also observe that in Wright's view any effort to slow up this process of urban decay would be "reactionary" in Marx's sense, an effort to turn back the clock of history. Dewey and Park and Jane Addams might then easily play the role in Wright's system that the utopian socialists did in Marx's: poor, beguiled, innocent reformers, ignorant of the vast, impersonal forces of urban history, unaware of the fact that in an age of live television, live conversation is outmoded. Wright himself would then emerge by contrast as the city-destroyer, the urban revolutionary, as opposed to the urban reformer: the man who, like Marx, went to the root of the matter instead of flitting about the trunk, the branches or the leaves of urban distress. The transformation of the city that Wright sought would come about, as he put it in another quasi-Marxian remark, "by evolution certainly—by bloodshed maybe."[31]

Although Wright held that the great effect of modern technology was decentralization—the kind of decentralization that makes the old city anachronistic—he was not content to decentralize indefinitely in conformity with the supposed laws of history. At some point in the process as Wright conceived it, the city planner must put things together, and therefore the double-barreled slogan of Wright's planning was "decenter and reintegrate."[32] Reintegration would have to be carried out according to the principles and with the tools of his organic architecture,[33] because philosophy, economics, religion, and art had all failed us, and because politics had been prostituted in a drift toward conformity.[34] Wright's reintegration is such, he tells us, that were we to carry it out "we might live indefinitely," much as Marx conceived his struggle against capitalism as man's step toward an era of perpetual, idyllic peace. And not only the figure of Marx, but that of Emerson, comes to mind when we hear that in Wright's utopia each man will be "a whole man, living a full life" in security.[35]

How is this Wrightian millenium to be designed? The first step is of course to decentralize, to spring man from the trap and cage of the crowded city into the countryside, assuring no less than an acre to each man, woman, and child, seeing that there were (in 1958 by Wright's calculation) about fifty-seven green acres for each human being in America. Spreading thin laterally would be the watchword. Obviously then, the agglomeration of human beings, the chief feature of cities according to some sociologists, would disappear completely. Broadacre City, the city of the future, would be "everywhere and nowhere,"[36] the city which embraces the country and becomes the nation.[37] And therefore, it is a city only by courtesy, by virtue of a very faint family resemblance to what we now call cities. For this reason, it is fair to call Wright an anti-urbanist in

198

spite of his protestation that he was trying to improve cities, for what he tried to do was to improve them into being non-cities. As in Howells' Altruria, there might be a city in Wright's utopia but not "in our meaning." Wright himself admitted that "the eventual city . . . will be so greatly different from the ancient city or from any city of today that we will probably fail to recognize its coming as the city at all."[38]

XIII

THE LEGACY OF FEAR

THE FACT that our most distinguished intellectuals have been on the whole sharply critical of urban life helps explain America's lethargy in confronting the massive problems of the contemporary city in a rational way. It is not the only element in the explanation, but the fact that so many of our intellectuals have been so antipathetic toward urban life has had a profound, even though not numerically measurable, effect on popular consciousness. It is not simply that the American city has been criticized by intellectuals. That in itself might have been a force in the direction of urban reform, a force of gadflies. It is rather that the literary attack has so often been an attack on American city life as such. Since *the city as such* is an abstract concept about which ordinary people do not think clearly and systematically, whatever general ideas they have on the subject are therefore likely to be influenced, and almost formed, by the writing of those who aspire to a higher level of abstraction. It takes something of an ideologue to construct an elaborate theory which unites, say, the city, science, the machine, commerce, industry, rationality, foreigners, the Jews, and the absence of community spirit into one frightening entity which is to be distrusted, feared, and voted against. Even where the novelist or philosopher exploits feelings of antipathy toward the city that already exist, he often raises them from an inchoate level and in this way creates a more formidable rendering of the popular mind's own prejudices. This, of course, is a hypothesis which would require a study as long as the present one for its confirmation in detail, but it has great initial plausibility. Not all of the actors in our story have had the power of the Presidency at their command, but it is well to keep in mind that Jefferson did seriously influence the life of the nation with his talk about cancers on the body politic, and that the image of the city as a tumor or wen was not likely to have originated with an uneducated Virginia farmer. John Dewey's favorable view of pre-urban America has obviously had a great influence on the kind of education several generations of urban Americans have received. And Jane Addams' image of the city as a unit whose organic character had been destroyed must have communicated itself to many, in spite of their ignorance of the long line of philosophers upon whom she was relying when she spoke in these organismic terms. And think of all the Americans to whom the works of Emerson have been available, to say nothing of those who followed the exploits of Natty Bumpo in James Fenimore Cooper's novels as they imbibed his heady brew of romantic animosity toward the city.

Even Henry Ford, who thought of history as bunk and "wouldn't give a nickel for all the history in the world" was probably influenced by the pastoralism of Longfellow's *Tales of a Wayside Inn* when he reconstructed that Massachusetts relic of the past. And he or his ghost-writers on the *Dearborn Independent* wrote a prose that is redolent of the tradition we have been examining.[1] Ford may have found Emerson's words too big, but his assistants did not, judging by the Emersonian ring of some of Ford's anti-urban sentiments in the *Independent*. The city, we read there, lacks a soul; it is artificial; it is not a community; it is a pestiferous growth; it should be abandoned for the country; it is absolutely dependent on the country; it is doomed to extinction; "the ultimate solution will be the abandonment of the City, its abandonment as a blunder"; and "we shall solve the City Problem by leaving the City."[2] An anti-urban ideology may arise from the same feelings that underlie popular attitudes, but the ideology can logically refine these feelings and give them a more respectable and authoritative form. The fact that so many intellectual figures who occupy our national pantheon said more in opposition to city life than they said in praise of it is

201

responsible for the fact that today's city planner in America finds no powerful intellectual tradition of love for the city to which he can appeal. He has needed a verbal tradition, but most of the verbalists have been on the other side. Henry Ford (or his ghost-writer) expressed a related point with accuracy when he said for an earlier generation: "When we all stand up and sing, 'My Country 'Tis of Thee,' we seldom think of the cities. Indeed in that old national hymn there are no references to the city at all . . . the country is THE country. The real United States lies outside the cities."[3] Interestingly enough, Ford paid no attention to the fourth stanza of "America the Beautiful":

> O beautiful for patriot dream
> That sees beyond the years
> Thine alabaster cities gleam
> Undimmed by human tears!

Nor did Ford pay any attention to Walt Whitman's exclamation in *Song of Myself:*

> This is the city and I am one of the citizens,
> Whatever interests the rest interests me,
>   politics, wars, markets, newspapers, schools,
> The mayor and councils, banks, tariffs,
>   steamships, factories, stocks, stores,
>   real estate and personal estate.

Whitman could sing this in the same song that also expressed his love for the countryside, since Whitman was large and, as he said, contained multitudes, unlike many of the writers we have been studying. The American attitude toward the city might have been different if Whitman's magnanimity had predominated. That attitude might also have been different if European Marxism had been more popular in the United States, and if native socialism had not been so agrarian in sympathy. Because in that case, a powerful pro-urban intellectual force would have been more active among ordinary people, and those who spoke of the idiocy of *urban* life might not have had as much of the field to themselves. And if our literary Bohemians of the twenties had been more effective, that too might have changed the picture, for they might have done more to make city life seem more exciting and even lovable to some. In fact, many of them have also turned their backs on the American city. According to one historian of Greenwich Village, some of its most ardent residents have come to speak like Emersonians: "Max Eastman believes that every true Bohemian has in him a touch of the poet and that few poets, if born in the country, can endure city life. 'You leave the city if you have any poetry in you,' he thinks. Floyd Dell believes the same, asking in effect, 'Who would live in the city when he can live in the country?' Malcolm Cowley, a satisfied resident of Sherman, Connecticut, also echoes this. Another writer puts it more specifically: 'It was all right to live and love on MacDougal Street, but once you got married nine-tenths of your reason for living in the Village was gone—and besides, who would want to bring up children on MacDougal Street?"[4] And while on this subject one may ask where William Faulkner lives. And where did Ernest Hemingway live at the end of his life?

Not only has the anti-urbanism of our intellectual tradition directly influenced the popular mind, but the tradition has probably had an even greater effect on ordinary Americans as it has been transmitted by writers who flourish somewhere between the highest reaches of our culture and the popular mind. In his discussion of Henry James' *Bostonians,* Philip Rahv has remarked that in the figure of Basil Ransom, James created "with remarkable prescience" a type of intellectual whose criticism of the modern urban world resembles that of Southern agrarians in the twentieth century.[5] The doctrines of the Southern agrarians resemble Royce's provincialism even though they veer from it in some respects.[6] And in spite of Howells' ironic handling of Colonel Woodburn in *A Hazard of New Fortunes,* the Colonel's views, like Basil Ransom's, also anticipate those of latter-day agrarians.[7] It is well to keep in mind, then, that the ideas of major writers may well influence the ordinary man's attitudes toward the city, as well as the attitudes of writers who manage to reach the ordinary man by virtue of the great popularity of their books. Two examples of the second phenomenon deserve special attention—the later historical work of Van Wyck Brooks and Lewis Mumford's studies of the city.

Probably the most striking example of the impact of anti-urbanism on the writing of popular literary history in our time may be found in the writings of Brooks, who combines native nostalgia with Spenglerian speculation in his depiction of the decline of Boston letters in the nineteenth century. He believes that the movement of the Boston mind followed a "culture-cycle" from a happy "culture-city" to a suburb, as it were, of a "world-city," New York; that Boston was at first the home of a homogeneous, intensely religious people who lived close to the soil and who possessed deep feeling for home and fatherland, but that later its collective mind became more detached from the soil and hence less powerful and vital. What is this but a version of Hegel's doctrine of the self-estranged mind, explicitly presented as such by Royce and implicitly advocated by many of the writers in whom Brooks had to steep himself while composing his history of American letters? Curiously enough, Brooks singles out Henry James as the symbol of Boston's surrender to New York: "Overintelligent, fragile, cautious and doubtful, the soul of the culture-city loses the self-confidence and joy that have marked its early development—it is filled with a presentiment of the end; and the culture city itself surrenders to the world-city—Boston surrenders to New York—which stands for cosmopolitan deracination."[8] There is irony and error in Brooks' association of Henry James with New York's deracination because we know that, in New York, James sorely missed the kind of "organic social relations" that Brooks extols. And we have sampled enough of Santayana's feelings on such matters to see why he, in spite of his distaste for Spengler's system,[9] could have used the same metaphor as Brooks in his description of Boston's passage "from summer to winter, from the 'flowering of New England' to its industrialization."[10]

And is it not certain that part of the American tradition of anti-urbanism is represented by Lewis Mumford, the most learned of all writers to turn his attention to the nature and destiny of Manhattan? For Mumford is not only a writer on cities, he is a student of American literature and has therefore had more than an ordinary opportunity to breathe the atmosphere we have been describing. More than any contemporary writer, Mumford works at the intersection of our two main topics: the American intellectual and the American city. His complaints about the city, like those of Frank Lloyd Wright, are quickly located in the literary and philosophical tradition previously discussed.

Mumford, like the Brook Farmer, Elizabeth Peabody, thinks that cities and their walls originated in and encouraged war. Like Emerson he thinks that the city has destroyed the whole human being, and like Emerson he is moved to decry the aggressive masculinity of the city. Even Mumford's psychoanalytic geometrizing about the woman's soft container, symbolizing the neolithic period by contrast to the phallic digging weapons of paleolithic times,[11] has its counterpart in Emerson's notion that the city is made up of sharp mathematical lines while the country is the scene of the curving horizon and soft clouds. And Emerson, more than all the figures treated in this book, would have agreed with Mumford's persistent attack on a "civilization geared to expansion by strictly rational and scientific means," and with his disparagement of those who "at bottom . . . are the victims of a quasi-scientific metaphysics incapable of interpreting organic processes or furthering the development of human life."[12] Like so many earlier critics of the city, Mumford is enthralled by the notion of the organism, by Emerson's and Coleridge's view that there is an invidious distinction to be drawn between mechanically imposed form and organic form that grows from within. And so it is not surprising that he should fall into the metaphor of the "cancerous tumors" afflicting the city.[13]

Turning from Mumford's links with the tradition of anti-urbanism that preceded the Civil War, we also find that he has a kinship with the critics of the gilded city, with Henry Adams and Henry James. He cites Adams with unqualified approval for his prophecies of the "almost automatic" disintegration, annihilation, and extermination toward which our cities are rushing.[14] In Mumford's criticism of the American metropolis, we also find Adams' nostalgia for the seventeenth- and eighteenth-century New England town, and for its architectural progenitors in the Middle Ages. Like Henry James and Frank Lloyd Wright, Mumford decries not only the visual chaos of the contemporary urban scene, the lack of lasting monuments, and the senseless motion, but he even views the skyscraper office building as "symbolically a sort of vertical human filing case, with uniform windows, a uniform facade, uniform accommodations, rising floor by floor in competition for light and air and above all financial prestige with other skyscrapers."[15] Since the spread of Megalopolis, Mumford has become even more antipathetic to the American city than Henry James, and now regards the urban background of skyscrapers to be merely the reflection of a civilization whose purposes "have become progressively more empty and trivial, more infantile and primitive, more barbarous and massively irrational." These final epithets of disgust and alarm are like those of the literary naturalists, so that Mumford manages to absorb and reflect almost every variety of anti-urban feeling since the Civil War.

While Mumford shares some of the impulses of the Age of Reform, he shares very little of its optimism. After devoting about a quarter of a million words of his *City in History* to about five thousand years of urban origins and transformations, he devotes only the remaining sixteen pages of his book to some of the city's favorable prospects. After the poor city is battered in page after page, a little ray of hope for it emerges on page 560. "Yet in the midst of this disintegration, fresh nodules of growth have appeared. This pattern necessarily is based on radically different premises from those of the ancient citadel builders or those of their modern counterparts, the rocket constructors and nuclear exterminators. If we can distinguish the main outlines of this multi-dimensional, life-oriented economy, we should also be able to describe the nature and the functions of the emerging city and the future pattern of human settlement. Above all, we should anticipate the next act in the human drama, provided mankind escapes the death-trap our blind commitment to a lop-sided, power-oriented, anti-organic technology has set for it."[16]

What are these fresh nodules of growth? The first, says Mumford, is the fact that the city fosters international peace by bringing together in one comparatively small place people of all races and cultures, along with their customs, their costumes, and their cuisines. In reporting this, Mumford cites a favorable remark of Henry James about the cosmopolitanism of London as a force for international peace. He might have also cited Jane Addams, who in 1904 expressed the hope that the "internationalism engendered in the immigrant quarters of American cities might be recognized as an effective instrument in the cause of peace," adding that "it is always a pleasure to recall the hearty assent given to it by Professor William James."[17] But a comparison of Mumford's optimism with that of Jane Addams and William James brings home to us how faint his optimism is.

According to Mumford, along with foreign-language groups, the museum is another urban nodule of growth because it represents the city's retentiveness, its capacity to hold records and monuments, which is for Mumford "one of the greatest values of the big city."[18] But he goes on to say, in agreement with Frank Lloyd Wright, that the city need no longer perform certain tasks that it once performed. Many of the city's original functions which demanded physical contact of people have been made unnecessary by swift transportation, electronic transmission, mechanical manifolding and world-wide distribution. It is true that, instead of going all the way with Frank Lloyd Wright and concluding, on the basis of this fact, that the city ought to be dispersed once and for all into a non-city, Mumford does draw back. Let cities retain those functions which absolutely require physical agglomeration, he says, and let them surrender those which don't. They may then become more ethereal, more invisible, by electronically spreading their wares over an entire region, as when an interlibrary loan system distributes microfilm and slides.

But identifying the city's nodules of growth with Italian restaurants, Polish dances, the Metropolitan Museum of Art and the New

York Public Library is hardly a matter of cheering at the top of your lungs for the city. And Mumford would be the first to admit that he is not an urban cheerleader. His suggestion that the city become more ethereal by sharing its books and paintings with smaller places is not very different from Howells' idea that cities should be abandoned for regional capitals, which were just as vaguely described as Mumford's future city. True, Howells did not have our present-day methods of electronic communication and aerial transportation in mind, but he did look forward to the day when speeding electrified trains would hurry artists from their hamlets to the regional capitals as they temporarily abandoned their "obligatories" for their "voluntaries." In short, Mumford's work is the most thorough, unrelenting, contemporary expression of the tradition under consideration. If he adds anything of general significance to that tradition, it is perhaps a greater insistence than some of his predecessors that he is working under the aegis of something called an organic philosophy. "No organic improvement is possible without a re-organization of [the city's] processes, functions and purposes, and a re-distribution of its population, in units that favor two-way intercourse, I-and-Thou relationships, and local control over local needs." And like John Dewey, his predecessor in urging a renewal of localism, Mumford appeals in the end to the organicist Emerson. Dewey concluded *The Public and its Problems* by citing the Concord philosopher's remark that we lie in the lap of an immense intelligence. Mumford concludes his mammoth labors on the city in history by recalling a similar Emersonian observation: "Our civilization and these ideas are reducing the earth to a brain. See how by telegraph and steam the earth is anthropolized."[19] In the history of the critique of the American city much changes but much remains the same. Let us now review the phases of the development we have witnessed.

CHAPTER

XIV

THE OUTLINES OF A TRADITION

WITH Frank Lloyd Wright's city to end all cities, we reached the climax of anti-urbanism; and it will now be useful to recapitulate the history of more than a century and a half of reflection on American city life and to highlight certain stages in the development.

The story opens with a relatively irenic age so far as the literature on the city is concerned. It is a period in which the American city, being very small and as yet nothing like a dominant force in our national life, aroused little hostility and little ideological debate between leading writers. To demonstrate this, one need only recall the views of Franklin the city-builder, of Crèvecoeur the celebrant of rural life, and of Jefferson the most articulate of American eighteenth-century writers on the problems of urbanization. Franklin, the bustling, busy urbanite, felt no inconsistency about being an agrarian pamphleteer; Crèvecoeur, the sentimental agrarian, was able to admire the American cities he knew; and the polemical Jefferson himself came at the end of his life to think that America might well have cities, in spite of his earlier attack on them in the *Notes on Virginia*. He despised the manners and principles of the urban mob as he knew it in Europe, and he hoped to keep that mob from crossing the Atlantic intact. He viewed the city as a cancer on the body politic, but he was conciliatory about the claims of the city in his later years. Not out of any love for it, but out of concern for the national interest. The country and its yeomen Jefferson loved all his life. In his old age he felt himself forced to accept the manufacturing city as a necessity after the War of 1812. This shift was made easier because Jefferson was not imprisoned by any elaborate philosophical framework that prevented him from recognizing the economic and political values of the city as an instrument of national defense and welfare: no metaphysical preconceptions forced him to view the city in a hostile manner. On the contrary, his later acceptance of the city's claims allowed him to adopt an attitude toward it which was more typical of the Enlightenment whose child he was.

However, the very War of 1812 that led Jefferson to reassess his views was followed by an enormous expansion of the American city, inaugurating a major phase of urban civilization between the Revolution and the Civil War. By 1860, the urban population was eleven times what it had been in 1820. This age of urban expansion, as William Dean Howells later observed, was not that of the statesman or the politician in the history of popular ideals, but rather that of the literary man. And the literary man had fallen under the spell of romanticism, which in America, as in Europe, entailed a variety of anti-urbanism that was not merely a human response to the horrors of the Industrial Revolution, but a theorem in a philosophical system which deprecated artificiality and science, feared technology as the enemy of sensibility, and regarded the American city as a threat to basic values. Emerson was the high priest of this movement. In his first philosophical work, *Nature,* he assailed the city at the very midpoint of the interval in which the urban population had increased eleven times. He shared Jefferson's dismay about aspects of city life which had become even more troubling in the second quarter of the nineteenth century. Communing across the Atlantic with writers who had already confronted a more fully developed city, he derived from them a metaphysics which permitted him to view the city as artificial and curtailed, unnatural, inferior to the wilderness, and destructive of poetry, philosophy, and solitude.

We know, of course, that Emerson, who was wary of consistency, also extolled the application of science and the virtues of civilization, the need for sociability and the advantages of specialization in spite of his distrust of science, his passion for the wilderness, and his desire to live the life of the whole man. But the preponderant impression he gives is that of one who feared the city, harped on the failings of State Street's commercialism, shuddered when he approached New York, regarded the city as a haven of liars and as a place of debased moral standards. His friend Thoreau and other associates in the transcendentalist movement went even further in their distaste for the city, for they were more opposed than Emerson to civilization as such. Thoreau's *Walden* is a prose poem in praise of the isolated individual, living in nature and free of *all* social attachments. The intellectual conversation and genial clubbiness that Emerson admired so much could not lure Thoreau into Boston. He was, as Henry James said, essentially a sylvan personage.

No matter how much they feared the effects of urbanization, romancers who followed Jefferson in our story had seen only the American beginnings of a troubling development. But like Jefferson they saw disturbing omens in the streets of Liverpool, London, Paris, and Rome of what might come to America. And being romancers, they characteristically resorted to the dream as a vehicle for expressing their feelings. Unlike Schiller, that avatar of romanticism in his "Greetings to the New Century," they did not flee from the realities of urban life to *happy* urban dreams. Their dreams of the city were rather nightmares in which they confronted ghostly cities, cities of crime, sin, poverty, and degradation. When they luridly portrayed foreign cities, they expressed their anxieties about what the American city might become. These pictures carried the American romancers' greetings to the new century that would begin in America with the Civil War. In their pictures they sketched the urban scenes they foresaw with a dread such as the prescient de Tocqueville, with a fuller knowledge of European cities, had voiced in 1835. While Hawthorne advocated the more dramatic course of purifying cities by burning them to the ground periodically, de Tocqueville urged the creation of a national armed force that would be able to repress the excesses of the urban rabble. So, pre-Civil War optimists and pessimists, deists and transcendentalists, empiricists and idealists, all composed their ideological differences while joining in an intellectual crusade against the American city. Even before the really great burst of post-Civil War urbanization began, the nation had been treated to a morbid critique of the city by its literary men, its philosophers, and its most penetrating visitor.

When Howells came to the Civil War in his illuminating tale of American images of greatness, he noted a brief period in which the military man took the national stage before being rudely replaced by the urban millionaires. At the time, the literary man was also forced to take a back seat, but from this position he was still able to witness an urban spurt whose magnitude exceeded anything his predecessors had seen or complained about. Between 1860 and 1900, the urban population quadrupled as the rural population merely doubled: between 1790 and 1890, the urban population increased one hundred and thirty-nine times while the total population had grown only sixteen times. The countryside was being drained of people; New England farms were being deserted; and the elevated railroad, trolley cars, cable cars, subways, telephones, and skyscrapers began to move into the city, bringing in their jarring wake what was then nervously called "American nervousness." New York had become the metropolis, and from that point on, when a writer referred indefinitely to the American city, he invariably referred to Manhattan. Some of the first writers to react sharply to this new world were, as Daniel Aaron has pointed out, men who looked at civilization with agrarian eyes—Walt Whitman and Mark Twain.[1] The same Whitman who was enchanted by Broadway in 1868, and who wrote "Crossing Brooklyn Ferry," looked through his "moral microscope" in 1871 and saw "cities, crowded with petty grotesques, malformations, phantoms, playing meaningless antics."[2]

But for purposes of this story, even more interesting responses to the new city may be found in the writings of Henry Adams and Henry James, who reacted less with pre-war agrarian feeling than with a respect for the values of urban civilization itself. Adams and James were members of cultivated families, one with Boston and the other with Albany wealth in his background, and for both of them the new American city created profound spiritual problems.

212

Because they lived in the period of the American city's undisputed supremacy, they could no longer speak of it as a remote phenomenon of the future or as something in Europe alone. They were refined, civilized, indeed urban men, whose distress with the American city was more significant because they were not opposed to cities in principle. They, therefore, demonstrate what a hard time the American city suffered at the hands of nineteenth-century American intellectuals. For here at last were two *city* types, neither of them professional romanticists or agrarians, who found the American metropolis sadly wanting in different ways. Adams in old age succumbed to the virus of anti-Semitism in his discussion of the city's defects, and to nostalgia for the days of the Virgin in medieval France. James was dismayed by the lack of historic monuments, by the decline of civility, by the absence of organic social relations, by the absence of elevating conversation, and by the absence of the King's English. In New York, where he found all these things wanting, he longed for the whole national consciousness of the Swiss and the Scot, and he too looked at the past as a place of refuge from the chaos he saw. One must not forget, of course, that James' novel *The Princess Casamassima* represents a marvelous effort to penetrate the depths of London, and that his admiring essay on that city was an effort to express his love for it and its people. But the more one remembers James' concern with London, the more one realizes how very different his attitude toward the American city was. After his harsh handling of the Boston reformers in *The Bostonians,* the American city did not provide him with any serious material for a full-length novel because, as F. O. Matthiessen has pointed out, he found neither the uptown nor the downtown of New York sufficiently interesting. In *The Princess Casamassima* he saw the crushing, oppressive effects of the British metropolis, but he could never bring himself to feel much affectionate concern for those who lived in the American metropolis.

On the other hand, the literary realists and naturalists, Howells and Norris and Dreiser, who expressed a sympathetic interest in the inhabitants of the American city, could be as devastating as James in their estimate of the city itself. Dreiser came to Chicago and then to New York in a state of awe and wonder, with great expectations; but he ended his life thinking that New York was a handsome woman with a cruel mouth. Norris left New York City in disgust for California. And William Dean Howells shared the anti-urbanism of Henry George, Laurence Gronlund, Tolstoy and William Morris. In spite of Howells' democratic socialism, realism, and scientific attitude, even he finally called for the dismantling of the American city and its replacement by curiously blank capitals to which officials and artists would make periodic visits. The predominant form of social life in his utopia would be that of villages and hamlets in which neighborliness and close family ties would unite all in a spirit of love. The traveler from Altruria told his American friends, "I do not think you will find anything so remarkable in our civilization, if you will conceive of it as the outgrowth of the neighborly instinct. In fact, neighborliness is the essence of Altrurianism. If you will imagine having the same feeling toward all," he explained to Mrs. Makely, the New York socialite, "as you have toward your next door neighbor."

Howells' book of 1894 continued with an exchange which outlined about a half-century of thinking on city life by sociologists and social workers. In response to the Altrurian's praise of neighborliness, Mrs. Makely exclaimed: "My next door neighbor! . . . But I don't *know* the people next door! We live in a large apartment house, some forty families, and I assure you I do not know a soul among them." The Altrurian looked at her in puzzlement as Mrs. Makely went on to admit that "sometimes it *does* seem rather hard. One day the people on the same landing with us, lost one of their children, and I should never have been a whit the wiser, if my cook hadn't happened to mention it. The servants all know each other; they meet in the back elevator, and get acquainted. I don't encourage it. You can't tell what kind of families they belong to." The Altrurian persisted and asked, "But surely you have friends in the city whom you think of as your neighbors?" And Mrs. Makely persisted and said, "No, I can't say that I have . . . I have my visiting list, but I shouldn't think of anybody on *that* as a neighbor." At this point Howells reports that the Altrurian looked so blank and baffled that he, Howells, could hardly help laughing. The Altrurian then said that he would not know how to explain Altruria to Mrs. Makely. But Mrs. Makely had a ready urban answer: "Well . . . if it's anything like neighborliness, as I've seen it in small places, deliver me from it! I like being independent. That's why I like the city. You're let alone." And now a lonely country lad breaks into the exchange to report: "I was down in New York, once, and I went through some of the streets and houses where the poor people live . . . and they seemed to know each other, and to be quite neighborly." At which point the irrepressible Mrs. Makely asks him whether he would like to live all messed up with other people in that way. And he replies, "Well, I thought it was better than living as we do in the country, so far apart that we never see each other, hardly. And it seems to be better than not having neighbors at all."[3]

Howells' Altruria, then, was somewhere between an isolated farm and an overcrowded tenement, neighborly and friendly, bent on combining the best of both worlds. But while Howells called for the removal of cities so that genuine neighborliness could be encouraged, a generation of reforming social workers, social scientists, and social philosophers all set themselves the task of accomplishing the same result within the city as it was known in the twentieth century. They did not adopt Howells' drastic methods of city destruction; they did not abandon the American city to its fate in the manner of Henry Adams, Henry James, and Theodore Dreiser. They wanted to be neighborly while they were let alone. Their patron saint was Henry James' brother, William, who was not driven by the sight of the American city to Europe or to the past. William James' hope and optimism allowed him to view the urbanization of America in a way that might encourage Americans to do something about urban problems. He did not worship the great cities of Western Europe. The blackness and the age of everything in Florence disgusted him in 1875 and the yellow-brown, stale spaciousness that he saw in London in 1889 filled him with a desire never to see England's capital again. With Emerson he looked to an American future, but the future he saw, unlike Emerson's, was filled with people in American cities living decent lives. Even New York at the turn of the century could send William James into ecstasy while it made his brother shiver and caused his friend William Dean Howells to call for its destruction. Skyscrapers, noise, movement, the subway—all were viewed by William James with characteristic whoops of pleasure.

There was, however, a deeper strain in James' thinking which was even more important in forming the attitudes of a whole generation of younger thinkers, among them Dewey, Jane Addams and Robert Park; and that was James' hatred of bigness, his great need for communication, his desire to go behind the faces of men, to overcome blindness about other people's thoughts and feelings. It was James' outgoing and yet penetrating spirit that heralded a pragmatic phase in urban thinking, in which educators, sociologists, and social workers joined forces in an effort to check the uncontrolled growth and impersonality of the American city. One dominant note in their typically progressive thinking was opposition to giantism, the desire to cut this vast force down to manageable size. And their conception of size was affected by a certain degree of nostalgia for the American village. They did not flee the metropolis for this village, but they wanted to decompose the city into spiritual units that would emulate village life. This is evident in Park's idealization of the primary group, in Jane Addams' hope that the settlement house would help fill the urban void, and in Dewey's plea for a revival of localism in his *Public and its Problems*. All of these figures in the Age of Reform stressed the importance of community and communication in re-creating a livable urban life, but they sought to inject into the city the kind of face-to-face community they knew in their own small villages and towns in the nineteenth century, before the radio, the automobile, the airplane and television made less neighborly forms of communication possible. Josiah Royce, on the other hand, looked to the province as a place in which the self-estrangement of the Hegelian spirit might be diminished.

The cause of communitarianism was not helped by the rushing development of technology. The forces for localism or provincialism were not favored by the march of Megalopolis from the centers of cities, through its suburbs, into the countryside and on to the outskirts of other cities, as it surrounded 31,000,000 people in a supercity along the eastern seaboard by 1960. No wonder Frank Lloyd Wright saw the primary group and face-to-face relations as a thing of the past. No wonder he spoke in strident tones about the search for village-scale community as a lost cause in the middle of the twentieth century. For him the American city had come to an end, brought there by the evolution of the forces that had once ushered it into existence. Technology, which had brought men together into cities would now disperse them, he warned—gradually by means of urban sprawl, instantly by bombs. Wright's Broadacre City was a return to the model of the self-sufficient homestead distributed uniformly over the vast, continental United States. With Wright this tale of more than a century and a half of intellectual anti-urbanism reached a climax.

In this narrative of anti-urban attitudes in America, a number of complaints and fears have persisted throughout the one hundred and seventy-five year period. Fears and doubts about the activities of the city mob, and about the unwieldy and corrupt political character of the city, continue from Jefferson through the early twentieth-century reformers and social critics. Also, distrust of commerce and disapproval of the accumulation of money, those evils continuously condemned by classical, biblical, and medieval writers onward, are still prominent and persistent in the minds of our nineteenth-century thinkers. Those who are burdened with this ancient distrust divide into the romantically inclined, who would most of the time imaginatively dispense with commerce and technology, and the more realistic reformers, who look for social control of both while being ready to recognize their benefits. As American intellectuals came in contact with the industrialization of the city,

217

they issued a series of complaints about the bad city air, the dust, the noise, the dirt, the miserable crowding, the accumulated poverty and beggary, the monotony of the buildings—looking like senseless chunks—and the monotony of the industrial jobs. As industrialization increased and after attempts to grapple with its biological and social effects, we find the reformers questioning whether the modern city is not too complex and too big to deal with effectively.

There are some striking shifts from the early reflections on the city to the later ones. The view that the city is artificial in its very nature and essence is mostly abandoned. Meanwhile, Jefferson's early view is sustained and elaborated: that the city is a malignant social form; over and over again the figure of the city's being a cancer or a tumor is used. The other shift of concern is from the fear of earlier thinkers about city people being especially vulnerable to infections and communicable diseases, a fear which medical science has so rapidly been making obsolete.

Complaints about the modern American city which emerge after the Civil War are: that it is not civilized enough and is too provincial compared to cities in Europe; that the modern commercial and industrial city destroys valuable forms of social life and substitutes nothing as socially valuable in their place; that city life is *too* mobile, both physically and socially; that life in the city is also too spectatorial but that there is too little that is especially worth looking at, little that is sensuously pleasing or artistic. And finally, after the Civil War, there is a great deal more complaint about the difficulties the individual encounters in the modern city. Our writers suggest that being alone in this kind of city has terrors that the country, or the country town, as they knew it, did not possess. They mention over and over again that there is in the city too much impersonality, too little genuine communication, too many immigrants, too many complete strangers, and too little continuity of face-to-face relations for the sound and full development of character. Although the large majority of our thinkers after the Civil War chose to live in cities for long periods in their lives, and were stimulated and fascinated by the freedom and variety of social life there, by the unexpected opportunities, by the range of human adaptations and achievements, still they all expressed grave psychological reservations about modern city life; and many of them were as much repelled by the smell, the sight, and the sound of our commercial and industrial cities as by the way of life they represented.

Considering the tidal wave of forces that rapidly inundated American cities during about a century and a half, it is no wonder that they should not have taken on all the characteristics of stable social settlements. Instead they retained or developed many of the characteristics of the socially fluid frontier. The vast, unsettled continent of the United States was continuously inviting the population to disperse westward into rural areas, while at the same time the combined forces of capitalism, industrialization, rapidly increasing population, and immigration from the ends of the earth were producing urban concentration. After the Civil War, while people began pouring into the cities, the autonomy of cities was being more and more undermined, not only by the advance of nation-wide capitalism and industrialization, but also by the full development of the national state. Moreover, an increasingly strong undertow in the direction of suburban dispersion began in the early years of the twentieth century to drain the vitality of the central city, and to create ill-defined metropolitan areas. And finally, the rapid technological advances in building, transportation, and communication hastened the detachment of individuals from any one fixed, permanent locality or social group.

Confronted with these constantly shifting urban developments over the relatively short span of a century and a half, American intellectuals developed conflicting or antipathetic attitudes and created no solid tradition of love for the American city. Instead they celebrated life in the wilderness, on Virginia farms, in exurban Concord, in isolated Walden, in nineteenth-century London, in the English countryside, in conversational Washington, in American villages and suburbs, in primary groups, in Broadacre City. The celebration of the city was left to chambers of commerce, to boosters and to literary sentimentalists from Dr. Holmes to O. Henry. To the most gifted intellectuals—by literary and philosophical standards—New York was certainly not what London was to Dr. Johnson, what Paris was to a long line of French writers, what Athens was to Aristotle. If distinguished American intellectuals came to the American metropolis to live, they did not always stay to live the good life; and some of them sedulously avoided our urban centers.

Readers who may feel that this story is based on an excessively narrow selection of writers and thinkers should remember that they represent some of our most distinctive intellectual and literary movements: the empiricism of the Enlightenment, transcendentalism before the Civil War, realism and naturalism in literature, post-Civil War pragmatism, idealism and naturalism in philosophy, and functionalism in architecture. Readers who think that we have not aimed high enough in our choice of American intellects should remember that other readers will find in these pages the names of our greatest philosopher, our greatest political thinker, our greatest essayist, our greatest theorist of education, our greatest novelist, our greatest historian, our greatest autobiographer, our greatest social worker, and our greatest architect—most of them worrying or throwing up their hands about one of the most distinctive features of our national life. And that is a fact worth recording and pondering.

ROMANTICISM IS NOT ENOUGH

How shall we explain this persistent distrust of the American city? Surely it is puzzling, or should be. First of all, because we think of the city as a place in which intellectuals habitually congregate. Secondly, because we know that urbanization has been increasing constantly in America for the last one hundred and seventy-five years, and may wonder why our most celebrated writers have so often shown animus toward it, why representatives of some of our most distinctive intellectual movements have been so critical of one of our most distinctive social developments. And thirdly because the intellectual traditions of other western countries, for example, France, have not been as anti-urban in feeling and ideology. The fact of intellectual antipathy and ambivalence toward the city seems to cry for some kind of explanation on several counts. Why, we may reasonably ask, is there so much criticism of the American city in American thought from Jefferson to Wright?

When one asks this question, one often hears in reply that something called "romanticism" is responsible for the phenomenon. But if the previous chapters show anything, they show that this is a mistaken view. And it is mistaken, not because it is wholly false, but because it is not wholly true. It offers too simple an explanation. The desire to explain the phenomenon in terms of espousal of one large global "ism" is, of course, standard among idealistic historians who are directly or indirectly influenced by Hegel, and who invariably seek to account for historical phenomena by referring to a spirit which dominates an age or country and which realizes or actualizes itself in the historical process. Yet such a mode of explanation is not offered only by official Hegelians. It is often proposed by those who would disavow any connection with the tradition of absolute idealism, perhaps without full recognition of the similarity between their approach and that of a philosopher from whom they might well wish to disassociate themselves. Such unconscious idealists, as they might be called, view our intellectual history as the perpetuation or working out of premises accepted in our early national life. Bertrand Russell once facetiously observed that Americans are given to the idea that their history is explained as the result of their being—in Lincoln's words—dedicated to a proposition. And while the prevalence of economic determinism in American historical thought of the twentieth century shows how inaccurate this is as an account of the habits of our professional historians, there is truth in the observation as applied to the effort to explain the persistent intellectual criticism of the American city simply as the outgrowth of romanticism.

On such a model of explanation, we ask why certain intellectuals all share a critical attitude toward the American city and we answer by saying that they all subscribed to the same romantic *Weltanschauung*. But we cannot successfully explain intellectual anti-urbanism in this monistic way. The American city has been so vast, so varied, and so much in flux that it has provided men either in fact or in their imaginations with a variety of things to dislike. The American city has been thought by American intellectuals to be: too big, too noisy, too dusky, too dirty, too smelly, too commercial, too crowded, too full of immigrants, too full of Jews, too full of Irishmen, Italians, Poles, too industrial, too pushing, too mobile, too fast, too artificial, destructive of conversation, destructive of communication, too greedy, too capitalistic, too full of automobiles, too full of smog, too full of dust, too heartless, too intellectual, too scientific, insufficiently poetic, too lacking in manners, too mechanical, destructive of family, tribal and patriotic feeling. And just because different intellectuals have disliked the city for so many different reasons, it is unlikely that one simple hypothesis will provide *the* explanation of why American thinkers have found the city objectionable. Nevertheless, the temptation to offer such simple hypotheses is great, for it is natural to seek in the various reasons given for disliking the city some central thread, some unifying ground for dislike. And so it is that an historian will often seize upon romanticism in an ultimately futile effort to subsume all the anti-urban complaints under one broad belief or doctrine. But while such an explanation may often be correct in the case of a given intellectual, especially if he is Emerson or Thoreau, the difficulty begins when one goes further and argues that *all* criticism of the city may be explained in this way.

An examination of the various American writers who have expressed antipathy to the American city makes abundantly clear that we cannot string so many intellectual beads on even so powerful an intellectual cord. If by romanticism we understand at least an attachment to the wilderness, a love of spontaneity as against reason, of the heart as against the head, of poetry as against calculation, then it is simply not true to say that all American writers who have chosen to attack the main features of the American city have done so because they view it as inferior to the wilderness. Henry James and John Dewey are notable cases in point. As we have seen, James was disturbed by some of the distinctively urban features of New York, and Dewey expressed the gravest concern about the impact of American urbanization. But they were not led to adopt their attitudes by a preference for the American wilderness. If Henry James disliked New York, it was not because he loved the soil, but because New York lacked the society, the civilization, and the brilliance he admired so much. It lacked history, organic social relations, and most of all, elevated conversation. And John Dewey's distaste for the American city in the twenties was not that of a tiller, a sower, or a reaper. It was primarily the distaste of a man who valued social intelligence and face-to-face human relationships, and who was deeply committed to believing in the importance of scientific communication in the conduct of the good life.

It is true, of course, that the tenets and attitudes of romanticism have dominated a good deal of our literary practice and our esthetic

223

theory. Having been instructed by the illuminating studies of Richard Chase, Harry Levin, the late F. O. Matthiessen, Perry Miller, and Henry Nash Smith, among others, we know that many of our American writers have been dreaming romancers more often than novelists in one sense of the latter word, and that they were deeply affected by the intellectual wave called "romanticism." But that wave had been damped, as the physicists say, by the end of the nineteenth century. Therefore, reference to romanticism will help explain the opposition of only certain writers to the city, namely those who lived when the energy of the wave was at its highest and before it encountered certain powerful counterwaves in our intellectual history. The fact is that the heritage of romanticism is not inescapable in American life: scratch an American writer and you won't always find a Natty Bumpo. It is wrong to suppose that resident in the American tradition there is one intellectual pull or impulse away from civilization that can explain *all* criticism of the city. That is why the study of the history of intellectual attitudes toward the city is not simply a chapter in the study of intellectual attitudes toward nature. If the citation of John Dewey is not sufficient to make the point, and if Henry James be eliminated as a counter-example because he was an expatriate, then William Dean Howells may be cited as a stay-at-home artist whose opposition to the American city cannot be construed as the product of a romantic admiration for nature in the sense of the forest or the wilderness, nor the product of a resolution to be savagely natural. Howells wanted to "bang the babes of romance about" and yet he wrote in *A Traveler from Altruria* and *Through the Eye of the Needle,* two of the most anti-urban tracts ever to be produced by an influential American literary man.

And what about Theodore Dreiser who, after a long career of excited literary concern with the city, came to think of the nation's metropolis as a sinister place? Surely Dreiser, like Howells, was not an agrarian or a romanticist. Nor was Henry Adams, who despised New York because he thought it gave more power to immigrant Jews than it did to him, "American of Americans, with Heaven

knew how many Puritans and Patriots behind him." Richard Hofstadter rightly points out that the same distrust of the city that was
conspicuous among the Agrarian Populists was also common among
Henry Adams' class of solid and respectable gentlemen—his brother
Brooks, Henry Cabot Lodge, Theodore Roosevelt, John Hay and
Albert J. Beveridge—who, as Hofstadter puts it, were "in all obvious respects the antithesis of the Populists."[1] These gentlemen
did not imagine themselves to be doctrinaire partisans of the agrarian's soil, or of the forest as against the city.

It must be repeated that if one were to prepare a list of reasons
why American intellectuals have in fact distrusted or disliked the
American city, it would be impossible to summarize or give the gist
of the whole of it by the use of the magic word "romanticism."
The concept of romanticism, at least in one of its many senses, will
not be able to embrace all of the anti-urban pejoratives. If one
construes it as a revolt against civilization in the name of untouched
nature, it is impossible to subsume under that rubric Henry James'
complaint that New York was destructive of good conversation.
The point is that we cannot make out a case for an exclusively
romantic theory of anti-urbanism, simply because many objections
to the American city have not been made—either explicitly or implicitly—in the name of nature's virtues as against those of civilization. Some of them have been made in the name of civilization itself. Therefore, we must conclude when we study the literature of
anti-urbanism that there are different reasons for the different expressions of anti-urbanism, and that some of these reasons are in a
sense opposed to each other. The American city has been criticized
by writers who doubted or despised the values of civilization, as well
as by writers who were intensely dedicated to civilized life. In short,
the American city has been caught in the crossfire of two powerful
antagonists—primitivists and sophisticates; and no mechanical recitation of the misleading aphorism that like effects are produced by
like causes can gainsay this fact. Indeed this fact makes it easier to
see why antipathy to the American metropolis has been so persistent,
why it weathered even the great change in intellectual climate that

came with the Civil War. In spite of a rapid reversal of intellectual winds, the city continued to be buffeted by them.

It is undoubtedly true that many of our pre-Civil War intellectuals were critical of the city because of their affiliation with romanticism. Writers like Thoreau, Emerson, Hawthorne, Poe and Melville used stock romantic arguments against the American city and voiced stock romantic feelings about its defects. But we cannot understand this phase of the story without bearing in mind certain social facts about the nation at that time. Just to the extent to which it was primarily non-urban in its way of life, literary and philosophical critics of the city could speak more plausibly of life in the wilderness as a viable alternative to life in the city. Hence a stereotyped romantic attack on the American city was retailable by Thoreau and Emerson as well as by lesser writers like James Fenimore Cooper, William Gilmore Simms, and William Cullen Bryant; and by painters like Asher Durand and Thomas Cole. The artistic defense of an undefiled nature against the encroachments of civilization made more sense in a period when there were fantastic amounts of undefiled nature to which a romantic writer and his readers could flee, than it could have made at a later date. We must recognize therefore that a fuller explanation of this pre-Civil War, romantic anti-urbanism would take into account the fact that it reached its zenith in rural America. In a predominantly rural country, romantic criticism of the city acquired considerable plausibility. Emerson's highly metaphysical attack on urban life derived its popularity in part from the fact that it was published at a time when large numbers of people *could* abandon the city for vast tracts of untouched nature. This does not mean that traditional romanticism can be expressed only in a period which is preponderantly nonurban, but it does suggest that it can flourish as the preponderant intellectual style only under such circumstances.

After the Civil War, however, doctrinaire love of the wilderness was not a serious factor in the animadversions on the American city that we find in Henry Adams, Henry James, William Dean Howells, Theodore Dreiser, and John Dewey. Of all the later figures treated

226

in this study, only Frank Norris and Wright clearly returned to romanticism in their attacks on the city. And when a late nineteenth-century critic of the American city like Henry Adams gave reasons for disliking the city that coincided with those adduced by Emerson —they both despised commercialism—it would be absurd to speak of Adams as "to that extent" a romanticist in an effort to save the theory that romanticism is *the* explanation of anti-urbanism. To attack the city on romantic grounds is to attack it in a stereotyped way, to bring to bear the full weight of romantic ideology. Some elements in that ideology, like the distrust of commerce, may turn up in other critiques, but however much these other critiques *share* with the romantic critique, they do not, merely by virtue of that sharing, become romantic or even partly so. One might just as well say that anyone who ever took a political position that coincided with that of a Communist was "to that extent" a Communist. A similar level of absurdity might be reached if one were to call George Santayana a crypto-romantic because he fled Boston and hated New York, or if one were to speak similarly of T. S. Eliot because he thought of the modern city as a wasteland.

After the Civil War the American city was attacked by leading intellectuals on grounds that were, if anything, almost anti-romantic. Even Frank Lloyd Wright said he opposed citification in the name of civilization.[2] The American city was no longer abandoned for the forest by figures like Henry Adams, Henry James, William Dean Howells, and John Dewey. *If the American city was then found wanting, it was found wanting not because it was too civilized but rather because it was not civilized enough.* For the generation of post-Civil War intellectuals, for realists and pragmatists and naturalists, American city life was not deficient because it was artificial, rational, self-conscious or effete. On the contrary, it was too wild, too vulgar, too ostentatious, too uncontrolled, too gaudy, too full of things that disturbed the sensibility of the fastidious like Henry James and George Santayana, and too chaotic for scientifically oriented minds like Dewey who sought a planned social order.

It was this anti-romanticism that may have helped to produce in

227

American writers a more positive attitude toward the European city at the end of the nineteenth century than that which had predominated before the Civil War. In the early part of the century many romanticists preferred the American city on moral grounds to what they regarded as depraved European centers like Liverpool, London, Rome, and Paris, even when they preferred these European cities on esthetic grounds. But the American city in the Gilded Age was often fled by men of sensibility for what they regarded as the more refined, more sophisticated and better-planned cities of Europe. The same forces that urbanized the country helped make literary and philosophical romanticism a less popular doctrine among major intellectuals after the Civil War, and helped replace it by criticism of the city that diverged sharply from Rousseauian or Thoreauvian romanticism. When Henry James and John Dewey lamented the decline of urban conversation and communication, and when Henry Adams found himself lost in New York, they were giving voice to their common feeling that the more advanced forms of human intelligence and sensibility were missing from New York; they were not lamenting the absence of the more primitive experiences that Thoreau missed in the city. The social workers who criticized the later nineteenth-century American city did not mean to praise it when they referred to "the city wilderness." Stephen Crane did not mean to praise the city in *Maggie* when he likened it to a jungle, nor did Upton Sinclair. Edith Wharton did not mean to praise upper-class New Yorkers when she said in *The Age of Innocence* that they resembled primitives in their ritualistic behavior. The critique of the city had shifted radically from the days when a romantic would have prayed for the city's transformation into a wilderness or a jungle. Even Lewis Mumford, that latter-day admirer of Emerson, complains that Megalopolis is too primitive and too barbaric.

The history of the critique of the American city, then, is divisible into two fundamental contrasting stages: one in which romanticism was employed in attacking the city for being overcivilized; and another stage in which the city was accused of being undercivilized by anti-, or at least non-romantics. The shift from a predominantly rural society to an urban one linked the promise and the possibilities of civilization with urbanization; and after the Civil War, intellectuals were more respectful of those possibilities. But they were not satisfied with mere possibilities. Urban intellectuals therefore turned upon the American city and citicized it for not living up to its possibilities and its promise; and as a result we find the growth of a city-based attack on the city itself, all in the name of the very things that a real romanticist would have scorned: science, sophistication, and order.

Of course, a great deal of urban reform was prompted by a desire to recapture the spirit of earlier village life. But village life as conceived by Dewey, Park, and Jane Addams was not purely impulsive, purely instinctual, purely of the heart. It was not part of untouched nature: it was not life in the forest or the wilderness. Santayana, a sharp critic of the American city, conceived of the pre-barbaric rural city as a place in which the life of reason could best be lived, and one of Howells' characters exclaimed: "Think of a city operated by science, as every city might be now, without one of the wretched animals tamed by savage man, and still perpetuated by the savage man for the awkward and imperfect uses of a barbarous society! A city without a horse, where electricity brought every man and everything silently to the door."[3] The "capitals" in Howells' Altruria were also to be freed of the romantic horse in the same scientific spirit. In this qualified nostalgia for the village—imagine a horseless village in nineteenth-century America!—one may find an ingredient of romanticism as conceived by *some* writers, without doubt. But we must avoid defining "romanticism" so broadly as to include under it any attitude which is critical of the city, for then, of course, every anti-urbanist will be by definition a romanticist and the concept will become useless to us as an explanatory device. Romanticism was not the presiding spirit of anti-urbanism after the Civil War, if we think of romanticism as antipathetic to science and technology, as celebrating nature after the fashion of Emerson when he said that he found something more dear and connate in the wilderness than in streets or villages. For romanticism in this sense was certainly not the spirit of Howells, who acknowledged his fear of loneliness in the country and his love of village streets. Nor was it the spirit in which Dewey, Henry James, Robert Park, Jane Addams, Theodore Dreiser, and Frank Lloyd Wright criticized the cities they knew.

Although the nation was stricken in its early history with a severe attack of Natty Bumpoism, by a serious case of intellectual hostility to the city in the name of nature, the fact that later varieties of anti-urbanism were often motivated by opposed considerations indicates that romantic anti-urbanism cannot be regarded as a permanent feature of the American mind. And once we see this, we are liberated from a mythical view of our intellectual past, and a stultifying view of our intellectual future. The tendency to see this country's mind as traditionally romantic is the product of a misguided philosophy of history and a failure to assess the facts of intellectual life after the Civil War. For at that time it became evident that romanticism was not a permanent affliction of the American intelligentsia. If able men continued to criticize the city sharply, it was primarily on other grounds. They recognized that at last America had developed complicated centers of culture and civilization but had not done enough to realize their potentialities. After the Civil War anti-urbanism was therefore more rational, less metaphysical, and less silly than meanderings about the supreme virtue of spontaneity, the heart, and the forest. We are not *all* heirs of Natty Bumpo, thank God, and we can escape that part of our so-called romantic heritage if we face the facts of history and the world about us.

XVI

IDEOLOGY, PREJUDICE, AND REASONABLE CRITICISM

ONCE it is recognized that not all writers who criticized the American city did so in the name of a romantic attachment to the forest, irrationality, spontaneity, and the unaided heart, it becomes easier to take some literary and philosophical attacks on the city more seriously. Or at any rate, it becomes more difficult to dismiss them all as irresponsible, just as it becomes more difficult to dismiss them all as the product of racism, nativism, or anti-Semitism when one realizes that many American writers criticized the city without being gripped by irrational prejudice. Many of the ideas previously encountered are neither irrational nor so remote as to have no bearing whatsoever on our contemporary urban predicament. One cannot treat them all as if they were like outmoded physical theories or astrological views, or seventeenth-century sermons, or proofs of the existence of universals and physical objects, having merely historical interest. The American city is a subject of intense concern today, and it is natural, therefore, that as concerted an onslaught on it as the one we have witnessed should stimulate at least some degree of critical reaction. On the other hand, it would be impossible at this point to evaluate all of the arguments and feelings that have been exposed to view. Instead we shall consider some of the main animadversions in the literature, in an effort to see which are intellectually dead, and which remain alive in this age of urban distress.

Before turning to some of the most typical criticisms, it is well to remark that very few of our thinkers provide us with complaints that rest on reflections of a scientific, or allegedly scientific, character.[1] Our thinkers have not been biologists, economists, or demographers who cite statistical evidence to justify their criticism of city life. In fact, when they do approach the problem in this way, or in a rudimentary version of this way, as in the case of Henry Adams, they are least persuasive. Henry Adams' view that the decline of urban civilization is an example of the lugubrious workings of the second law of thermodynamics is perhaps the closest thing to a scientific argument that we have met, but it need not concern us very seriously. If the universe is growing colder and colder, and more and more scattered, *that* would militate against the continued existence of all life and not merely against the continued existence of urban life. If the sun were to go out, the farms and the wilderness as well as the city would disappear, and it would even become impossible to reconstruct Adams' beloved age of Mont-Saint-Michel and Chartres.[2] Moreover, nothing that a city-dweller could do would halt the process. To predict that the whole universe itself is going to a frozen Hell is not to advance an argument which the city-lover must answer with special care. If Adams' theory is as "deterministic" as he says it is, it could not support a corrective critique of any human mistakes. If our will is bound and we are doomed from eternity to see our cities decay, we shall see them decay—and that will be the end of it. The serious question raised by a view like Adams' is whether, given the amount of energy available to us at any given time, we should spend it in cities or not; and on this question the laws of thermodynamics tell us nothing. Here Adams' prejudices were more relevant than his theories. And his prejudices, in spite of being expressed in a fine prose style, are no more worthy of a reasoned reply than those of, say Josiah Strong, who, in his writings at the end of the nineteenth century, catered to a less fastidious class of readers by encouraging their fear that Anglo-Saxon supremacy would be destroyed by the urban mob.[3]

The arguments against the city which are worth our serious attention today are neither those that foolishly appeal to irrelevant metaphysics, nor those based on unreasoned prejudice against Jews, Catholics, and foreigners. In general, the more high-flown and metaphysical the anti-urban argument, the less cogent it is; but the more it expresses a writer's direct feelings and knowledge about the common trials of urban living, the more it is likely to strike a resonant note even in the most doctrinaire and sentimental city-lover. Let us examine some attacks which rest on metaphysically founded moral doctrines.

Underlying many critiques of the American city is the ancient imperative: Follow nature. The argument built upon this imperative has been relatively simple so far as it affects the city. Man ought to follow nature, but life in the city does not follow nature; therefore, life in the city is wicked. This is not the place for a play-back of the age-old philosophical controversies over "Follow nature" and allied doctrines, but it is worth reminding ourselves of the classical philosophical objections to this doctrine. As Emerson pointed out, the word "nature" has two main senses. According to one it refers to the totality of things, processes, and events in the universe; according to another it refers to the universe as it would be if no human being ever touched it or interfered with its behavior. But to be told that we should follow nature in the first sense is not very meaningful, since we cannot help following it in that sense. As parts of nature ourselves, we are subject to its laws, physical, biological, chemical, and psychological, and therefore we follow it as a matter of necessity. And while to be told that we should always follow it in the second sense is not a wholly clear doctrine, if it means something to the effect that we should do whatever "nature" does, we must recall a relevant observation of John Stuart Mill. He once remarked that "nearly all the things which men are hanged or imprisoned for doing to one another are nature's every day performances . . . Nature impales men, breaks them as if on the wheel, casts them to be devoured by wild beasts, burns them to death, crushes them with stones like the first Christian martyr, starves them with hunger, freezes them with cold, poisons them by the quick or slow venom of her exhalations, and has hundreds of other hideous deaths in reserve, such as the ingenious cruelty of a Nabis or a Domitian never surpassed."[4]

If the argument from nature against the city was not dead at the time Emerson published his essay on nature in 1836, it certainly was by the time Mill composed his about fifteen years later. It is true, of course, that a wise man will bear in mind the consequences of his actions, and that he will abandon or dismantle cities if he can be shown that they are inevitably evil, beyond repair, and worse than any alternative home. But the attack on the city via the simple command to follow nature is philosophically unconvincing. It should be repeated, however, that a refusal to guide oneself by this philosophical maxim does not mean that one abandons natural and social science. One merely refuses to be bullied into anti-urbanism by muddled or indefensible metaphysics in the service of a questionable moral philosophy.

Those romantics who urged city-dwellers to follow nature and abandon the city were opposed at the end of the nineteenth century by sociologists, philosophers, and social workers who refused to call the city unnatural, and who insisted that its development was governed by empirical regularities and hence subject to scientific study. But they also insisted that the city could not be viewed as a mere spatial unit or as a mere political unit, and following Park they advocated an ecological approach.[5] Their point of view was not built on any moral idea that residents of the city should somehow imitate the processes of untouched nature. It was rather a protest against construing nature so narrowly as to exclude the city. And when such writers spoke of the city as an organism, they did not fall into the errors of certain theorists who thought that the city was literally an organism or a person.[6] This is evident even in the first serious study of urban sociology to be published in this country, a section of Albion Small's and George Vincent's *Introduction to the Study of Society* of 1894. Such empirically minded sociologists recognized that a scientific student of urban problems may well acknowledge the interconnections of the major aspects of city life without literally treating the city as an organism, a person, or a mysterious whole.[7] It was rather Emerson, in his most anti-urban, most anti-scientific mood, who wrote in *Nature* that "empirical science is apt

234

to cloud the sight, and by the very knowledge of functions and processes to bereave the student of the manly contemplation of the whole." But a distinguished contemporary sociologist has reminded us that "the contemplation of 'wholes' has never taken root in the United States as a fundamental scientific attitude. American social scientists . . . could not remain wholly satisfied with the ecstatic self-immersion into 'wholeness' or the undifferentiated sense of the interconnectedness of all things."[8] There are thus two traditions of organicism in American thought, one of which is metaphysical and romantic in tendency, and which leads from Emerson to Lewis Mumford; while the other leads to a more empirical and more rational attitude toward the problems of the city, one which need not neglect esthetic and social values.

Organicism in its more metaphysical mood has been applied to the city mainly with critical intent. Its most common use has been in the metaphor of the city as a cancer on the body of the state; but more recently Lewis Mumford has come up with the idea that the city is a neurotic person. Now there is no objection to the use of a lively metaphor in serious writing, and many an important fact has been uncovered by the imaginative use of analogy. But in the history of American thought about the city, the organic metaphor has often been used to cloak the absence of hard, empirical reflection on the problems of urban life. If there is anything that scares the American today, it is cancer and mental disease; and the idea that the city is literally or figuratively afflicted with them is not calculated to lead the debates about the value of city life into a serious and sober context. Not even when such language is accompanied by assurances that urban pathologists are able to cure it by ruthless surgery, or that its psychopathologists can cure it by making it ethereal and invisible.

Urban studies need clearer talk about communication; and more communication in direct, simple prose, accompanied by solid scientific investigation and self-conscious formulation of the values that city planners are seeking to realize in the American city. They do not need "wholistic," "organic" metaphysics of the kind that Mum-

235

ford has urged them to cultivate. Indeed, one finds it hard to make any sense whatever out of this effort to harness organic metaphysics to the problems of the city today. Mumford believes that the whole future of urban culture rests on our capacity to develop "a more organic world picture, which shall do justice to all the dimensions of living organisms and living personalities."[9] And in his book of Emersonian title, *The Conduct of Life,* he announces that "the new philosophy will treat every part of human experience, from the enduring structure of the physical world to the briefest incarnation of divinity, as an aspect of an inter-related and progressively integrating whole. It will restore the normal hierarchy of the organic functions, placing the part at the service of the whole, and the lower function at the command of the higher: thus it will establish once more the primacy of the person, and the function of man himself as the interpreter and director—not the passive mirror and ultimate victim—of the forces that have brought him into existence."[10] But one need not be a Philistine or a positivist to be puzzled about how the development of such a philosophy will help us improve our cities. Moreover, if anything is likely to slow up and perhaps permanently impede the improvement of our cities, it is the insistence that they cannot be improved before we construct a world-view according to such blurry blueprints. It is one thing to make no small architectural plans, but it is another to make grandiose metaphysical ones and then insist that the reconstruction of the city must await the reconstruction of metaphysics in accordance with one's incomprehensible instructions. If organic metaphysics is not dead, it ought to be; moreover it can contribute nothing of value to our understanding and solution of urban problems.

As we have already suggested, the tradition of anti-urbanism in American writing is at its best when it conveys esthetic, psychological, and moral ideas, and impressions of the city's defects. Whatever one's opinion of the metaphysics of the American city's critics, from Emerson to Mumford, one must acknowledge that they have often reacted to the city with sensibility and insight that did them much more credit than their organic philosophies. Therefore, the city planner would make a grave mistake if he were to dismiss that tradition, if he were to treat it as a point of view from which nothing could be learned, if he were to forget it or disregard it. Those who must live in today's American city or who like to live in it, can profit by taking seriously the urban criticism of our great writers, for it was deep and many-sided. It was not only esthetic but also moral. Henry James spoke most profoundly for those who saw the city as a scene of chaos as it presented itself to "the painter's eye." It lacked order, structure, history, and dignity in 1907, and these virtues have not been miraculously supplied in the age of urban sprawl and suburban slums. But the city, as Robert Park said, is a state of mind as well as an esthetic object, and many of the distinguished critics of the American city have found psychological and moral fault with it.

All of our thinkers suggest that some degree of stability and continuity are necessary for the development of culture in the individual and in society—continuity primarily in social associations so that communication is easy, spontaneous and complete. Park and Dewey both distinguished between societies organized simply for economic purposes, and those capable of corporate action based on mutual understanding and deliberate two-way communication designed to satisfy civilized human needs. They both suggest that the modern American city, in undermining the primary group, has interfered with the full development and education of the individual, and with the maintenance of communities capable of genuinely democratic action. In their view, if the primary groups lose much of their effectiveness in the supercity, neither the full development of the individual's consciousness, nor the evolution of a democratic community is possible. It is still a grave question what social institutions in our urban centers can adequately supplement the faltering family, church, and neighborhood in an effort to strengthen communication. If we look to the school, the college, and the university, they must be vastly expanded and redirected to this massive role without in the process eliminating genuine two-way, intimate communication. There are, therefore, still many reasonable doubts

237

about the psychological environment of the modern city in America. When Jefferson warned of the dangers of what he called the city mob, when Emerson complained of the city's conventionalism, when John Dewey lamented the decline of neighborliness, all of them thought of the city as a place in which certain basic human values were being subverted, values which ought to be cherished today as they were in the eighteenth century of Jefferson, the nineteenth century of Emerson, and the twentieth century of Dewey. And what are these values? Jefferson's worry about the mobs of the city arose from doubt about the American city's capacity to educate its inhabitants in a way that would preserve and extend the democratic process. And when Emerson worried about the growth of conventionalism in the city, he was thinking in part, as were his contemporaries Søren Kierkegaard and John Stuart Mill, about the increase in conformity, about the decline of individuality which was proportional to the increase of urbanization. Although Dewey's main concern was with the improvement of human communication within the city, by communication he did not mean the exchange of information alone. He valued the capacity to share feelings and experiences, the capacity to discuss with, to learn from and intelligently persuade others, and to *live* with them in the profoundest sense.

Who can deny in 1962, then, that the great problem of the American city is to demonstrate at least three things: first, that it can solve the problem of education for the millions of people who are entering its gates, that it can absorb the Negro and the Puerto Rican, as it has other groups, into its economy and the democratic process; second, that it can foster individuality, the capacity and the right of the human being to develop into a rounded personality concerned with more than merely commercial values; and third, that it can be more than a vast prison of unconnected cells in which people of different occupations, color, class, or creed fail to understand one another on the basic human issues of social life, let alone agree with one another.

The moral message of the intellectual critic of the city today is

238

not fundamentally different from what it was in the age of Jefferson, Emerson, and Dewey. For today's serious thinker must also build upon a respect for the fundamental values of education, individuality, and easy communication among men. But, unlike his predecessors, he cannot deceive himself about the *place* in which those values must be realized today. The wilderness, the isolated farm, the plantation, the self-contained New England town, the detached neighborhood are things of the American past. All the world's a city now and there is no escaping urbanization, not even in outer space.

NOTES

NOTES

CHAPTER I: OPENING THEME

1. The phrase was used by Herman Melville in his review of Nathaniel Hawthorne's *Mosses from an Old Manse*.

2. See the section, "The Nature of the City," in Paul K. Hatt and Albert J. Reiss, Jr., eds., *Cities and Societies: The Revised Reader in Urban Sociology* (Glencoe, Ill., 1957), esp. pp. 17–21.

CHAPTER II: THE IRENIC AGE: Franklin, Crèvecoeur, and Jefferson

1. Richard Hofstadter, *The Age of Reform: From Bryan to F.D.R.* (New York, 1956), p. 27; Carl Van Doren, *Benjamin Franklin* (New York, 1952), pp. 177–178.

2. Henry Adams, *History of the United States of America During the First Administration of Thomas Jefferson* (New York, 1909), vol. I, ch. 1.

3. *Ibid.*, p. 28.

4. Gilbert Chinard, *Thomas Jefferson: The Apostle of Americanism* (Boston, 1939), p. 166.

5. Carl Bridenbaugh, *Cities in Revolt: Urban Life in America, 1743–1756* (New York, 1955), p. 419.

6. Benjamin Franklin, *The Autobiography of Benjamin Franklin*, edited by Max Farrand (Berkeley and Los Angeles, 1949), pp. 79–80.

7. *Ibid.*, p. 150.

8. J. Hector St. John Crèvecoeur, *Letters from an American Farmer*, reprinted from original edition, preface by W. P. Trent, introduction by Ludwig Lewisohn (London and New York, 1908), p. 20.

9. *Ibid.*, p. 15.

10. D. H. Lawrence, *Studies in Classic American Literature* (New York, 1955), p. 23. The original edition was published in New York in 1923.

11. *Ibid.*, p. 38.

12. *Ibid.*, p. 33.

13. Crèvecoeur, *Letters*, p. 26.

14. Lawrence, *Studies*, p. 32.

15. Crèvecoeur, *Letters*, p. 26.

16. Ralph H. Gabriel, "Crèvecoeur and His Times," introduction to J. Hector St. John Crèvecoeur, *Sketches of Eighteenth Century America* (New Haven, 1925), p. 2.

17. Crèvecoeur, *Letters*, appendix II, pp. 349–351.

18. Crèvecoeur, *Sketches*, p. 54.

19. *Works of Thomas Jefferson*, edited by P. L. Ford (New York, 1904), IV, 86.

20. A. W. Griswold, *Farming and Democracy* (New York, 1948); see especially ch. ii, "The Jeffersonian Ideal." For a very informative discussion of the literary and philosophical backgrounds of agrarianism from the classics to the eighteenth century, see Paul H. Johnstone, "In Praise of Husbandry," *Agricultural History*, 11:80–95 (1937), and "Turnips and Romanticism," *Agricultural History*, 12:224–255 (1938). Also see C. E. Eisinger, "The Free-hold Concept in Eighteenth Century American Letters," *William and Mary Quarterly*, 3rd ser., 4:42–59 (1947).

21. Letter to Lithgow, *Works*, IV, 86–88, note.

22. Chinard, *Thomas Jefferson*, pp. 159–175; see also Marie Kimball, "Jefferson in Paris," *North American Review*, 248:75 (1939).

23. Letter to Anne Willing Bingham, Paris, Feb. 7, 1787, *The Papers of Thomas Jefferson*, edited by J. P. Boyd, XI (Princeton, 1955), 122–123.

24. Letter to Charles Bellini, *Papers of Thomas Jefferson*, VIII (Princeton, 1953), 568–570.

25. *Works*, IX, 146–147.

26. See *Territorial Papers of the United States*, edited by C. E. Carter (Washington, 1934–1952), vol. VII, *The Territory of Indiana, 1800–1810*, p. 88; also *The Writings of Thomas Jefferson* (Washington, 1907), XI, 66–67. We are indebted to Professor J. Reps of Cornell University for calling this material to our attention. See his article, "Thomas Jefferson's Checkerboard Towns," *Journal of the Society of Architectural Historians*, 20:108–114 (1961).

27. *Works*, XI, 503–504.

28. Richard Hofstadter has pointed out that Jefferson was not the prisoner of any elaborate social philosophy involving the city, not even the philosophy of the physiocrats, which V. L. Parrington thought was central to Jefferson's thinking. See Parrington, *Main Currents in American Thought* (New York, 1930), I, 346, and Hofstadter, "Parrington and the Jeffersonian Tradition," *Journal of the History of Ideas*, 2:391–400 (1941).

29. *Works*, XI, 537–538.

30. *Writings*, XV, 469.

CHAPTER III: METAPHYSICS AGAINST THE CITY: The Age of Emerson

1. A. F. Weber, *The Growth of Cities in the Nineteenth Century: A Study in Statistics* (New York, 1899); Arthur M. Schlesinger, "The City in American Civilization," *Paths to the Present* (New York, 1949), p. 216.

2. Schlesinger, *Paths to the Present*, p. 216.

3. *Ibid.*, pp. 217–218.

4. *Ibid.*, p. 223.

5. John A. Kouwenhoven, *The Columbia Historical Portrait of New York: An Essay in Graphic History* (New York, 1953), p. 196.

METAPHYSICS AGAINST THE CITY

6. E. Porter Belden, *New-York: Past, Present, and Future* (New York, 1849), p. 45.
7. *Ibid.*, p. 76.
8. Alexis de Tocqueville, *Democracy in America* (New York, 1945), I, 290.
9. *Ibid.*, pp. 289–290, note.
10. Quoted in Sherman Paul, *Emerson's Angle of Vision: Man and Nature in American Experience* (Cambridge, 1952), p. 38. In this work one may find a helpful discussion of the impact of Coleridge on Emerson's distinction between Reason and Understanding.
11. *Journals of Ralph Waldo Emerson*, edited by E. W. Emerson and W. E. Forbes (Boston, 1909–1914), V, 310–311; see Paul, *Emerson's Angle of Vision*, pp. 79–82.
12. *The Complete Works of Ralph Waldo Emerson*, edited by E. W. Emerson (Boston, 1903–1904), I, 66–67.
13. *Ibid.*, VII, 161–166; X, 265; XI, 121–123.
14. *Ibid.*, VII, 31–32.
15. *Ibid.*, p. 244.
16. *Ibid.*, pp. 424–425.
17. *Ibid.*; VI, 149.
18. *Ibid.*, VII, 10–11.
19. *Ibid.*, VI, 56–57.
20. *Ibid.*, p. 148.
21. *Ibid.*, p. 97.
22. Bliss Perry, ed., *The Heart of Emerson's Journals* (Boston, 1937), p. 208.
23. Emerson, *Works*, XII, 453.
24. Walter Muir Whitehill, *Boston: A Topographical History* (Cambridge, 1959), pp. 99, 103–104, 106.
25. *Works*, VI, 153.
26. *Ibid.*, pp. 155–156.
27. *Ibid.*, VII, 140.
28. *Ibid.*, I, 9.
29. Perry, *Heart of Emerson's Journals*, p. 88.
30. *Works*, I, 10.
31. *The Correspondence of Thomas Carlyle and Ralph Waldo Emerson* (Boston, 1883), I, 269–270.
32. Perry, *Heart of Emerson's Journals*, p. 264.
33. *Works*, I, 10.
34. *Ibid.*, p. 31.
35. *Ibid.*, p. 341.
36. *Ibid.*, p. 342.
37. *Ibid.*, VII, 153–154.
38. *Ibid.*, X, 477.
39. *Ibid.*, pp. 481–482.

40. *Ibid.,* I, 347–348.

41. Henry David Thoreau, *Walden,* in *The Writings of H. D. Thoreau* (Boston, 1904), II, 144.

42. "Walking," *Writings,* IX, 267.

43. Elizabeth Palmer Peabody, "Plan of the West Roxbury Community," *The Dial,* January 1842, pp. 361–372; see esp. pp. 361–362 and p. 372. The article is reprinted in part in Perry Miller, *The Transcendentalists: An Anthology* (Cambridge, 1950), pp. 465–469.

44. See Miller, *The Transcendentalists,* pp. 464–465.

45. Emerson, *Works,* III, 253–254.

46. Ralph Barton Perry, *The Thought and Character of William James* (Boston, 1935), I, 73, 69, 44, 56.

47. Perry Miller, *Consciousness in Concord* (Boston, 1958), p. 46.

48. *Writings,* IX, 51.

CHAPTER IV: BAD DREAMS OF THE CITY: Melville, Hawthorne, and Poe

1. Harry Levin, *The Power of Blackness* (New York, 1958), pp. 234–235. This book is indispensable for the study of anti-urbanism in Melville, Poe, and Hawthorne. See also Leo Marx's interesting study of Hawthorne's "imagery of technology" in "The Machine in the Garden," *New England Quarterly,* 29:27–42 (1956); and Perry Miller's penetrating essay on the romanticism of early nineteenth-century American literature, "Nature and the National Ego," in his *Errand into the Wilderness* (Cambridge, 1956), pp. 204–216.

2. *Redburn,* in *The Works of Herman Melville,* V (London, 1922), 161.

3. William H. Gilman, *Melville's Early Life and Redburn* (New York, 1951), p. 216.

4. *Redburn,* p. 303.

5. *Ibid.,* p. 272.

6. *Ibid.,* pp. 258, 260.

7. *Pierre, Or, The Ambiguities,* in *The Works of Herman Melville,* IX (London, 1922), 4.

8. *Ibid.,* p. 9.

9. *Ibid.,* p. 16.

10. *Ibid.,* p. 33.

11. *Ibid.,* p. 321.

12. *Ibid.,* p. 322.

13. *Ibid.,* pp. 98, 127, and 403, to mention only a few.

14. *Ibid.,* p. 16.

15. Gilman, *Melville's Early Life,* pp. 239–240; see John Higham, *Strangers in the Land: Patterns of American Nativism, 1860–1925* (New Brunswick, New Jersey, 1955), p. 21.

16. Perry, *Heart of Emerson's Journals,* p. 317.

17. Gilman, *Melville's Early Life,* p. 238.

18. *Redburn*, pp. 259–260.

19. Henry A. Murray, Introduction to *Pierre* (New York, 1949), pp. xxvi-xxvii. Our italics.

20. F. O. Matthiessen, *American Renaissance: Art and Expression in the Age of Emerson and Whitman* (New York, 1941), p. 468.

21. *The Blithedale Romance*, in *The Works of Nathaniel Hawthorne*, V (Boston, 1882), 391.

22. *Ibid.*, p. 486.

23. *Ibid.*, p. 487.

24. *Ibid.*, pp. 491–492.

25. Levin, *Power of Blackness*, p. 86.

26. *Blithedale Romance*, p. 487.

27. *Ibid.*, p. 421.

28. Quoted in Perry Miller, *The Raven and the Whale: The War of Words and Wits in the Era of Poe and Melville* (New York, 1956), p. 89.

29. Levin, *Power of Blackness*, p. 43.

30. Hawthorne, *Works*, I, 220, 227.

31. *Ibid.*, III, 624, 631, 641.

32. *Ibid.*, V, 541, 588.

33. *The Letters of Henry James*, selected and edited by Percy Lubbock (New York, 1920), I, 72.

34. *The Marble Faun*, in Hawthorne, *Works*, VI, 346–347.

35. *Ibid.*, p. 341.

36. Edward H. Davidson, *Poe: A Critical Study* (Cambridge, 1957), p. 269.

37. *Ibid.*, pp. 118–120.

38. Edgar Allan Poe, *Doings of Gotham*, edited by J. E. Spannuth and T. O. Mabbott (Pottsville, Pennsylvania, 1929), pp. 25–26. The editors wonder whether "portentous" should not be replaced by "pretentious"; see also Killis Campbell, *The Mind of Poe and Other Studies* (Cambridge, 1933), pp. 106, 119, 123–124.

39. Poe, *Doings of Gotham*, pp. 40–41.

40. *Ibid.*, p. 32.

41. *Ibid.*, pp. 59–60.

42. *Ibid.*, p. 61.

43. *The Complete Works of Edgar Allan Poe*, edited by James A. Harrison (New York, 1902), VI, 208–209.

44. *Ibid.*, pp. 212–213.

45. *Ibid.*, p. 138.

CHAPTER V: THE DISPLACED PATRICIAN: Henry Adams

1. Schlesinger, *Paths to the Present*, p. 225.

2. Max I. Baym, "Henry Adams and the Critics," *The American Scholar*, 15:79–89 (1945–1946); also *The French Education of Henry Adams* (New York, 1951), esp. ch. vii.

NOTES TO CHAPTER V

3. William H. Jordy, *Henry Adams: Scientific Historian* (New Haven, 1952), pp. 155 ff., 247 ff.
4. Adams, *History*, I, 147.
5. *Ibid.*, p. 148.
6. *Ibid.*, p. 138.
7. *Ibid.;* see also Henry Adams's *John Randolph* (Boston, 1882), pp. 6–8.
8. Adams, *History*, I, 87.
9. *Ibid.*, p. 117.
10. *Ibid.*, p. 130. Jordy, *Henry Adams*, p. 76, suggests that Adams, like Macaulay, exaggerated the primitiveness of the past.
11. Adams, *History*, I, 184.
12. Jordy, *Henry Adams*, passim.
13. Henry Adams, *The Education of Henry Adams* (Boston, 1918), p. 238; Edward N. Saveth, *American Historians and European Immigrants, 1875–1925* (New York, 1948), ch. iii; Oscar Handlin, "American Views of the Jew at the Opening of the Twentieth Century," *Publications of the American Jewish Historical Society*, no. 40, part 4, p. 330 (June 1951).
14. *The Education of Henry Adams*, p. 241.
15. *Ibid.*, p. 247.
16. *Ibid.*, pp. 51–52.
17. *Letters of Henry Adams*, edited by Worthington C. Ford (Boston, 1930), I, 6.
18. *Ibid.*, p. 228.
19. *Ibid.*, p. 288.
20. *Ibid.*, II, 80; Saveth, *American Historians and European Immigrants*, pp. 67–68.
21. Saveth, p. 94; see also Harold Dean Cater, *Henry Adams and His Friends: A Collection of His Unpublished Letters* (Boston, 1947), pp. 353–354.
22. *Letters*, II, 314.
23. Cater, *Henry Adams and His Friends*, p. 369.
24. *Letters*, II, 414.
25. *Ibid.*, p. 466.
26. *Education*, p. 26.
27. *Ibid.*, p. 9.
28. *Ibid.*, pp. 10–11.
29. *Ibid.*, p. 62.
30. *Ibid.*, p. 63.
31. *Ibid.*, p. 35.
32. *Ibid.*, p. 52.
33. *Ibid.*, p. 309.
34. *Letters*, I, 399.
35. *Education*, p. 73.

36. *Ibid.,* p. 195; see T. S. Eliot's review of the *Education* in *The Athenaeum,* May 23, 1919, pp. 361–362.

37. *Education,* p. 90.

38. *Letters,* I, 118.

39. *Education,* pp. 403–405.

40. *Ibid.,* p. 77.

41. *Ibid.,* p. 79.

42. *Ibid.,* p. 410.

43. *Letters,* I, 90.

44. *Ibid.,* p. 91.

45. *Ibid.,* p. 96.

46. *Ibid.,* p. 99.

47. *Ibid.*

48. *Ibid.,* p. 111

49. Cater, *Henry Adams and His Friends,* pp. 22–23.

50. *Letters,* I, 313.

51. *Ibid.,* p. 322.

52. *Letters,* II, 3.

53. Cater, *Henry Adams and His Friends,* p. 341.

54. *Ibid.,* p. 344.

55. *Ibid.,* p. 350.

56. *Letters,* I, 130.

57. *Ibid.,* p. 319.

58. Cater, *Henry Adams and His Friends,* p. 461.

59. *Ibid.,* pp. 490–491.

60. *Letters,* II, 317.

61. *Education,* p. 256.

62. *Ibid.,* p. 317.

63. *Ibid.*

64. *Letters,* I, 302.

65. *Ibid.*

66. Ernest Samuels, *Henry Adams: The Middle Years* (Cambridge, 1958), p. 79.

67. *Education,* p. 48.

68. *Letters,* II, 620.

69. *Education,* pp. 499–500.

70. Henry Adams, *Mont-Saint-Michel and Chartres* (Boston, 1932), pp. vii-viii (editor's note).

71. *Ibid.,* p. 381.

72. *Ibid.,* p. 380.

73. *Letters,* II, 46.

CHAPTER VI: THE VISITING MIND: Henry James

1. James Bryce, *The American Commonwealth,* 2nd ed., rev. (New York, 1908), I, 681, 673.

NOTES TO CHAPTER VI

2. Leon Edel, *Henry James, the Untried Years, 1843–1870* (Philadelphia, 1953), p. 336.

3. *Ibid.*, p. 156.

4. Quoted by F. O. Matthiessen, "The Ambassadors," in F. W. Dupee, ed., *The Question of Henry James* (New York, 1945), p. 225.

5. Edel, *Henry James*, pp. 81–82, 86, 88, 90.

6. *Ibid.*, p. 141.

7. *Ibid.*, pp. 191–192.

8. Henry James, *Hawthorne* (New York, 1880), p. 12.

9. *The Notebooks of Henry James*, edited by F. O. Matthiessen and Kenneth B. Murdock (New York, 1947), p. 43.

10. Henry James, *The Art of Travel*, edited with an introduction by Morton Dauwen Zabel (New York, 1958), pp. 329, 333, 354.

11. Quoted in Edel, *Henry James*, p. 302.

12. *The Letters of Henry James*, selected and edited by Percy Lubbock (New York, 1920), I, 48.

13. *The Art of Travel*, p. 217.

14. *Letters*, I, 41–42, 51. George Santayana reported in *The Middle Span* (New York, 1945), pp. 39–40, that James once told him an anecdote about Prosper Mérimée wondering at James for choosing to live in England and finding that a good background for his inspiration. Mérimée said to James: "Vous vivez parmi des gens moins fins que vous."

15. *Letters*, I, 22.

16. Edel, *Henry James*, pp. 283–284.

17. Matthiessen, "The Ambassadors," in *The Question of Henry James*, pp. 227–228.

18. Edel, *Henry James*, p. 196.

19. *Letters*, I, 54–55.

20. *Ibid.*, pp. 15–16.

21. Preface to *The Princess Casamassima* (London, 1921).

22. *The Princess Casamassima*, I, 314.

23. *Ibid.*, II, 340.

24. *Ibid.*, pp. 3–4, 17.

25. *Letters*, I, 28.

26. *Princess Casamassima*, II, 107–111.

27. Henry James, *Essays in London and Elsewhere* (New York, 1893), p. 5.

28. *Ibid.*, p. 12.

29. *Ibid.*, p. 27.

30. *Ibid.*, p. 12.

31. *Ibid.*, p. 14.

32. *Ibid.*, pp. 27–28.

33. *Views and Reviews by Henry James*, edited with an introduction by Leroy Phillips (Boston, 1908), p. 102.

34. *The Notebooks of Henry James*, pp. 25, 33.

35. *Letters*, I, 99.
36. *The American Scene* (New York, 1946), p. 355.
37. *Ibid.*, pp. 355, 359–360, 339.
38. *Ibid.*, pp. 342–343.
39. *Ibid.*, p. 73.
40. *Ibid.*, pp. 139, 143.
41. *Ibid.*, pp. 76–77, 92, 95–96.
42. *Ibid.*, pp. 83–84.
43. *Ibid.*, pp. 85–87, 275, 279–280.
44. *The American Novels and Stories of Henry James*, edited with an introduction by F. O. Matthiessen (New York, 1947), pp. 867, 869, 877, 981–982.
45. *Ibid.* See Matthiessen's introduction for an elaboration of this point.
46. Edmund Wilson, "The Ambiguity of Henry James," in Dupee, ed., *The Question of Henry James*, pp. 172–173.

CHAPTER VII: THE AMBIVALENT URBANITE: William Dean Howells
1. Edwin H. Cady, *The Road to Realism: The Early Years, 1837–1885, of William Dean Howells* (Syracuse, New York, 1956), ch. ix; Edwin H. Cady, *The Realist at War: The Mature Years, 1885–1920, of William Dean Howells* (Syracuse, New York, 1958), ch. i; Everett Carter, *Howells and the Age of Realism* (Philadelphia and New York, 1954), ch. iii.
2. William Dean Howells, *A Traveler from Altruria* (New York, 1957), p. 138. The original edition was published in New York in 1894.
3. William Dean Howells, *Suburban Sketches* (Boston, 1875), pp. 69–72; pp. 113–114. In 1875 Howells worried even about "the encounter of the Irish and the Chinese now rapidly approaching each other from opposite shores of the continent" and asked nervously, "Shall we be crushed in the collision of these superior races?"
4. Daniel Aaron, *Men of Good Hope: A Story of American Progressives* (New York, 1951), pp. 184–185; Van Wyck Brooks, *Howells: His Life and World* (New York, 1959), p. 268; *Life in Letters of William Dean Howells*, edited by Mildred Howells (New York, 1928), II, 70.
5. See Aaron, *Men of Good Hope*, p. 185. See also George Arms and William M. Gibson, " 'Silas Lapham,' 'Daisy Miller' and the Jews," *New England Quarterly*, 16:118–122 (1943); and *Mark Twain—Howells Letters: The Correspondence of Samuel L. Clemens and William D. Howells, 1872–1910*, edited by Henry Nash Smith and William M. Gibson (Cambridge, Mass., 1960), II, 555.
6. *Life in Letters of William Dean Howells*, II, 1.
7. Cady, *The Realist at War*, p. 182.
8. *Ibid.*, p. 141.
9. Howells, *Suburban Sketches*, pp. 250–251, 241.
10. Carter, *Howells and the Age of Realism*, p. 119.
11. Cady, *The Road to Realism*, p. 93.

12. Quoted by Mildred Howells, *Life in Letters of William Dean Howells,* I, 13. In *Suburban Sketches* Howells said that "he is but a poor creature who does not hate the village where he was born."

13. *Life in Letters of William Dean Howells,* I, 29.

14. *Ibid.,* p. 30.

15. *Ibid.,* p. 31.

16. William Dean Howells, *Literary Friends and Acquaintance: A Personal Retrospect of American Authorship* (New York, 1901), pp. 68, 88.

17. Cady, *The Road to Realism,* p. 119.

18. *Ibid.,* ch. ix, passim.

19. *Life in Letters of William Dean Howells,* I, 362.

20. Cady, *The Realist at War,* p. 3.

21. *Ibid.,* p. 6; see also George Arthur Dunlap, *The City in the American Novel, 1789–1900* (Philadelphia, 1934), p. 84.

22. William Dean Howells, *The Minister's Charge, or the Apprenticeship of Lemuel Barker* (Boston, 1887), p. 458.

23. Carter, *Howells and the Age of Realism,* pp. 194, 206.

24. *Life in Letters of William Dean Howells,* II, 7.

25. *Ibid.,* p. 18.

26. Cady, *The Realist at War,* p. 182.

27. *Letters of Henry James,* I, 165.

28. Quoted in Carter, *Howells and the Age of Realism,* p. 60.

29. William Dean Howells, *A Hazard of New Fortunes,* Everyman ed. (New York, 1952), p. 339.

30. *Ibid.,* p. 19.

31. *Ibid.,* pp. 251–252.

32. *Ibid.,* pp. 160–161.

33. Aaron, *Men of Good Hope,* p. 187.

34. Lawrence Gronlund, *The Cooperative Commonwealth: An Exposition of Modern Socialism,* 3rd ed. (London, 1891), p. 116. It is interesting to observe that Gronlund changed his point of view on the city by the time his book, *The New Economy: A Peaceable Solution of the Social Problem* (New York, 1907) appeared; see p. 192 thereof.

35. Henry George, *Social Problems* (New York, 1886), pp. 317–318.

36. William Dean Howells, *The World of Chance* (New York, 1893), pp. 12–13.

37. *Ibid.,* p. 153; see also Brooks, *Howells,* p. 195. Reminiscing in 1900 about New York in 1860, Howells said that "at that day the skyscrapers were not yet, and there was a fine regularity in the streets that these brute bulks have robbed of all shapeliness," *Literary Friends and Acquaintance,* p. 77. And in *The Coast of Bohemia* (New York, 1893), one of Howells's characters on arriving in New York comes upon the following sounds, sights and smells: "the street was full of cars and carts and carriages, all going every which way, with a din of bells, and wheels and hoofs that was as if crushed to one clangorous mass by the superior uproar of the railroad trains

coming and going on a sort of street-roof overhead. A sickening odor came from the mud of the gutters and the horses and people, and as if a wave of repulsion had struck against every sense in her, the girl turned and fled from the sight and sound and smell of it all" (p. 64). Howells was an enemy of the urban horse, it would appear, and believed that the city could be made as clean as the country "simply by the elimination of the horse, an animal which we [Altrurians] should be as much surprised to find in the streets of a town as the plesiosaurus or the pterodactyl." *A Traveler from Altruria*, p. 189.

38. *The World of Chance*, p. 116.

39. *A Traveler from Altruria*, p. 174.

40. *Ibid.*, p. 182.

41. *Ibid.*, pp. 187–188.

42. *Ibid.*, p. 190.

43. William Dean Howells, *Through the Eye of the Needle: A Romance* (New York, 1907), p. 3.

44. *A Hazard of New Fortunes*, p. 79.

45. *Through the Eye of the Needle*, pp. 10–11.

46. See, for example, Aaron, *Men of Good Hope*, ch. vi, passim.

47. *The Minister's Charge*, p. 3.

48. "Folks rust out living alone. It's human nature to want to get together," says young Camp, the country lad, in *A Traveler from Altruria*, p. 124.

49. *Life in Letters of William Dean Howells*, II, 69.

50. *Ibid.*, p. 150.

51. This was cut from the pages of *Their Silver Wedding Journey* of 1899. See Brooks, *Howells*, p. 237.

52. William Dean Howells, *Hither and Thither in Germany* (New York, 1920), pp. 115–116.

CHAPTER VIII: DISAPPOINTMENT IN NEW YORK: Frank Norris and Theodore Dreiser

1. Franklin Walker, *Frank Norris: A Biography* (New York, 1932), p. 89.

2. Frank Norris, *McTeague: A Story of San Francisco* (New York, 1899).

3. *Ibid.*, p. 353.

4. Ernest Marchand, *Frank Norris, A Study* (Stanford, 1942), p. 142.

5. Frank Norris, *The Octopus: A Story of California* (New York, 1901), p. 402.

6. *Ibid.*, p. 144.

7. Walker, *Frank Norris*, p. 166.

8. *Ibid.*, pp. 171–172.

9. "A Plea for Romantic Fiction," *Complete Edition of Frank Norris* (New York, 1928), VII, 167.

10. Quoted in Walker, *Frank Norris*, p. 209.

11. "New York as a Literary Centre," *Complete Edition of Frank Norris*, VII, 71–76.

12. "Salt and Sincerity," *ibid.*, p. 208.

13. Theodore Dreiser, *A Hoosier Holiday* (New York, 1916), p. 365.

14. Kenneth S. Lynn, *The Dream of Success: A Study of the Modern American Imagination* (Boston, 1955), ch. i.

15. David Brion Davis, "Dreiser and Naturalism Revisited," in *The Stature of Theodore Dreiser*, edited by Alfred Kazin and Charles Shapiro (Bloomington, Indiana, 1955), pp. 225–236.

16. Theodore Dreiser, *Dawn* (New York, 1931), p. 78.

17. *Ibid.*, p. 105.

18. *Ibid.*, pp. 116–117.

19. *Ibid.*, p. 156.

20. Theodore Dreiser, *The Titan* (New York, 1914), ch. ii, passim.

21. *Dawn*, pp. 159–163.

22. *A Hoosier Holiday*, p. 228.

23. *Dawn*, p. 298.

24. *Ibid.*, p. 327.

25. *A Hoosier Holiday*, p. 229.

26. F. O. Matthiessen, *Theodore Dreiser* (New York, 1951), p. 57.

27. *Dawn*, p. 296.

28. Theodore Dreiser, *Newspaper Days* (New York, 1922), p. 1.

29. *Ibid.*, p. 20.

30. *Ibid.*, p. 107.

31. *Ibid.*, p. 183.

32. *Ibid.*, pp. 217–218.

33. *Ibid.*, p. 352.

34. *Ibid.*, pp. 451–452.

35. *Ibid.*, p. 458.

36. *Ibid.*, p. 470.

37. *Ibid.*, p. 474.

38. *Ibid.*, p. 479.

39. *Ibid.*, pp. 480–482.

40. *Ibid.*, p. 487.

41. *The Color of a Great City* (New York, 1923), p. v.

42. *Ibid.*, p. 154.

43. *Ibid.*, p. 233.

44. *Ibid.*, p. 2.

45. Theodore Dreiser, *A Traveler at Forty* (New York, 1913), p. 512.

46. *Ibid.*, p. 79.

47. Matthiessen, *Theodore Dreiser*, p. 216.

CHAPTER IX: PRAGMATISM AND SOCIAL WORK: William James and Jane Addams

1. Ralph Barton Perry, *The Thought and Character of William James* (Boston, 1935), I, 352.

2. *Ibid.*, pp. 352–353.

PRAGMATISM AND SOCIAL WORK

3. *Ibid.*, p. 351.
4. *Ibid.*, p. 412.
5. *Ibid.*, p. 226.
6. *Ibid.*, p. 351.
7. *Ibid.*, p. 389.
8. *Ibid.*, p. 225.
9. *Ibid.*, p. 350.
10. *Ibid.*, p. 349.
11. *Ibid.*, II, 254–255.
12. *The Letters of William James*, edited by Henry James (Boston, 1920), II, 264.
13. William James, *Talks to Teachers on Psychology: And to Students on Some of Life's Ideals* (New York, 1899), p. 234.
14. *Ibid.*, p. 248.
15. Quoted by James, *ibid.*, pp. 251–252.
16. Quoted in William James, *Pragmatism: A New Name for Some Old Ways of Thinking* (New York, 1907), p. 24.
17. *Ibid.*, pp. 32–33.
18. See Lewis Feuer's article, "John Dewey and the Back to the People Movement in American Thought," *Journal of the History of Ideas*, 20:545–568 (1959).
19. *Letters of William James*, II, 90.
20. Jane Addams, *Twenty Years at Hull House, With Autobiographical Notes* (New York, 1912), pp. 111–112.
21. Oscar Handlin, *The Uprooted* (Boston, 1951)
22. Jane Addams, *The Spirit of Youth and the City Streets* (New York, 1911), p. 9 and passim.
23. *Twenty Years at Hull House*, p. 195.
24. Jane Addams, *Democracy and Social Ethics* (New York, 1902), pp. 206–207.
25. *Twenty Years at Hull House*, p. 37.
26. Jane Addams, "The Objective Value of a Social Settlement," *Philanthropy and Social Progress*, edited with an introduction by Henry C. Adams (New York, 1893), pp. 28–31.
27. *Twenty Years at Hull House*, pp. 118, 368.
28. *Ibid.*, p. 127. For Tolstoy's attack on the organic philosophy, see especially *What Shall We Do Then?*, in *Works*, Illus. Sterling ed., translated by Leo Wiener (Boston, 1904), XVII, 218–223.
29. *Twenty Years at Hull House*, p. 125.
30. *Ibid.*, p. 151.
31. *Ibid.*, p. 309.
32. *Ibid.*, p. 346.
33. *Ibid.*, p. 247.
34. *The Spirit of Youth and the City Streets*, p. 4; ch. i, passim; *Democracy and Social Ethics*, pp. 51–56.

35. *The Spirit of Youth and the City Streets*, p. 134.
36. *Democracy and Social Ethics*, p. 209.
37. James Weber Linn, *Jane Addams* (New York, 1935), p. 117.

CHAPTER X: THE PLEA FOR COMMUNITY: Robert Park and John Dewey

1. Robert Ezra Park, *Human Communities: The City and Human Ecology* (Glencoe, Ill., 1952), p. 75.
2. Edward Shils, *The Present State of American Sociology* (Glencoe, Ill., 1948), p. 7.
3. Robert Ezra Park, "An Autobiographical Note," in his *Race and Culture* (Glencoe, Ill., 1950), pp. v–ix, passim. See also E. W. Burgess, "In Memoriam: Robert E. Park, 1864–1944," *American Journal of Sociology*, 49 (March 1944). For the relations of Park, Dewey, and Franklin Ford, see Perry, *The Thought and Character of William James*, II, 518; Morton White, *The Origin of Dewey's Instrumentalism* (New York, 1943), pp. 100–102; also the article by Lewis S. Feuer, "John Dewey and the Back to the People Movement in American Thought," *Journal of the History of Ideas*, 20:545–568 (1959).
4. Park, *Race and Culture*, pp. vi–vii.
5. William James, *Talks to Teachers on Psychology: And to Students on Some of Life's Ideals* (New York, 1899), pp. 263–264.
6. Park, *Race and Culture*, pp. vi–vii.
7. *Ibid.*, p. ix.
8. See Georg Simmel's famous essay, "The Metropolis and Mental Life," in which he identifies the large city as a place which values the head rather than the heart (in a manner reminiscent of Emerson), which accentuates the importance of money, mathematical exactness and impersonality, punctuality, reserve and a blasé attitude. Also, on Simmel's view, the city grants "the individual a kind and amount of personal freedom which has no analogy whatsoever under other conditions." The essay has been translated by Kurt H. Wolff and appears in his *Sociology of Georg Simmel* (Glencoe, Ill., 1950); reprinted in Hatt and Reiss, eds., *Cities and Society*, pp. 635–646.
9. See Maurice Stein, *The Eclipse of Community* (Princeton, 1960), p. 16.
10. Park, *Human Communities*, p. 74.
11. *Ibid.*, pp. 47–48.
12. *Ibid.*, p. 60.
13. *Ibid.*, pp. 88–89.
14. *Ibid.*, p. 13.
15. *Ibid.*, p. 14.
16. Robert E. Park and Ernest W. Burgess, *Introduction to the Science of Sociology* (Chicago, 1921), p. 42.
17. Park, *Human Communities*, p. 45.
18. *Ibid.*, p. 218. This is a reprint of the contribution that Park and

THE PLEA FOR COMMUNITY

Newcomb made to R. D. McKenzie's *The Metropolitan Community* (New York, 1933).
19. *Ibid.*, p. 47.
20. Robert E. Park, *Society* (Glencoe, Ill., 1955), pp. 93–94.
21. *Human Communities*, p. 34.
22. *Ibid.*, p. 59.
23. *Ibid.*, pp. 60–63.
24. *Ibid.*, p. 68.
25. *Ibid.*, p. 72.
26. *Ibid.*, p. 73.
27. *Ibid.*, p. 74.
28. Everett C. Hughes, preface to Park, *Human Communities*, p. 6.
29. *Human Communities*, p. 24.
30. Park, *Race and Culture*, p. 14.
31. Hughes, preface to Park, *Human Communities*, p. 6.
32. *Human Communities*, p. 140.
33. *Ibid.*, pp. 140–141.
34. *Ibid.*, pp. 46–47; Park and Burgess, *Introduction to Sociology*, pp. 286–287.
35. Park, *Race and Culture*, p. 22.
36. Thorstein Veblen, *Theory of the Leisure Class*, Modern Library ed. (New York, 1934), pp. 86–87.
37. Park and Burgess, *Introduction to Sociology*, pp. 956–957.
38. See "Biography of John Dewey," edited by Jane M. Dewey, in P. A. Schilpp, ed., *The Philosophy of John Dewey* (Evanston and Chicago, 1939), pp. 3–45.
39. John Dewey, *The School and Society*, rev. ed. (Chicago, 1923), p. 6. See also Morton White, *Social Thought in America: The Revolt Against Formalism* (New York, 1949; rev. ed., Boston, 1957), chapter vii.
40. Dewey, *School and Society*, p. 7.
41. *Ibid.*, pp. 7–8.
42. *Ibid.*, p. 9.
43. *Ibid.*, p. 11.
44. *Ibid.*, p. 12.
45. Patrick Geddes, *Cities in Evolution: An Introduction to the Town Planning Movement and to the Study of Civics* (London, 1915), pp. 48–49.
46. *Ibid.*, p. 83.
47. Charles Horton Cooley, *Social Organization* (New York, 1909), p. 23.
48. *Ibid.*, pp. 26–27.
49. John Dewey, *The Public and its Problems* (New York, 1927), p. 98.
50. *Ibid.*, p. 184.
51. *Ibid.*, p. 211.
52. *Ibid.*, p. 214.
53. *Ibid.*, pp. 217–218.
54. *Ibid.*, p. 218.

257

55. *Ibid.*, p. 219.

56. *Ibid.*

57. *The Living Thoughts of Thomas Jefferson*, presented by John Dewey, with an introductory essay (New York, 1940), pp. 21–23.

58. Frederick C. Howe, *The City: The Hope of Democracy* (New York, 1905), p. 204.

59. Frederick C. Howe, *The Confessions of a Reformer* (New York, 1925), pp. 339–340.

CHAPTER XI: PROVINCIALISM AND ALIENATION: An Aside on Josiah Royce and George Santayana

1. Christopher Tunnard and Henry Hope Reed, *American Skyline* (New York, 1956), pp. 194, 200–201. The original edition was published in Boston in 1955.

2. Josiah Royce, *Race Questions, Provincialism and Other American Problems* (New York, 1908), p. 73. Also see Royce's *California, From the Conquest in 1846 to the Second Vigilance Committee in San Francisco: A Study of American Character* (Boston and New York, 1886), esp. pp. 499–501 and ch. v, passim.

3. Royce, *Race Questions*, p. 74.

4. *Ibid.*, p. 80, et seq. See also Gustave LeBon, *The Crowd* (New York, 1896), a translation of *Psychologie des foules* (Paris, 1895).

5. Josiah Royce, *The Philosophy of Loyalty* (New York, 1908), p. 239.

6. *Ibid.*, p. 241.

7. *Ibid.*, p. 242.

8. In his *Economic and Political Manuscripts* of 1844 the young Marx wrote: "In what does this alienation of labour consist? First, that the work is *external* to the worker, that it is not a part of his nature, that consequently he does not fulfil himself in his work but denies himself, has a feeling of misery, not of well-being, does not develop freely a physical and mental energy, but is physically exhausted and mentally debased. The worker therefore feels himself at home only during his leisure, whereas at work he feels homeless. His work is not voluntary, but imposed, *forced labour*." Marx also said: "The object produced by labour, its product, now stands opposed to it as an *alien* being, as a *power independent* of the producer." See Karl Marx, *Selected Writings in Sociology and Social Philosophy*, edited by T. B. Bottomore and M. Rubel (London, 1956), p. 169, p. 171.

9. Royce, *Philosophy of Loyalty*, p. 242.

10. *Ibid.*, p. 245. Italics his.

11. Josiah Royce, *The Hope of the Great Community* (New York, 1916), p. 46. See also Royce, *The Problem of Christianity* (New York, 1913), vol. I, lecture II, "The Idea of the Universal Community." Howells' minister in *The Minister's Charge* preaches his sermon on the Pauline text: "Remember them that are in bonds as bound with them." See Cady, *The Realist at War*, p. 6.

ARCHITECTURE AGAINST THE CITY

12. See Stuart Gerry Brown's helpful introductory essay in his volume of selections, *The Social Philosophy of Josiah Royce* (Syracuse, N.Y., 1950), p. 4.

13. Royce, *Race Questions,* p. 97.

14. *Ibid.,* pp. 97–98.

15. See Tunnard and Reed, *American Skyline,* pp. 194, 200–201.

16. George Santayana, *The Background of My Life* (New York, 1944), esp. pp. 68, 88, 162, 180.

17. *Ibid.,* pp. 226–227.

18. George Santayana, *The Middle Span* (New York, 1945), pp. 6–7.

19. Santayana, *The Background of My Life,* p. 230.

20. *The Philosophy of George Santayana,* edited by P. A. Schilpp, (Evanston and Chicago, 1940), pp. 560–561.

21. *Ibid.,* p. 538. Santayana's critics were the late Irwin Edman and Professor Milton K. Munitz.

22. John Dewey's review of *The Philosophy of George Santayana,* in *Mind,* n.s., 50:379, note (1941).

23. Santayana, *The Middle Span,* pp. 25–26.

24. *Ibid.,* p. 22.

25. *Ibid.,* pp. 35–36.

26. Santayana, *The Background of My Life,* p. 131.

27. *Ibid.,* p. 100.

28. *Ibid.,* p. 230.

29. *Ibid.,* p. 298.

30. George Santayana, *My Host the World* (New York, 1953), p. 140.

31. *Ibid.*

CHAPTER XII: ARCHITECTURE AGAINST THE CITY: Frank Lloyd Wright

1. Frank Lloyd Wright, *An Autobiography* (New York, 1943).

2. R. P. Adams, "Architecture and the Romantic Tradition: Coleridge to Wright," *American Quarterly,* 9:46–62 (1957).

3. Louis Sullivan, *Kindergarten Chats and Other Writings* (New York, 1947), pp. 132–133.

4. *Ibid.,* p. 146.

5. Louis Sullivan, *The Autobiography of An Idea* (New York, 1949), pp. 98–99.

6. Sullivan, *Kindergarten Chats,* p. 115.

7. Frank Lloyd Wright, *The Living City* (New York, 1958), p. 34.

8. *Ibid.,* p. 111.

9. *Ibid.,* p. 97.

10. *Ibid.,* pp. 67–68.

11. *Ibid.,* p. 31.

12. Wright, *Autobiography,* p. 17.

13. *Ibid.,* p. 28.

259

14. Adams, *American Quarterly*, 9:46–62 (1957).
15. On Wright's organicism the following is a random sample of passages: *Autobiography*, pp. 142, 144, 146–147, 168, 194, 241, 271, 312, 314, 341; *The Living City*, pp. 39, 45, 48–49, 91, 140–142, 145–146, 206, 218.
16. *The Living City*, p. 52.
17. *Ibid.*, p. 55.
18. *Autobiography*, p. 461.
19. *Ibid.*, p. 462.
20. *Ibid.*, pp. 95–102.
21. *Ibid.*, pp. 22, 113.
22. *The Living City*, p. 33.
23. *Autobiography*, p. 242.
24. *Ibid.*, p. 485.
25. *Ibid.*, p. 281.
26. Lewis Mumford, "A Phoenix Too Infrequent," *From the Ground Up* (New York, 1956), p. 86.
27. *Autobiography*, p. 319; see also *The Living City*, pp. 67 ff.
28. *Autobiography*, p. 320; also p. 350.
29. *The Living City*, p. 87.
30. *Autobiography*, p. 320.
31. *Ibid.*, p. 328.
32. *The Living City*, p. 72.
33. *Ibid.*, p. 64.
34. *Ibid.*, p. 77.
35. *Ibid.*, p. 78.
36. *Autobiography*, p. 548.
37. *The Living City*, p. 119.
38. *Autobiography*, pp. 319–320.

CHAPTER XIII: THE LEGACY OF FEAR

1. See Roger Burlingame, *Henry Ford: A Great Life in Brief* (New York, 1955), pp. 3, 11–13, 103–106.
2. Henry Ford, *Ford Ideals: Being a Selection from 'Mr. Ford's Page' in The Dearborn Independent* (Dearborn, Michigan, 1922); see especially the sections entitled "The Farmer—Nature's Partner," pp. 124–128; "The Modern City—A Pestiferous Growth," pp. 154–158; "The Exodus from the Cities," pp. 425–428; "The Small Town," pp. 293–296.
3. *Ibid.*, p. 127.
4. Allen Churchill, *The Improper Bohemians: A Re-creation of Greenwich Village in its Heyday* (New York, 1959), p. 329.
5. Philip Rahv, introduction to Henry James, *The Bostonians* (New York, 1945), p. ix.
6. Stuart Gerry Brown, "Introductory Essay," *The Social Philosophy of Josiah Royce*, p. 6.
7. Cady, *The Realist at War*, p. 106.

8. Brooks, *The Flowering of New England: 1815–1865*, new and rev. ed. (New York, 1937), p. 527.
9. See his review of the *Decline of the West*, in *New Adelphi*, 2:210–214 (1929).
10. Santayana, *The Background of My Life*, p. 48.
11. Lewis Mumford, *The City in History: Its Origins, Its Transformations, and Its Prospects* (New York, 1961), p. 15.
12. *Ibid.*, p. 554.
13. *Ibid.*, pp. 543, 560.
14. *Ibid.*, p. 558.
15. *Ibid.*, p. 535.
16. *Ibid.*, p. 560.
17. Addams, *Twenty Years at Hull House*, p. 308.
18. Mumford, *The City in History*, p. 562.
19. *Ibid.*, pp. 566–567. See also Mumford's *The Conduct of Life* (New York, 1951), p. 298, where Emerson is praised even more enthusiastically for "his crystalline vision and his sense of life's capacity for self-renewal."

CH. XIV: THE OUTLINES OF A TRADITION

1. Aaron, *Men of Good Hope*, p. 172.
2. *Ibid.*, for quotation from Whitman.
3. Howells, *A Traveler from Altruria*, pp. 123–124.

CHAPTER XV: ROMANTICISM IS NOT ENOUGH

1. Hofstadter, *The Age of Reform*, p. 91.
2. Wright, *The Living City*, p. 55.
3. Howells, *The World of Chance*, p. 297.

CHAPTER XVI: IDEOLOGY, PREJUDICE, AND REASONABLE CRITICISM

1. Such as one finds, for example, in Elmer T. Peterson, ed., *Cities Are Abnormal* (Norman, Okla., 1946).
2. See *Letters of William James*, II, 344; also Jordy, *Henry Adams: Scientific Historian*, p. 214, et seq.
3. See Josiah Strong, *Our Country* (New York, 1885), ch. x; *The New Era* (New York, 1893), ch. ix. The subject of the city's impact on religious thinkers and institutions is a vast one. See the studies of A. I. Abell, *The Urban Impact on American Protestantism 1865–1900* (Cambridge, Mass., 1943) and H. F. May, *Protestant Church and Industrial America* (New York, 1949).
4. John Stuart Mill, "Nature," in *Three Essays on Religion* (New York, 1874), pp. 28–29.
5. See Louis Wirth, "Human Ecology," *American Journal of Sociology*, 50 (1945); R. D. McKenzie, "The Fields and Problems of Demography, Human Geography, and Human Ecology," in L. L. Bernard, ed., *The Fields*

NOTES TO CHAPTER XVI

and Methods of Sociology (New York, 1934); also Edward Shils, *The Present State of American Sociology* (Glencoe, Ill., 1948), p. 9, note 6.

6. See the extremely useful monograph by F. W. Coker, *Organismic Theories of the State: Nineteenth Century Interpretations of the State as Organism or as Person,* Columbia University Studies in History, Economics, and Public Law, vol. 38, no. 2 (New York, 1910), in which the more sophisticated and the more absurd theories are both analyzed.

7. Albion W. Small and George E. Vincent, *An Introduction to the Science of Society* (New York, 1894), p. 93.

8. Shils, *Present State of American Sociology,* p. 12.

9. Mumford, *The City in History,* p. 567.

10. Mumford, *The Conduct of Life,* p. 226.

ACKNOWLEDGMENTS

Grateful acknowledgment is made to the following for permission to quote from the works indicated:

Charles Scribner's Sons: Henry James, *The American Scene*.

Charles Scribner's Sons and Paul R. Reynolds and Son: *The Letters of Henry James*, edited by Percy Lubbock.

Duell, Sloan and Pearce, Inc.: Frank Lloyd Wright, *An Autobiography*. Copyright 1943 by Frank Lloyd Wright.

Houghton Mifflin Company: *The Education of Henry Adams, Henry Adams and His Friends*, compiled by Harold Dean Cater, and *Letters of Henry Adams, 1858–1891* and *1892–1918*, edited by Worthington C. Ford.

Holt, Rinehart and Winston, Inc.: John Dewey, *The Public and its Problems*.

The American Institute of Architects: Louis H. Sullivan, *The Autobiography of an Idea*.

The Free Press of Glencoe, Inc.: Robert Ezra Park, *Race and Culture* and *Human Communities*.

Professor Paul A. Schilpp and the Open Court Publishing Company: *The Philosophy of George Santayana*.

We also acknowledge permission to quote material from *Newspaper Days* by Theodore Dreiser. Copyright 1922 by Boni & Liveright, Inc. Copyright 1949 by Helen Dreiser. Reprinted by permission of the World Publishing Company.

Parts of Chapters XIV and XVI of the present work appeared originally in *Daedalus*, Winter 1961, pp. 166–179, in our article "The American Intellectual versus the American City" (copyright 1961 by Morton and Lucia White), which was reprinted in *The Future Metropolis*, edited by Lloyd Rodwin (1961), and in *The Chicago Sun-Times* for May 20, 1962.

Parts of Chapter XV were delivered by one of the authors as a paper to a conference on "The City in History," held at Harvard University in the summer of 1961.

INDEX

Aaron, Daniel, 107, 212
Adams, Brooks, 61, 67, 225
Adams, Charles Francis, 61
Adams, Henry, 2, 3, 55–74, 81, 132,
 139, 143, 184, 191, 212–213, 215,
 224–225, 226, 227, 228, 232; *The
 History of the United States*, 8, 56–
 58, 59, 60; on Philadelphia, 8; *The
 Education of Henry Adams*, 55, 59,
 60, 62, 65, 66; *Mont-Saint-Michel
 and Chartres*, 58, 73; *Democracy*, 70–
 71; compared to Howells, 95, 96, 97,
 107; compared to Addams, 147, 148;
 and Wright, 195; Mumford and, 205–
 206
Adams, Richard P., 191
Addams, Jane, 3, 94, 139, 146–154,
 155, 157, 164, 170 172, 176, 178,
 179, 196, 197, 201, 207, 216, 229,
 230; *The Spirit of Youth and the
 City Streets*, 152
Age of Reform, the, 3, 139, 176, 206,
 216
Agrarianism, 13, 15, 54, 56, 203, 212–
 213, 224, 225
Albany, 7
Aldrich, Thomas Bailey, 103
Alienation, doctrine of: and Park, 165;
 and Royce, 181, 217; and Santayana,
 187; and Brooks, 204
American Scene The, 87–88, 140, 143
Anti-Semitism, 231, 232; in Adams, 58–
 59, 60, 61, 65, 66, 67–68, 69, 71–72,
 97, 195, 213, 224; in Santayana, 184,
 186, 187; in Wright, 195
Artificiality of the city, 210, 218, 227;
 Emerson on, 26, 29, 30, 36, 210;
 Elizabeth Peabody on, 31; Haw-
 thorne on, 43–44, 46; Park on, 164;
 Henry Ford on, 201
Austin, Benjamin, 13, 17, 18
*Autobiography of Benjamin Franklin,
 The*, 6, 9–10

Balzac, Honoré de, 132, 134

Baym, Max, 55
Beard, Charles, 168
Belden, E. P., 22–23
Bellamy, Edward, 108, 109
Bellini, Charles, 16
Berlin, 61, 66
Beveridge, Albert J., 225
Bingham, Mrs. William, 15–16
Blithedale Romance, The, 41–42, 51,
 104
Boston: in 1800, 7, 57; Emerson and,
 27–28, 211; Hawthorne and, 41–42,
 43–44; Adams and, 59, 60–62, 70,
 71; Henry James and, 78–79, 94, 213;
 Howells and, 100, 101–102, 104; San-
 tayana and, 183–184; 204; Sullivan
 and, 191–192; Brooks and, 204
Bostonians, The, 78, 83, 203, 213
Brook Farm, 31–33, 41, 44, 149
Brooks, Van Wyck, 204
Bryant, William Cullen, 226
Bryce, James, Viscount, 75–76, 149
Burgess, Ernest W., 160, 166
Businessmen: in Henry James' view, 86,
 92–93, 94; in Howells' view, 95–96,
 97–98, 100, 112–113, 119, 212; in
 Norris's view, 118–119

Cambridge: Henry James and, 79;
 Howells and, 101; William James
 and, 141
Cameron, Elizabeth, 68
Carlyle, Thomas, 29
Carter, Everett, 102
Charleston, 7
Chase, Richard, 224
Chicago, 141, 155; Dreiser and, 125–
 131, 171, 214; Addams and, 149–154;
 Park and, 158, 160, 165–166; Dewey
 and, 171, 174; Wright and, 190;
 Sullivan and, 192
Chinard, Gilbert, 15
Cincinnati, 7, 21
Civilization, the city as manifestation
 of, 227, 228–229, 230; Emerson's

265

INDEX

Octopus, The, 118–121
Organicism, 234–235; Adams and, 73; Addams and, 150, 151, 201; Park and, 160; Wright and, 194, 198; Mumford and, 205, 208

Palfrey, John Gorham, 66
Paris: Jefferson on, 13, 15–16; Adams on, 65, 68, 71; Henry James on, 79–80, 83–84
Park, Robert, 3, 139, 146, 155–167, 170, 171, 174, 176, 178, 180, 196, 197, 216, 229, 230, 234, 237; "Community Organization and Juvenile Delinquency" 161; "Community Organization and the Romantic Temper," 162
Peabody, Elizabeth, 31, 205
Philadelphia: in 1800, 7, 8–10, 57; Franklin and, 9–10; Jefferson on, 8, 19; after War of 1812, 21; de Tocqueville on, 23–24; Henry James and, 75, 90
Pierre, 39–41, 44, 104
Pittsburgh, 21
Poe, Edgar Allan, 2, 3, 36–37, 46–52, 58, 100, 226; "The City in the Sea," 46–47; "Al Araaf," 47; "The Man of the Crowd," 47–49, 50; "The Murders in the Rue Morgue," 49, 50; Doings of Gotham, 50; "The Mystery of Marie Rogêt," 51; "Mellonta Tauta," 51–52; "Some Words with a Mummy," 52; "Philosophy of Furniture," 53
Population growth: in 1800, 7, 57; in 1860, 21–22, 210; after Civil War, 54, 219; in the twentieth century, 189; by 1900, 212
Populist movement, 54, 139
Princess Casamassima, The, 82–84, 85, 104, 213
Provincialism, 179–183, 188, 189, 203, 216, 217
Public and its Problems, The, 156, 168, 172, 175, 180, 189, 208, 216
Pulitzer, Joseph, 121, 133–134

Quincy, 62–64, 70, 71, 73

Rahv, Philip, 203
Redburn, 37–39, 40, 44
Reed, Henry Hope, 180
Reformism, 4, 41, 153, 215, 217–218, 229; Emerson on, 32; Howells and,

102, 104; Addams and, 146; Dewey and, 146; Park and, 162
Regional city: Howells' proposals for, 107, 113, 180, 194, 208, 214; Mumford's proposals for, 183
Riley, James Whitcomb, 123
Ripley, George, 31
Romanticism and the city, 1, 19–20, 34, 54, 210, 211, 213, 217, 221–230, 231, 235; Adams and, 55, 57–58; Howells and, 104–105; Norris and, 121, 124; Dreiser and, 129; Addams and, 151, 152; Park and, 162, 164; Royce and, 179, 183; Santayana and, 185; Sullivan and, 191; Wright and, 194
Rome: Hawthorne on, 44–45, 79; Adams on, 65; Henry James on, 79; William James on, 140
Roosevelt, Theodore, 225
Rousseau, Jean-Jacques, 11, 138, 148, 151, 228
Royce, Josiah, 132, 136, 178, 179–183, 189, 203, 204, 216–217; The Philosophy of Loyalty, 181; Santayana and, 187–188
Rush, Benjamin, 16–17
Ruskin, John, 108
Russell, Bertrand, 222

Santayana, George, 179, 183–188, 204, 227, 229
Schiller, J. C. F., 211
Schlesinger, Arthur M., 21, 54
School and Society, The, 168, 170, 172, 173
Science, 210, 231–232; Emerson on, 25–26, 210, 234–235; Henry James and, 89, Howells and, 100, 229; Dewey and, 168, 171
Short, William, 19
Simmel, Georg, 158, 164
Simms, William Gilmore, 226
Sinclair, Upton, 228
Sister Carrie, 126, 130–131, 133, 138, 149, 190
Skyscrapers: Henry James on, 85, 89–90, 94; Howells on, 110; Wright on, 194–195; Mumford on, 206; by 1900, 212; William James on, 216
Sloan, John, 125
Slums, 54; Norris' view, 121–122, 124, 145; Addams' view, 148, 149; Park's view, 159, 160
Small Albion, 234
Smith, Henry Nash, 224

269